STUDY GUIDE

to accompany

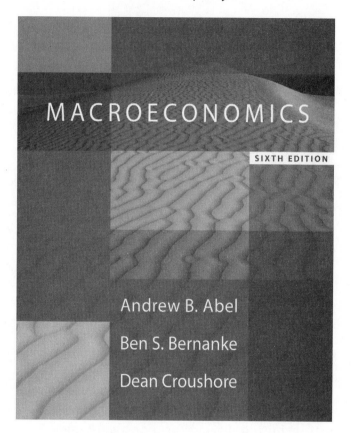

MACROECONOMICS

SIXTH EDITION

Andrew B. Abel

Ben S. Bernanke

Dean Croushore

Dean Croushore

Robins School of Business
University of Richmond

PEARSON

Addison
Wesley

Boston   San Francisco   New York
London   Toronto   Sydney   Tokyo   Singapore   Madrid
Mexico City   Munich   Paris   Cape Town   Hong Kong   Montreal

Reproduced by Pearson Addison Wesley from electronic files supplied by author.

Copyright © 2008 Pearson Education, Inc.
Publishing as Pearson Addison Wesley, 75 Arlington Street, Boston, MA 02116

ISBN-13   978-0-321-48219-8
ISBN-10   0-321-48219-0

3 4 5 6 BB 10 09 08

Contents

Chapter 1
Introduction to Macroeconomics

■ Introduction

The purpose of this chapter is to give you a general introduction to the main concepts in macroeconomics. In Section 1.1, the major issues in macroeconomics are discussed—growth, business cycles, unemployment, inflation, the international economy, macroeconomic policy, and aggregation. Section 1.2 discusses the major things that macroeconomists do—forecasting, analysis, research, and data development. Then Section 1.3 covers the subject of why economists disagree and talks about the textbook's approach to covering material, given that there's so much disagreement.

Though many instructors will blow through this chapter quickly, you shouldn't. You should spend some time looking at all the data in this chapter and trying to understand what it's all about. This will help you later on when you go through the rest of the textbook. You should know that most macroeconomists are very motivated by looking at data. They want to explain how the world works and why the data behave the way they do. Figures like those shown in Section 1.1 provide economists with what they call "stylized facts" about how the economy behaves. Then the economists try to think up models that are consistent with the data.

■ Outline

I. **What Macroeconomics is About (Sec. 1.1)**
   A) Long-run economic growth
      1. Growth of output in United States over time
         a. Figure 1.1: Output of United States since 1869
         b. Note decline in output in recessions; increase in output in some wars
      2. Sources of growth—population, average labor productivity growth
      3. Average labor productivity
         a. Average labor productivity: output produced per unit of labor input
         b. Figure 1.2: Average labor productivity of United States since 1900
         c. Average labor productivity growth:
            1) About 2.5% per year from 1949 to 1973
            2) 1.1% per year from 1973 to 1995
            3) 2.0% per year from 1995 to 2005
   B) Business cycles
      1. Business cycle: Short-run contractions and expansions in economic activity
      2. Downward phase is called a recession

C) Unemployment
   1. Unemployment: the number of people who are available for work and actively seeking work but cannot find jobs
   2. U.S. experience shown in Fig. 1.3
   3. Recessions cause unemployment rate to rise

D) Inflation
   1. U.S. experience shown in Fig. 1.4
   2. Deflation: when prices of most goods and services decline
   3. Inflation rate: the percentage increase in the level of prices
   4. Hyperinflation: an extremely high rate of inflation

E) The international economy
   1. Open vs. closed economies
      a. Open economy: an economy that has extensive trading and financial relationships with other national economies
      b. Closed economy: an economy that does not interact economically with the rest of the world
   2. Trade imbalances
      a. U.S. experience shown in Fig. 1.5
      b. Trade surplus: exports exceed imports
      c. Trade deficit: imports exceed exports

F) Macroeconomic policy
   1. Fiscal policy: government spending and taxation
      a. Effects of changes in federal budget
      b. U.S. experience in Fig. 1.6
      c. Relation to trade deficit?
   2. Monetary policy: growth of money supply; determined by central bank; the Fed in U.S.

G) Aggregation
   1. Aggregation: summing individual economic variables to obtain economywide totals
   2. Distinguishes microeconomics (disaggregated) from macroeconomics (aggregated)

II. What Macroeconomists Do (Sec. 1.2)

A) Macroeconomic forecasting
   1. Relatively few economists make forecasts
   2. Forecasting is very difficult

B) Macroeconomic analysis
   1. Private and public sector economists—analyze current conditions
   2. Does having lots of economists ensure good macroeconomic policies? No, because politicians, not economists, make major decisions

C) Macroeconomic research
   1. Goal: to make general statements about how the economy works
   2. Theoretical and empirical research are necessary for forecasting and economic analysis
   3. Economic theory: a set of ideas about the economy, organized in a logical framework
   4. Economic model: a simplified description of some aspect of the economy

5. Usefulness of economic theory or models depends on reasonableness of assumptions, possibility of being applied to real problems, empirically testable implications, theoretical results consistent with real-world data

6. Box 1.1: Developing and Testing an Economic Theory

   a. Step 1: State the research question

   b. Step 2: Make provisional assumptions

   c. Step 3: Work out the implications of the theory

   d. Step 4: Conduct an empirical analysis to compare the implications of the theory with the data

   e. Step 5: Evaluate the results of your comparisons

D) Data development—very important for making data more useful

III. Why Macroeconomists Disagree (Sec. 1.3)

A) Positive vs. normative analysis

   1. Positive analysis: examines the economic consequences of a policy

   2. Normative analysis: determines whether a policy should be used

B) Classicals vs. Keynesians

   1. The classical approach

      a. The economy works well on its own

      b. The "invisible hand": the idea that if there are free markets and individuals conduct their economic affairs in their own best interests, the overall economy will work well

      c. Wages and prices adjust rapidly to get to equilibrium

         1) Equilibrium: a situation in which the quantities demanded and supplied are equal

         2) Changes in wages and prices are signals that coordinate people's actions

      d. Result: Government should have only a limited role in the economy

   2. The Keynesian approach

      a. The Great Depression: Classical theory failed because high unemployment was persistent

      b. Keynes: Persistent unemployment occurs because wages and prices adjust slowly, so markets remain out of equilibrium for long periods

      c. Conclusion: Government should intervene to restore full employment

   3. The evolution of the classical–Keynesian debate

      a. Keynesians dominated from WWII to 1970

      b. Stagflation led to a classical comeback in the 1970s

      c. Last 30 years: excellent research with both approaches

C) A unified approach to macroeconomics

   1. Textbook uses a single model to present both classical and Keynesian ideas

   2. Three markets: goods, assets, and labor

   3. Model starts with microfoundations: individual behavior

   4. Long run: wages and prices are perfectly flexible

   5. Short run: Classical case—flexible wages and prices; Keynesian case—wages and prices are slow to adjust

■ Multiple Choice Questions

1. Which of the following is *not* a topic of macroeconomics?
    (a) Why nations have different rates of growth.
    (b) What causes inflation and what can be done about it.
    (c) What factors contribute to the presence of monopolies in the economy.
    (d) Why unemployment periodically reaches very high levels.

2. Which of the following factors are most important for determining the economic growth of a country?
    (a) The country's level of resources
    (b) The independence of the country's central bank
    (c) The country's rates of saving and investment
    (d) The level of sophistication of a country's financial markets

3. The amount of output produced per unit of labor input is called
    (a) marginal revenue product of labor.
    (b) average labor productivity.
    (c) a util.
    (d) unit labor cost.

4. The business cycle describes the
    (a) progression of an industry's structure from monopoly to perfect competition.
    (b) progression of an industry's structure from perfect competition to monopoly.
    (c) expansion and contraction of an individual industry within the economy.
    (d) expansion and contraction of economic activity in the economy as a whole.

5. Recessions
    (a) don't occur in developed countries like the United States.
    (b) cause the unemployment rate to increase.
    (c) never last more than two consecutive quarters.
    (d) are always followed by long periods of high rates of real economic growth.

6. When national output declines, the economy is said to be in
    (a) an expansion.
    (b) a deflation.
    (c) a recovery.
    (d) a recession.

7. If a county has 3,293 unemployed people and 73,177 in its labor force, then the county's unemployment rate equals
    (a) 22.2%.
    (b) 2.2%.
    (c) 4.5%.
    (d) 0.45%.

8. The average price of goods in the United States
    (a) was relatively constant over the 1800–1945 period.
    (b) was relatively constant over the decade of the 1980s.
    (c) declined over the decade of the 1970s.
    (d) is always constant in the long run.

9. Historical evidence shows that consumer prices in the United States
    (a) declined between the 1920s and World War II, but increased afterward.
    (b) increased between the 1920s and World War II, but declined afterward.
    (c) have shown a continuous inflationary pattern since the 1920s.
    (d) have displayed no clear-cut trend since the 1920s.

10. The inflation rate is the
    (a) real interest rate minus the nominal interest rate.
    (b) percentage increase in the average level of prices over a year.
    (c) number of unemployed divided by the labor force.
    (d) labor force divided by the number of unemployed.

11. An economy that doesn't interact economically with the rest of the world is called
    (a) a non-open economy.
    (b) a newly industrializing economy.
    (c) a closed economy.
    (d) an autarky.

12. In most years during the 1980s and 1990s, the U.S. trade balance
    (a) was in equilibrium.
    (b) was a trade deficit.
    (c) was a trade surplus.
    (d) was cyclical, fluctuating annually between trade deficits and trade surpluses.

13. U.S. exports are goods and services
    (a) produced abroad and sold to Americans.
    (b) produced in the United States and sold to Americans.
    (c) produced abroad and sold to foreigners.
    (d) produced in the United States and sold to foreigners.

14. A country had imports of $50 billion, exports of $60 billion, and GDP of $300 billion. The trade surplus was what percent of GDP?
    (a) 3.3%
    (b) 10.0%
    (c) 16.7%
    (d) 20.0%

15. A country's monetary policy is controlled by
    (a) private citizens.
    (b) the central bank.
    (c) large banks.
    (d) the legislature.

16. Fiscal policy determines _____ while monetary policy determines _____.
    (a) government spending and taxation; the growth of the money supply
    (b) government's capital; government's investment
    (c) the rate of growth of the economy; the rate of growth of prices
    (d) the inflation rate; the rate of growth of prices

17. Which of the following fiscal policies do Keynesians recommend to help the economy recover from a recession?
    (a) An increase in government spending
    (b) An increase in taxes
    (c) An increase in the money supply
    (d) An increase in saving

18. The large government budget deficits of the 1980s and the early-to-mid–1990s coincided with
    (a) high inflation rates.
    (b) large trade deficits.
    (c) low unemployment rates.
    (d) Keynesian policies.

19. Since the Great Depression, the share of national income collected in taxes and spent by the federal government in the United States has
    (a) increased from less than 10% to more than 20%.
    (b) remained relatively stable at 15%.
    (c) remained relatively stable at 35%.
    (d) declined from about 40% to less than 15%.

20. The government of Anchovy collected receipts of $100 billion and had expenditures of $125 billion. Its GDP was $400 billion. The government's deficit was what percent of GDP?
    (a) 6.25%
    (b) 12.50%
    (c) 25.00%
    (d) 100.00%

21. The process of adding together individual economic variables to obtain economywide totals is called
    (a) macroeconomics.
    (b) aggregation.
    (c) agglomeration.
    (d) data development.

22. Testing a theory by comparing the theory's implications with data obtained in the real world is called
    (a) empirical analysis.
    (b) descriptive calibration.
    (c) historical variance analysis.
    (d) univariate analysis.

23. The principal distinction between positive analysis and normative analysis is that
    (a) positive analysis is useful and normative analysis is not useful.
    (b) positive analysis is optimistic and normative analysis is neutral.
    (c) economists always agree on the conclusions of positive analysis but could disagree on the conclusions of normative analysis.
    (d) positive analysis tells us "what is," but normative analysis tells us "what ought to be."

24. Which of the statements below is primarily normative in nature?
    (a) There is an unequal distribution of income in the United States.
    (b) The distribution of income is more unequal in the United States than it is in Japan.
    (c) The inequality of income that exists in the United States is partly caused by an unequal distribution of wealth.
    (d) The distribution of income in the United States should be more equal than it is.

25. Classical economists who assume the "invisible hand" works reasonably well do *not* argue that
    (a) the government should have a limited role in the economy.
    (b) government policies will be ineffective and counterproductive.
    (c) the government should actively intervene in the economy to eliminate business cycles.
    (d) wages and prices adjust quickly to bring the economy back to equilibrium.

26. The classical approach to macroeconomics assumes that
    (a) wages, but not prices, adjust quickly to balance quantities supplied and demanded in markets.
    (b) wages and prices adjust quickly to balance quantities supplied and demanded in markets.
    (c) prices, but not wages, adjust quickly to balance quantities supplied and demanded in markets.
    (d) neither wages nor prices adjust quickly to balance quantities supplied and demanded in markets.

27. Equilibrium in the economy means
    (a) unemployment is zero.
    (b) quantities demanded and supplied are equal in all markets.
    (c) prices aren't changing over time.
    (d) tax revenues equal government spending, so the government has no budget deficit.

28. John Maynard Keynes disagreed with the classical economists because he believed that
    (a) wages and prices adjust slowly.
    (b) international trade plays a major role in the macroeconomy.
    (c) government intervention in the economy cannot reduce business cycles.
    (d) unemployment will be eliminated quickly by the invisible hand of the market.

■ Review Questions

1. Identify and briefly describe six major topics studied by macroeconomists.

2. What is a recession? Briefly state the effect of a recession on the unemployment rate. Identify and briefly describe two macroeconomic policies that might be used to help pull the macroeconomy out of a recession. In the absence of government intervention, do classical or Keynesian economists believe the economy would recover quickly from a recession? Briefly explain.

3. Briefly describe the following tasks of macroeconomists: forecasting; analysis; research; and data development.

4. Why is macroeconomic forecasting so difficult? Does this difficulty mean economics is a worthless field of study?

5. What are the four major areas in which macroeconomists work? Give an example of a job in each.

6. Discuss the major differences between classical and Keynesian economists. Be sure to explain how they differ with regard to how quickly equilibrium is restored in the economy as well as what role they see for government action in restoring equilibrium.

7. Describe the evolution of the classical–Keynesian debate since World War II.

■ Numerical Problems

1. Starting from a year in which gross domestic product for the economy is $8,000 billion, calculate how much output the national economy would produce in each of the next five years if it continued to grow at its potential real growth rate of 3%.

   How much output would the economy produce in each year if it grew by 4% the first year, 2% the second year, 1% the third year, –1% the fourth year, and –3% the fifth year? (Note: A negative growth rate means output is declining.)

   By the fifth year, how far is output below its potential level?

2. Suppose there are 125 million people in the labor force.
   (a) Calculate the unemployment rate if 10 million people are unemployed.
   (b) Calculate the unemployment rate if the number of unemployed falls to 6 million.
   (c) If the unemployment rate is 6%, how many unemployed people are there?

3. Using the CPI measure of the price level, which is 100 in the base year of 2003, calculate the annual inflation rates for: a) 2004, when the index is 103.5; b) 2005, when the index is 104.5; c) 2006, when the index is 105.2.

■ Analytical Question

1. Determine whether each of the following is a positive or normative statement.
   (a) The Fed should lower interest rates to increase economic growth, because we're in a recession.
   (b) Higher government budget deficits cause higher interest rates.
   (c) The trade deficit should decline because of the fall in the value of the dollar.
   (d) Because of our high inflation rate, we must reduce the rate of money growth.
   (e) A generous unemployment insurance system is a primary cause of high unemployment in Europe.
   (f) Increased average labor productivity in a country should lead to faster growth.
   (g) Government budget deficits are too high in the United States and should be reduced.

■ Answers

Multiple Choice

1. c	7. c	13. d	19. a	24. d
2. c	8. a	14. a	20. a	25. c
3. b	9. a	15. b	21. b	26. b
4. d	10. b	16. a	22. a	27. b
5. b	11. c	17. a	23. d	28. a
6. d	12. b	18. b		

Review Questions

1. Macroeconomists study the causes and effects of the following macroeconomic events.
   (a) Long-run economic growth. Economists examine increases in real GDP (national output) over extended periods of time, living standards, and productivity growth.
   (b) Business cycles. Economists study the alternating periods of contraction and expansion in economic activity.
   (c) Unemployment. Unemployment is the inability of some people to find jobs, even though they are willing to work at market wages.
   (d) Inflation. Inflation is the rate of growth in the average price of goods and services.
   (e) The international economy. Economists study patterns of international trade and borrowing among nations, as well as trade imbalances.
   (f) Macroeconomic policy. Economists examine both fiscal and monetary policy. Fiscal policy consists of changes in government spending and taxation. Monetary policy represents changes in the money supply.

2. A recession is a time when the economy's output is growing very slowly or falling. The unemployment rate increases during recessions. Two macroeconomic policies that might be used to help pull the macroeconomy out of a recession are fiscal policy (increases in government spending or reductions in taxes) and monetary policy (increases in the money supply). Both classical and Keynesian economists believe the economy will recover from a recession in the absence of government intervention. However, classical economists believe the recovery will occur fairly quickly; Keynesians believe the recovery will occur slowly.

3. (a) Forecasting. Macroeconomists develop models to predict the future values of macroeconomic variables in one or more markets. These models are usually based on economic theory but are statistical in form and estimated using macroeconomic data.
   (b) Analysis. Macroeconomists analyze changes in macroeconomic policies as well as other changes in macroeconomic market conditions. This analysis is based on economic theory, uses analytic reasoning techniques, and may rely on forecasting models.
   (c) Research. The goal of macroeconomic research is to make general statements about how the economy works. Research economists formulate and test theories.
   (d) Data development. Macroeconomic data development provides the data needed in macroeconomic research, analysis, and forecasting. Most macroeconomic data are collected and published by the government.

4. Forecasting is difficult because our understanding of how the economy works is imperfect and because it's impossible to take into account all the factors that might affect future economic trends. This just means the field of economics is difficult and complex, not that it's worthless.

5. Forecasting, analysis, research, and data development. Forecasting: forecasting the stock market on Wall Street; analysis: analyzing the economy for the Federal Reserve; research: investigating the link between the trade deficit and the government budget deficit as a university professor; data development: working at the Bureau of Labor Statistics to develop better ways to measure unemployment.

6. Classical and Keynesian economists differ most with regard to how quickly they see wages and prices adjusting to restore equilibrium in the economy. Classical economists think that when the economy is out of equilibrium, wages and prices adjust quickly to restore equilibrium. As a result, there shouldn't be long periods of abnormally high unemployment. The quick return to equilibrium means there is no reason for government action. Keynesians, on the other hand, think wages and prices are slow to adjust. As a result, the economy may be out of equilibrium for some time, perhaps with high unemployment. To restore equilibrium quickly may necessitate some government action, such as increasing the government's demand for goods and services.

7. The Keynesian approach dominated macroeconomic theory and policy from World War II until about 1970. But stagflation in the 1970s undermined faith in the Keynesian approach, and classical macroeconomics made a comeback. Currently, excellent research is being conducted with both approaches.

Numerical Problems

1.

Potential Output	Actual Output
Year 1: $8,000 billion × 1.03 = $8,240 billion	$8,000 billion × 1.04 = $8,320 billion
Year 2: $8,240 billion × 1.03 = $8,487 billion	$8,320 billion × 1.02 = $8,486 billion
Year 3: $8,487 billion × 1.03 = $8,742 billion	$8,486 billion × 1.01 = $8,571 billion
Year 4: $8,742 billion × 1.03 = $9,004 billion	$8,571 billion × 0.99 = $8,486 billion
Year 5: $9,004 billion × 1.03 = $9,274 billion	$8,486 billion × 0.97 = $8,231 billion

[*Note:* Don't worry about rounding differences that arise in problems like this, because such differences depend on how many digits you carry over from one calculation to the next.]

Output is below potential output by [(9,274 – 8,231)/9,274] × 100% = 11.2%.

2. Use the formula: unemployment rate = number of people unemployed/number of people in labor force × 100%.

(a) 10/125 × 100% = 8%.

(b) 6/125 × 100% = 4.8%.

(c) Solve for y (where y is in millions) in the equation: 6% = y/125 × 100%, or y = 125 × 6/100 = 125 × .06 = 7.5.

3. The annual inflation rate = (price level in the current year – price level in the previous year)/price level in the previous year

(a) inflation in 2004 = (103.5 – 100)/100 × 100% = 3.5%.

(b) inflation in 2005 = (104.5 – 103.5)/103.5 × 100% = 1.0%.

(c) inflation in 2006 = (105.2 – 104.5)/104.5 × 100% = 0.7%.

Analytical Questions

1. (a) Normative
   (b) Positive
   (c) Positive
   (d) Normative
   (e) Positive
   (f) Positive
   (g) Normative

Chapter 2
The Measurement and Structure
of the National Economy

■ Introduction

Chapter 2 is all about numbers—those that describe the economy. First, Section 2.1 discusses the general idea of the national income accounts and talks about the relationships between key macroeconomic variables. Section 2.2 then goes into a detailed discussion of GDP (the main measure of output) and its components. Then, Section 2.3 talks about measures of saving and wealth, both for the private sector and for the government. Section 2.4 covers real GDP, price indexes, and inflation. Interest rates are discussed in Section 2.5.

You might think that all this accounting business is pretty dull, routine stuff, but it's been the focus of a lot of attention recently. As you'll learn in the chapter, counting all the economy's output and especially calculating the inflation rate is very tricky business. Many economists are convinced that we've been mismeasuring many of the macroeconomic variables, especially inflation. And that, in turn, has policymakers concerned.

As you go through this chapter, you may find some of the details of national income accounting somewhat tedious. But it helps to know how economic goods and services are counted in order to understand the concepts used later in the textbook. So immerse yourself in some of the details; it will pay off later.

■ Outline

I. **National Income Accounting: The Measurement of Production, Income, and Expenditure (Sec. 2.1)**

   A) National income accounts: an accounting framework used in measuring current economic activity

   B) Three alternative approaches give the same measurements

      1. Product approach: the amount of output produced
      2. Income approach: the incomes generated by production
      3. Expenditure approach: the amount of spending by purchasers

   C) Juice business example shows that all three approaches are equal

      1. Important concept in product approach: value added = value of output minus value of inputs purchased from other producers

D) Why are the three approaches equivalent?

   1. They must be, by definition

   2. Any output produced (product approach) is purchased by someone (expenditure approach) and results in income to someone (income approach)

   3. The fundamental identity of national income accounting:

$$\text{total production} = \text{total income} = \text{total expenditure} \tag{2.1}$$

II. Gross Domestic Product (Sec. 2.2)

A) The product approach to measuring GDP

   1. GDP is the market value of final goods and services newly produced within a nation during a fixed period of time

   2. Market value: allows adding together unlike items by valuing them at their market prices

      a. Problem: misses nonmarket items such as homemaking, the value of environmental quality, and natural resource depletion

      b. There is some adjustment to reflect the underground economy

      c. Government services (that aren't sold in markets) are valued at their cost of production

   3. Newly produced: counts only things produced in the given period; excludes things produced earlier

   4. Final goods and services

      a. Don't count intermediate goods and services (those used up in the production of other goods and services in the same period that they themselves were produced)

      b. Final goods and services are those that are not intermediate

      c. Capital goods (goods used to produce other goods) are final goods because they aren't used up in the same period that they are produced

      d. Inventory investment (the amount that inventories of unsold finished goods, goods in process, and raw materials have changed during the period) is also treated as a final good

      e. Adding up value added works well, because it automatically excludes intermediate goods

   5. GNP Versus GDP

      a. GNP (gross national product) = output produced by domestically owned factors of production

      GDP (gross domestic product) = output produced within a nation

      b. GDP = GNP – NFP (net factor payments from abroad) (2.2)

      c. NFP = payments to domestically owned factors located abroad minus payments to foreign factors located domestically

      d. Example: Engineering revenues for a road built by a U.S. company in Saudi Arabia is part of U.S. GNP (built by a U.S. factor of production), not U.S. GDP, and is part of Saudi GDP (built in Saudi Arabia), not Saudi GNP

      e. Difference between GNP and GDP is small for the United States, about 0.2%, but higher for countries that have many citizens working abroad

B) The expenditure approach to measuring GDP

   1. Measures total spending on final goods and services produced within a nation during a specified period of time

   2. Four main categories of spending: consumption (C), investment (I), government purchases of goods and services (G), and net exports (NX)

   3. $Y = C + I + G + NX$, the income-expenditure identity (2.3)

   4. Consumption: spending by domestic households on final goods and services (including those produced abroad)

     a. About 2/3 of U.S. GDP

     b. Three categories

        (1) Consumer durables (examples: cars, TV sets, furniture, major appliances)

        (2) Nondurable goods (examples: food, clothing, fuel)

        (3) Services (examples: education, health care, financial services, transportation)

5. Investment: spending for new capital goods (fixed investment) plus inventory investment

     a. About 1/6 of U.S. GDP

     b. Business (or nonresidential) fixed investment: spending by businesses on structures and equipment and software

     c. Residential fixed investment: spending on the construction of houses and apartment buildings

     d. Inventory investment: increases in firms' inventory holdings

6. Government purchases of goods and services: spending by the government on goods or services

     a. About 1/5 of U.S. GDP

     b. Most by state and local governments, not federal government

     c. Not all government expenditures are purchases of goods and services

        (1) Some are payments that are *not* made in exchange for current goods and services

        (2) One type is transfers, including Social Security payments, welfare, and unemployment benefits

        (3) Another type is interest payments on the government debt

     d. Some government spending is for capital goods that add to the nation's capital stock, such as highways, airports, bridges, and water and sewer systems

7. Net exports: exports minus imports

     a. Exports: goods produced in the country that are purchased by foreigners

     b. Imports: goods produced abroad that are purchased by residents in the country

     c. Imports are subtracted from GDP, as they represent goods produced abroad, and were included in consumption, investment, and government purchases

C) The income approach to measuring GDP

1. Adds up income generated by production (including profits and taxes paid to the government)

     a. National income = compensation of employees (including benefits) + proprietors' income + rental income of persons + corporate profits + net interest + taxes on production and imports + business current transfer payments + current surplus of government enterprises

     b. National income + statistical discrepancy = net national product

     c. Net national product + depreciation (the value of capital that wears out in the period) = gross national product (GNP)

     d. GNP – net factor payments (*NFP*) = GDP

2. Private sector and government sector income
   a. Private disposable income = income of the private sector = private sector income earned at home (*Y* or GDP) and abroad (*NFP*) + payments from the government sector (transfers, *TR*, and interest on government debt, *INT*) – taxes paid to government (*T*) = $Y + NFP + TR + INT - T$ (2.4)
   b. Government's net income = taxes – transfers – interest payments = $T - TR - INT$ (2.5)
   c. Private disposable income + government's net income = GDP + *NFP* = GNP

III. Saving and Wealth (Sec. 2.3)

A) Wealth
   1. Household wealth = a household's assets minus its liabilities
   2. National wealth = sum of all households', firms', and governments' wealth within the nation
   3. Saving by individuals, businesses, and government determine wealth

B) Measures of aggregate saving
   1. Saving = current income – current spending
   2. Saving rate = saving/current income
   3. Private saving = private disposable income – consumption

$$S_{pvt} = (Y + NFP - T + TR + INT) - C \qquad (2.6)$$

   4. Government saving = net government income – government purchases of goods and services

$$S_{govt} = (T - TR - INT) - G \qquad (2.7)$$

   a. Government saving = government budget surplus = government receipts – government outlays
   b. Government receipts = tax revenue (*T*)
   c. Government outlays = government purchases of goods and services (*G*) + transfers (*TR*) + interest payments on government debt (*INT*)
   d. Government budget deficit = $-S_{govt}$
   e. Despite the BEA's change in methods that explicitly recognize government investment, the text simplifies matters by counting government investment as government purchases, not investment. This avoids complications when the concepts are introduced and can be modified for further analysis later.

   5. National saving
   a. National saving = private saving + government saving
   b. $S = S_{pvt} + S_{govt}$
      $$= [Y + NFP - T + TR + INT - C] + [T - TR - INT - G] \qquad (2.8)$$
      $$= Y + NFP - C - G = GNP - C - G$$

C) The uses of private saving
   1. $S = I + (NX + NFP)$ (2.9)

   $S = I + CA$ (2.10)

   Derived from $S = Y + NFP - C - G$ and $Y = C + I + G + NX$

   $CA = NX + NFP$ = current account balance

2. $S_{pvt} = I + (-S_{govt}) + CA$ (2.11)

{using $S = S_{pvt} + S_{govt}$}

The uses-of-saving identity—saving is used in three ways:

  a. investment (I)

  b. government budget deficit ($-S_{govt}$)

  c. current account balance (CA)

D) Relating saving and wealth

  1. Stocks and flows

    a. Flow variables: measured per unit of time (GDP, income, saving, investment)

    b. Stock variables: measured at a point in time (quantity of money, value of houses, capital stock)

    c. Flow variables often equal rates of change of stock variables

  2. Wealth and saving as stock and flow (wealth is a stock, saving is a flow)

  3. National wealth: domestic physical assets + net foreign assets

    a. Country's domestic physical assets (capital goods and land)

    b. Country's net foreign assets = foreign assets (foreign stocks, bonds, and capital goods owned by domestic residents) minus foreign liabilities (domestic stocks, bonds, and capital goods owned by foreigners)

    c. Wealth matters because the economic well-being of a country depends on it

    d. Changes in national wealth

      (1) Change in value of existing assets and liabilities (change in price of financial assets, or depreciation of capital goods)

      (2) National saving ($S = I + CA$) raises wealth

    e. Comparison of U.S. saving and investment with other countries

      (1) The United States is a low-saving country; Japan is a high-saving country

      (2) U.S. investment exceeds U.S. saving, so we have a negative current-account balance

E) Application: Wealth Versus Saving

  1. The personal saving rate has declined dramatically in recent years (Fig. 2.1)

  2. We might not need to worry about the decline in the personal saving rate because:

    a. private saving is the relevant measure of saving

    b. the personal saving rate may be revised upward in the future (Fig. 2.2)

    c. the personal saving rate ignores capital gains; as people's wealth rises, their saving rate declines (Fig. 2.3)

IV. Real GDP, Price Indexes, and Inflation (Sec. 2.4)

A) Real GDP

  1. Nominal variables are those in dollar terms

  2. Problem: Do changes in nominal values reflect changes in prices or quantities?

  3. Real variables: adjust for price changes; reflect only quantity changes

  4. Example of computers and bicycles

  5. Nominal GDP is the dollar value of an economy's final output measured at current market prices

  6. Real GDP is an estimate of the value of an economy's final output, adjusting for changes in the overall price level

B) Price indexes
1. A price index measures the average level of prices for some specified set of goods and services, relative to the prices in a specified base year
2. GDP deflator = 100 × nominal GDP/real GDP
3. Note that base year $P = 100$
4. Consumer Price Index (CPI)
    a. Monthly index of consumer prices; index averages 100 in reference base period (1982 to 1984)
    b. Based on basket of goods in expenditure base period (2003 to 2004)
5. Box 2.2 on the computer revolution and chain-weighted GDP
    a. Choice of expenditure base period matters for GDP when prices and quantities of a good, such as computers, are changing rapidly
    b. BEA compromised by developing chain-weighted GDP
    c. Now, however, components of real GDP don't add up to real GDP, but discrepancy is usually small
6. Inflation
    a. Calculate inflation rate: $\pi_{t+1} = (P_{t+1} - P_t)/P_t = \Delta P_{t+1}/P_t$
    b. Text Fig. 2.4 shows the U.S. inflation rate since 1960 for the GDP deflator
7. Box 2.3: Does CPI inflation overstate increases in the cost of living?
    a. The Boskin Commission reported that the CPI was biased upwards by as much as one to two percentage points per year
    b. One problem is that adjusting the price measures for changes in the quality of goods is very difficult
    c. Another problem is that price indexes with fixed sets of goods don't reflect the substitution by consumers that goes on when one good becomes relatively cheaper than another; this problem is known as substitution bias
    d. If inflation is overstated, then real incomes are higher than we thought and we've overindexed payments like Social Security
    e. Latest research (July 2006) suggests bias is still 1% per year or higher

V. **Interest Rates (Sec. 2.5)**
A) Real Versus nominal interest rates
1. Interest rate: a rate of return promised by a borrower to a lender
2. Real interest rate: rate at which the real value of an asset increases over time
3. Nominal interest rate: rate at which the nominal value of an asset increases over time
4. Real interest rate $= i - \pi$ (2.12)
    Text Fig. 2.5 plots nominal and real interest rates for the United States since 1960

B) The expected real interest rate
1. $r = i - \pi^e$ (2.13)
2. If $\pi = \pi^e$, real interest rate = expected real interest rate

■ Multiple Choice Questions

1. The *value added* of a producer is the
    (a) total amount for which all its products sell minus its change in inventories.
    (b) value of its total sales once externalities are accounted for.
    (c) value of its output minus the value of the inputs it purchases from other producers.
    (d) quality-adjusted amount of its total sales less any commissions paid.

2. The product approach to calculating GDP
    (a) adds together the market values of final goods and services produced by domestic and foreign-owned factors of production within the nation in some time period.
    (b) includes the market value of goods and services produced by households for their own consumption but excludes the value of the underground economy.
    (c) is superior to the income approach because, unlike the income approach, it gives us the real value of output.
    (d) adds together the market values of final goods, intermediate goods, and goods added to inventories.

3. The A company collects bushels of wild berries, which it sells for $2 million to the B company to be made into jam. The B company's wild berry jam is sold for a total of $6 million. What is the total contribution to the country's GDP from companies A and B?
    (a) $2 million
    (b) $4 million
    (c) $6 million
    (d) $8 million

4. The fundamental identity of national income accounting tells us that
    (a) total production = total income = total expenditure.
    (b) total production = total income – total expenditure.
    (c) total production = total income + total expenditure.
    (d) total production < total income + total expenditure.

5. One problem with using market values to measure GDP is that
    (a) you cannot compare completely heterogeneous goods by using their dollar values.
    (b) some useful goods and services are not sold in markets.
    (c) prices for some goods change every year.
    (d) market values of exported goods are usually priced in foreign currencies.

6. Unlike final goods and services, intermediate goods and services
    (a) are purchased by businesses.
    (b) are purchased by government.
    (c) are not exported.
    (d) are completely used up in the current time period.

7. Underground activities in the economy are
   (a) excluded from measurements of the GDP because they are not beneficial to the nation.
   (b) excluded from measurements of GDP because there is no way of measuring them.
   (c) included in GDP if legal and excluded from GDP if illegal.
   (d) estimated and included in measurements of GDP.

8. Capital goods are
   (a) not counted in GDP as final goods.
   (b) not used to produce other goods.
   (c) used up in the same period that they are produced.
   (d) goods used to produce other goods.

9. Beautiful Boating purchases five new boats at $200,000 each to rent to vacationing fishermen. The firm sells its old boats to the public for $500,000. The net increase in GDP of these transactions was
   (a) $500,000.
   (b) $1,000,000.
   (c) $1,250,000.
   (d) $1,500,000.

10. Suppose Toyota built a new automobile plant in Mexico using Japanese management practices, American capital, and Mexican labor. Which of the following statements would be true?
    (a) The portion of output contributed by American capital would be included in American GDP.
    (b) The portion of output contributed by Japanese management would be included in both Japanese GNP and GDP.
    (c) The portion of output contributed by Japanese management would be included in neither Japanese GNP nor GDP.
    (d) The portion of output contributed by Mexican labor would be included in both Mexican GNP and GDP.

11. If $C = \$250$, $I = \$75$, $G = \$50$, $NX = \$20$, and $NFP = \$5$, what is GNP?
    (a) $405
    (b) $400
    (c) $395
    (d) $390

12. In using the expenditure approach to GNP, consumption includes
    (a) all final and intermediate goods consumed by domestic households and firms.
    (b) all final and intermediate goods consumed by domestic households produced at home, but not those produced abroad.
    (c) all final goods consumed by domestic households produced at home, but not those produced abroad.
    (d) all final goods consumed by domestic households produced at home and abroad.

13. Business fixed investment includes purchases of
    (a) capital equipment and structures.
    (b) land and energy.
    (c) long-term bonds.
    (d) inventories.

14. To calculate national income, we add compensation of employees, proprietor's income, rental income of persons, corporate profits, net interest, business current transfer payments, current surplus of government enterprises, and
    (a) statistical discrepancy.
    (b) net national product.
    (c) depreciation.
    (d) taxes on production and imports.

15. National income is equal to
    (a) GNP minus depreciation.
    (b) net national product minus statistical discrepancy.
    (c) GNP minus depreciation and taxes on production and imports.
    (d) net national product minus taxes on production and imports and employer contributions to Social Security.

16. Monica grows coconuts and catches fish. Last year she harvested 1,500 coconuts and 600 fish. She values one fish as worth three coconuts. She gave Rachel 300 coconuts and 100 fish for helping her to harvest coconuts and catch fish, all of which were consumed by Rachel. Monica set aside 200 fish to help with next year's harvest. In terms of fish, consumption would equal
    (a) 700 fish.
    (b) 900 fish.
    (c) 1,100 fish.
    (d) 2,700 fish.

17. Private saving is defined as
    (a) private disposable income minus consumption.
    (b) net national product minus consumption.
    (c) private disposable income minus consumption plus interest.
    (d) private disposable income minus consumption plus interest plus transfer payments.

18. Which of the following equations describes a government budget deficit?
    (a) $T - TR - INT < G$
    (b) $T - TR - INT > G$
    (c) $T + TR + INT < G$
    (d) $T + TR + INT > G$

19. If a local government collects taxes of $250,000 has $175,000 of government consumption expenditures, makes transfer payments of $75,000 and has no interest payments or investment, its budget would
    (a) show a surplus of $75,000.
    (b) show a surplus of $50,000.
    (c) be in balance with neither a surplus nor a deficit.
    (d) show a deficit of $75,000.

20. The government budget surplus equals
    (a) government purchases plus transfers.
    (b) government receipts minus outlays.
    (c) government outlays minus receipts.
    (d) government purchases minus transfers.

21. Private saving is $1,071.8 billion, investment is $1,287.2 billion, and the current account balance is –$135.4 billion. From the uses-of-saving identity, how much is government saving?
    (a) –$350.8 billion
    (b) –$80.0 billion
    (c) $80.0 billion
    (d) $350.8 billion

22. National saving is $717.8 billion, investment is $796.5 billion, and private saving is $986.9 billion. How much is the current account balance?
    (a) $269.1 billion
    (b) $78.7 billion
    (c) –$78.7 billion
    (d) –$269.1 billion

23. If the government deficit is $139 billion, gross private domestic investment is $633 billion, the current account balance is $188 billion, consumption spending is $1,504 billion, and government purchases equal $654 billion, then national saving equals
    (a) $404 billion.
    (b) $543 billion.
    (c) $682 billion.
    (d) $821 billion.

24. Saving is a _____ variable, and wealth is a _____ variable.
    (a) stock; flow
    (b) stock; stock
    (c) flow; flow
    (d) flow; stock

25. National wealth is the value of

(a) domestic and foreign physical and financial assets.

(b) domestic physical and financial assets.

(c) domestic physical assets plus net foreign physical and financial assets.

(d) net foreign assets.

26. Use the following information to answer this question about the country of Polity:

Good	Year 1 Quantity	Year 1 Price	Year 2 Quantity	Year 2 Price
Guns	4000	$4	4625	$6
Butter	5000	$3	5200	$2

Using Year 1 as the base year, what is the percent change in real output from Year 1 to Year 2?

(a) 8%

(b) 10%

(c) 12%

(d) 15%

27. Nominal GDP in 1970 was $1,015.5 billion, and in 1980 it was $2,732.0 billion. The GDP deflator is 42.0 for 1970 and 85.7 for 1980, where 1982 is the base year. Calculate the percent change in real GDP in the decade from 1970 to 1980. Round off to the nearest percentage point.

(a) 32%

(b) 104%

(c) 132%

(d) 169%

28. The consumer price index (CPI) is 311.1 for 1994 when using 1967 as the base year (1967 = 100). Now suppose we switch and use 1994 as the base year (1994 = 100). What is the CPI for 1967 with the new base year?

(a) 20.2

(b) 32.1

(c) 48.4

(d) 56.2

29. In the 1990s, the saving rate of wealthy households (those in the top 20% of the income distribution) _____ and the saving rate of poorer households _____.

(a) rose; fell

(b) rose; rose

(c) fell; rose

(d) fell; fell

30. If the nominal interest rate on a one-year loan was 7%, the expected inflation rate over the year was 3% and the actual inflation rate over the year turned out to be 3.5%, then the real interest rate equals

(a) 6.5%.

(b) 4.0%.

(c) 3.75%.

(d) 3.5%.

■ Review Questions

1. Identify and briefly describe the three approaches to measuring GDP.

2. State the fundamental identity of national income accounting.

3. Give an example of each of the following:
    (1) consumer durables
    (2) nondurable goods
    (3) services

4. Approximately what share of GDP do personal consumption expenditures represent?

5. Give an example of each of the following types of business fixed investment:
    (1) equipment
    (2) structures

6. Briefly describe the role that inventory investment plays in the income-expenditure identity.

7. Why are net exports added into the expenditure calculation of GDP?

8. How are net exports, net factor payments from abroad, and the current account balance related?

9. State the "uses-of-saving identity" and tell what it means.

10. What is chain-weighted real GDP? Why did the government switch to using chain-weighted indexes?

11. Does the CPI provide an accurate estimate of the cost of living? Discuss.

■ Numerical Problems

1. Use the following data to calculate national output using the expenditure approach and the income approach for the economy, and show that GDP has the same value when calculated by either approach. (Assume no statistical discrepancy.)

Consumption	$4,480 billion	Compensation to employees	$4,200 billion
Investment	980	Proprietors' income	420
Government purchases	1,400	Rental income of persons	70
Net exports	140	Corporate profits	490
		Net interest	420
		Taxes on production and imports	650
		Business current transfer payments	30
		Current surplus of government enterprises	20
		Consumption of fixed capital	770
		Factor income received from rest of world	140
		Payments of factor income to rest of world	70

2. Pete the Pizza Man produced $87,000 worth of pizzas in the past year. He paid $39,000 to employees, paid $11,000 for vegetables and other ingredients, and paid $5,000 in taxes. He began the year with ingredient inventories valued at $1,000 and ended the year with inventories valued at $2,000. What was Pete's (and his employees') total contribution to GDP this year?

3. Use the following data to calculate private saving, government saving, and national saving.

GDP	$7,000 billion
Net factor payments from abroad	−70
Consumption	4,480
Government purchases	1,400
Interest payments on government debt	210
Taxes	2,450
Transfers	1,050

4. For 2004 an economy had the following nominal quantities (in billions of dollars) and price indexes (1997 = 100) for each category of expenditure:

	Nominal Value	Price Index
Consumption	4,139.9	123.9
Fixed investment	789.1	108.6
Government purchases	1,131.8	119.7
Exports	640.5	110.8
Imports	670.1	109.6
Inventory investment	7.3	112.3

(a) Calculate the real quantity for each category (to one decimal point).

(b) Calculate nominal and real GDP (you may assume the real components add up to real GDP).

(c) Find the implicit price deflator (1997 = 100).

5. Nominal GDP in a country was $8,759.9 billion in 2003 and $9,254.6 billion in 2004. The GDP deflator was 102.86 for 2003 and 104.37 for 2004.

(a) What is the growth rate of nominal GDP between 2003 and 2004?

(b) What is the inflation rate from 2003 to 2004?

(c) What is the growth rate of real GDP from 2003 to 2004?

6. The country of Old Jersey produces milk and butter, and it has published the following macroeconomic data, where quantities are in gallons and prices are dollars per gallon:

	Year 1		Year 2	
Good	Quantity	Price	Quantity	Price
Milk	500	$2	900	$3
Butter	2,000	$1	3,000	$2

What was the growth rate of real GDP between Year 1 and Year 2? What was the inflation rate (using Year 1 as the base year)?

7.   If the CPI was 125 one year ago and increased to 150 today, what would be the inflation rate over the past year?

8.   Calculate the real interest rate if the nominal interest rate is 8% and the inflation rate is 5%.

■ Analytical Questions

1.   Would an increase in goods imported from a foreign subsidiary of a U.S. multinational firm, produced mostly with U.S.-owned capital and labor, increase GDP for the United States? Briefly explain.

2.   Could GDP increase while GNP declined? Briefly explain.

3.   If net exports were equal to 1% of a nation's GDP, is it fair to say that international trade is unimportant? Briefly explain.

■ Answers

Multiple Choice

1. c	7. d	13. a	19. c	25. c
2. a	8. d	14. d	20. b	26. b
3. c	9. b	15. b	21. c	27. a
4. a	10. d	16. b	22. c	28. b
5. b	11. b	17. a	23. d	29. c
6. d	12. d	18. a	24. d	30. d

Review Questions

1.   The three approaches to measuring GDP are called the product approach, the income approach, and the expenditure approach. The product approach adds together the market values of the goods and services produced within the borders of the nation's domestic economy during a specified time period (e.g., one-quarter of a year or one year). The income approach adds together the compensation to employees, interest income, rental income of persons, proprietors' income, and corporate profits earned from domestic production before taxes and depreciation, less net factor payments from abroad. The expenditure approach adds together consumption, investment, government purchases, and net exports to measure spending on all domestically produced goods and services.

2.   The fundamental identity of national income accounting is total production = total income = total expenditure.

3.   (1) Consumer durables are long-lived consumer goods, such as family automobiles, refrigerators, lawn mowers, home computers, and household furniture.
     (2) Nondurable goods are short-lived consumer goods, such as food, clothing, fuel, cosmetics, and prescription drugs.
     (3) Services include such things as education, medical services, legal advice, accounting, travel, and restaurant and hotel services.

4.   Personal consumption expenditures currently represent approximately two-thirds of GDP for the United States.

5. (1) Equipment includes tools and machines, such as harvesters for farms, printing presses for newspaper businesses, tractors for construction companies, cash registers for retail stores, office equipment, furniture, company-owned vehicles, and so on.

    (2) Structures include construction of facilities such as factory buildings, warehouses, retail store buildings, and so on.

6. The income-expenditure identity states that $Y = C + I + G + NX$. This equation suggests that all the goods and services produced are sold. If all the goods and services produced are not sold during the year, inventory investment increases by the amount of the unsold goods. From an accounting viewpoint the unsold goods are recorded as being sold to the firms that produced them, and they are counted as investment.

7. Net exports = exports – imports. Exports are added to the expenditure calculation of GDP because they represent foreign spending on goods and services produced in the domestic economy. Imports are subtracted because they were included in the figures for consumption, investment, or government purchases. Because GDP represents how much is produced by a country, we add exports to $C + I + G$ to represent goods produced domestically and sold to foreigners, and we subtract imports from $C + I + G$ because they represent goods produced abroad and purchased by domestic consumers, firms, or governments. So, total production equals $C + I + G + NX$.

8. $NX + NFP = CA$.

9. The following equation is the "uses-of-saving identity": $S_{pvt} = I + (-S_{govt}) + CA$. It means that private saving can be used for domestic investment, financing the government deficit, or investing abroad.

10. Chain-weighting methods calculate the growth of real output by averaging growth rates of real GDP using both the prior year and the current year as the base year. The BEA switched to a chain-weighted index primarily because there's no clear "right" year to choose as the base year. Also, chain weighting avoids the problem of historical growth rates being revised when the base year changes, as had been the case before 1996.

11. The CPI overstates increases in the cost of living because of changes in the quality of goods and services and because of substitution bias.

Numerical Problems

1. In the expenditure approach, national output is $Y = C + I + G + NX$, which totals $7,000 billion. The income approach is calculated by adding all the payments received by domestic resource suppliers (the first nine numbers in the last column), then subtracting the $70 billion of net factor payments from abroad ($140 billion factor income received minus $70 billion payments to the rest of the world), which also totals $7,000 billion.

2. $87,000 –$11,000 paid for intermediate goods + $1,000 change in inventories = $77,000.

3. The values of these variables can be calculated by plugging the appropriate data values into the following equations (where Y = GDP).

$$S_{pvt} = (Y + NFP - T + TR + INT) - C = \$1{,}260 \text{ billion.}$$

$$S_{govt} = (T - TR - INT) - G = -\$210 \text{ billion.}$$

$$S = S_{pvt} + S_{govt} = Y + NFP - C - G = \$1{,}050 \text{ billion.}$$

4. (a) Real C = 4,139.9/1.239 = 3,341.3; real fixed I = 789.1/1.086 = 726.6; real G = 1,131.8/1.197 = 945.5; real exports = 640.5/1.108 = 578.1; real imports = 670.1/1.096 = 611.4; real II = 7.3/1.123 = 6.5.

    (b) Add up the nominal quantities (but subtract imports) to get 6,038.5. Add up the real quantities (but subtract imports) in part (a) to get 4,986.6.

    (c) The implicit deflator is nominal GDP/real GDP × 100 = 6,038.5/4,986.6 × 100 = 121.1.

5. (a) 9,254.6/8,759.9 × 100 = 5.6%

    (b) [(104.37/102.86) − 1] × 100 = 1.5%

    (c) Real GDP (2003) = 8,759.9/1.0286 = 8,516.3

    Real GDP (2004) = 9,254.6/1.0437 = 8,867.1

    Growth rate = [(8,867.1/8,516.3) − 1] × 100% = 4.1%

    Note that the growth rate of nominal GDP (5.6%) equals the inflation rate (1.5%) plus the growth rate of real GDP (4.1%).

6. Real GDP (Year 1) = Year 1 quantities at Year 1 prices = (500 × $2) + (2,000 × $1) = $3,000

    Real GDP (Year 2) = Year 2 quantities at Year 1 prices = (900 × $2) + (3,000 × $1) = $4,800

    Growth rate of real GDP = [(4,800/3,000) − 1] × 100% = 60%

    Nominal GDP (Year 2) = Year 2 quantities at Year 2 prices = (900 × $3) + (3,000 × $2) = $8,700

    GDP deflator (Year 2) = (8,700/4,800) × 100 = 181.3

    Inflation rate = [(181.3/100) − 1] × 100% = 81.3%

7. If the CPI increased from 125 to 150, the inflation rate would be [(150 − 125)/125] × 100% = 20%.

8. Real interest rate = nominal interest rate − inflation rate = 8% − 5% = 3%.

Analytical Questions

1. No. Goods produced abroad, including goods produced with U.S.-owned factors of production, are not part of the GDP of the United States.

2. Yes. GDP = GNP − NFP, so GDP would increase if a decline in NFP exceeded the decline in GNP.

3. Even though net exports represent just 1% of GDP, net exports equal exports minus imports. A better measure of the importance of international trade would be to examine exports or imports separately. Exports and imports might each be a substantial fraction of GDP. So international trade in goods and services could be an important component of the economy, even though net exports aren't large.

Chapter 3
Productivity, Output, and Employment

■ Introduction

This chapter's main goal is to provide the background of a theoretical model of the economy that is developed throughout the textbook. The discussions of the labor market and production function developed in this chapter are the basic building blocks of everything that comes later. Section 3.1 begins the chapter by introducing the production function—the main determinant of output. Then, Section 3.2 discusses the demand for labor, showing how firms decide on how much labor to use based on the wage and the marginal product of labor. Section 3.3 then shows how people decide how much labor to supply. Demand and supply together determine equilibrium in the labor market, as Section 3.4 discusses. The section also shows how labor-market equilibrium then determines the economy's rate of full-employment output and what happens when there's a change in either the demand or supply of labor. Section 3.5 provides an introduction to unemployment—how it's measured, how long it lasts, and why it occurs. Finally, Section 3.6 shows the relationship between unemployment and output via Okun's law.

This is a long and very important chapter. It's the first chapter in which the main analytic device used throughout the chapter appears—a diagram in which equilibrium is found where two curves cross. You'll find the same basic diagram that appears here for the labor market also appears in other chapters for other markets. So be sure you understand why the labor-demand and labor-supply curves have the slopes they do, what shifts them, and how equilibrium is determined. You'll see a similar pattern in many other places in the textbook.

If you have trouble understanding some of the math in the chapter, be sure to work many of the numerical problems in this study guide and in the textbook. The more you work with things like calculating output using a production function or using Okun's law to determine the relationship between output and unemployment, the more comfortable and confident you'll be.

■ Outline

I. **How Much Does the Economy Produce? The Production Function (Sec. 3.1)**

    A) Factors of production

        1. Capital (K)

        2. Labor (N)

        3. Others (raw materials, land, energy)

        4. Productivity of factors depends on technology and management

    B) The production function

        1. $Y = AF(K, N)$ (3.1)

        2. Parameter A is "total factor productivity" (the effectiveness with which capital and labor are used)

C) Application: The production function of the U.S. economy and U.S. productivity growth
  1. Cobb-Douglas production function works well for U.S. economy:

$$Y = AK^{0.3}N^{0.7} \qquad\qquad (3.2)$$

  2. Data for U.S. economy—Table 3.1
  3. Productivity growth calculated using production function
    a. Productivity moves sharply from year to year
    b. Productivity grew slowly in the 1980s and the first half of the 1990s, but increased in the second half of the 1990s
D) The shape of the production function
  1. Two main properties of production functions
    a. Slopes upward: more of any input produces more output
    b. Slope becomes flatter as input rises: diminishing marginal product as input increases
  2. Graph production function (Y vs. one input; hold other input and A fixed)
    a. Marginal product of capital, $MPK = \Delta Y/\Delta K$ (Figure 3.1; Key Diagram 1; like text Figure 3.2)

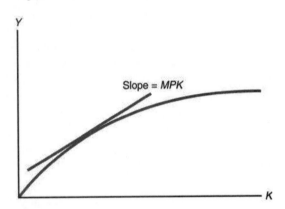

Figure 3.1

    (1) Equal to slope of production function graph (Y vs. K)
    (2) MPK always positive
    (3) Diminishing marginal productivity of capital—MPK declines as K rises
    b. Marginal product of labor, $MPN = \Delta Y/\Delta N$ (Figure 3.2; like text Figure 3.3)

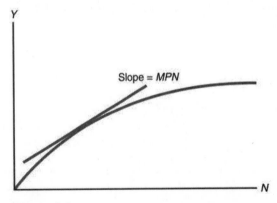

Figure 3.2

        (1) Equal to slope of production function graph (Y vs. N)
        (2) *MPN* always positive
        (3) Diminishing marginal productivity of labor

E) Supply shocks
    1. Supply shock = productivity shock = a change in an economy's production function
    2. Supply shocks affect the amount of output that can be produced for a given amount of inputs
    3. Shocks may be positive (increasing output) or negative (decreasing output)
    4. Examples: weather, inventions and innovations, government regulations, oil prices
    5. Supply shocks shift graph of production function (Figure 3.3; like text Figure 3.4)

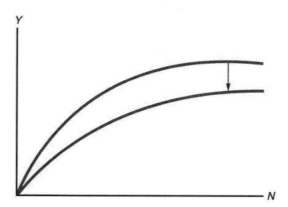

Figure 3.3

      a. Negative (adverse) shock: Usually slope of production function decreases at each level
        of input (for example, if shock causes parameter A to decline)
      b. Positive shock: Usually slope of production function increases at each level of output
        (for example, if parameter A increases)

II.   The Demand for Labor (Sec. 3.2)

A) How much labor do firms want to use?
    1. Assumptions
      a. Hold capital stock fixed—short-run analysis
      b. Workers are all alike
      c. Labor market is competitive
      d. Firms maximize profits

2. Analysis at the margin: costs and benefits of hiring one extra worker (Figure 3.4; like text Figure 3.5)

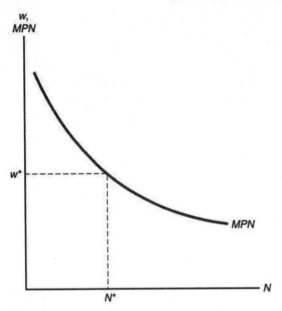

Figure 3.4

a. If real wage (w) > marginal product of labor (MPN), the firm is paying the marginal worker more than the worker produces, so the firm should reduce the number of workers to increase profits

b. If $w < MPN$, the marginal worker produces more than he or she is being paid, so the firm should increase the number of workers to increase profits

c. Firms' profits are highest when $w = MPN$

B) The marginal product of labor and labor demand: an example

1. Example: The Clip Joint—setting the nominal wage equal to the marginal revenue product of labor

$$MRPN = P \times MPN \tag{3.3}$$

2. $W = MRPN$ is the same condition as $w = MPN$, because $W = P \times w$ and $MRPN = P \times MPN$

3. A change in the wage

a. Begin at equilibrium where $W = MRPN$

b. A rise in the wage rate means $W > MRPN$, unless N is reduced so the $MRPN$ rises

c. A decline in the wage rate means $W < MRPN$, unless N rises so the $MRPN$ falls

C) The marginal product of labor and the labor demand curve

1. Labor demand curve shows relationship between the real wage rate and the quantity of labor demanded

2. It is the same as the MPN curve, because $w = MPN$ at equilibrium

3. So the labor demand curve is downward sloping; firms want to hire less labor, the higher the real wage

D) Factors that shift the labor demand curve

    1. Note: A change in the wage causes a movement along the labor demand curve, not a shift of the curve

    2. Supply shocks: Beneficial supply shock raises *MPN*, so shifts labor demand curve to the right; opposite for adverse supply shock

    3. Size of capital stock: Higher capital stock raises *MPN*, so shifts labor demand curve to the right; opposite for lower capital stock

E) Aggregate labor demand (Figure 3.5)

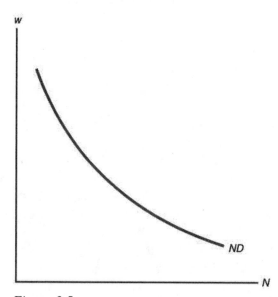

Figure 3.5

    1. Aggregate labor demand is the sum of all firms' labor demand

    2. Same factors (supply shocks, size of capital stock) that shift firms' labor demand cause shifts in aggregate labor demand

III.   The Supply of Labor (Sec. 3.3)

A) Supply of labor is determined by individuals

    1. Aggregate supply of labor is sum of individuals' labor supply

    2. Labor supply of individuals depends on labor-leisure choice

B) The income-leisure trade-off

    1. Utility depends on consumption and leisure

    2. Need to compare costs and benefits of working another day

      a. Costs: Loss of leisure time

      b. Benefits: More consumption, because income is higher

    3. If benefits of working another day exceed costs, work another day

    4. Keep working additional days until benefits equal costs

C) Real wages and labor supply
  1. An increase in the real wage has offsetting income and substitution effects
      a. Substitution effect of a higher real wage: Higher real wage encourages work, because the reward for working is higher
      b. Income effect of a higher real wage: Higher real wage increases income for the same amount of work time, and with higher income, the person can afford more leisure, so will supply less labor
  2. A pure substitution effect: a one-day rise in the real wage
     A temporary real wage increase has just a pure substitution effect, because the effect on wealth is negligible
  3. A pure income effect: winning the lottery
      a. Winning the lottery doesn't have a substitution effect, because it doesn't affect the reward for working
      b. But winning the lottery makes a person wealthier, so a person will both consume more goods and take more leisure; this is a pure income effect
  4. The substitution effect and the income effect together: a long-term increase in the real wage
      a. The reward to working is greater: a substitution effect toward more work
      b. But with a higher wage, a person doesn't need to work as much: an income effect toward less work
      c. The longer the high wage is expected to last, the stronger the income effect; thus labor supply will increase by less or decrease by more than for a temporary reduction in the real wage
  5. Empirical evidence on real wages and labor supply
      a. Overall result: Labor supply increases with a temporary rise in the real wage
      b. Labor supply falls with a permanent increase in the real wage

D) The labor supply curve (Figure 3.6; like text Figure 3.7)

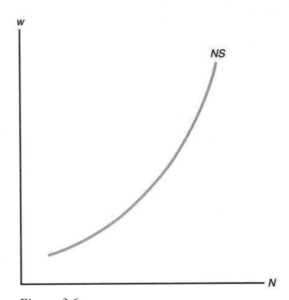

Figure 3.6

  1. Increase in the current real wage should raise quantity of labor supplied
  2. Labor supply curve relates quantity of labor supplied to real wage
  3. Labor supply curve slopes upward because higher wage encourages people to work more

E) Factors that shift the labor supply curve
  1. Wealth: Higher wealth reduces labor supply (shifts labor supply curve to the left)
  2. Expected future real wage: Higher expected future real wage is like an increase in wealth, so reduces labor supply (shifts labor supply curve to the left)

F) Aggregate labor supply
  1. Aggregate labor supply rises when current real wage rises
     a. Some people work more hours
     b. Other people enter labor force
     c. Result: Aggregate labor supply curve slopes upward
  2. Factors increasing labor supply
     a. Decrease in wealth
     b. Decrease in expected future real wage
     c. Increase in working-age population (higher birth rate, immigration)
     d. Increase in labor force participation (increased female labor participation, elimination of mandatory retirement)

G) Application: comparing U.S. and European labor markets
  1. Unemployment rates were similar in the U.S. and Europe in 1970s and 1980s, but are higher in Europe since then (Fig. 3.9)
  2. Research: three main reasons for higher unemployment rates in Europe (generous unemployment insurance systems, high tax rates, government policies that interfere with labor markets)
  3. European countries: more generous unemployment insurance
     a. Replacement rate = fraction of lost wages that a worker receives; higher in Europe than U.S.
     b. European workers get unemployment benefits for longer, so have incentive to remain unemployed
     c. The more turbulent economy of 1980s and 1990s led European job losers to take advantage of unemployment insurance system
     d. Ireland and Netherlands reformed their unemployment insurance systems, and unemployment rates fell significantly
  4. High income-tax rates in Europe also reduce incentive to work
  5. Government interference in labor markets in Europe affects demand for labor and sometimes supply of labor

IV. Labor Market Equilibrium (Sec. 3.4)

A) Equilibrium: Labor supply equals labor demand (Figure 3.7; Key Diagram 2; like text Figure 3.11)

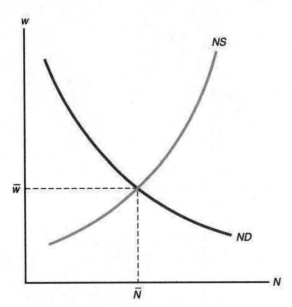

Figure 3.7

1. Classical model of the labor market—real wage adjusts quickly (later, in Chapter 11, look at other models of labor market in which real wage does not adjust quickly)
2. Determines full-employment level of employment $\overline{N}$ and market-clearing real wage $\overline{w}$
3. Factors that shift labor supply or labor demand affect $\overline{N}$ and $\overline{w}$
4. Problem with classical model: can't study unemployment

B) Full-employment output

1. Full-employment output = potential output = $\overline{Y}$ = level of output when labor market is in equilibrium
2. $\overline{Y} = AF(K, \overline{N})$ (3.4)
3. $\overline{Y}$ affected by changes in $\overline{N}$ or production function (example: supply shock, Fig. 3.11)

C) Application: output, employment, and the real wage during oil price shocks
1. Sharp oil price increases in 1973–74, 1979–80, 1990
2. Adverse supply shock—lowers labor demand, employment, the real wage, and the full-employment level of output
3. All three cases: U.S. economy entered recessions

D) Application: technical change and wage inequality
1. Two important features of U.S. real wages since 1970
    a. Slowdown in growth of real wages
    b. Increased wage inequality

2. Slowdown in productivity growth combined with increased labor force participation has kept real wages from rising as much as they did before 1970

3. Skill-biased technical change (such as computerization) has increased real wages of highly educated workers, but reduced real wages of unskilled workers (shown graphically)

V.   Unemployment (Sec. 3.5)

A) Measuring unemployment

1. Categories: employed, unemployed, not in the labor force

2. Labor Force = Employed + Unemployed

3. Unemployment Rate = Unemployed/Labor Force

4. Table 3.4 shows current data

5. Participation Rate = Labor Force/Adult Population

6. Employment Ratio = Employed/Adult Population

B) Changes in employment status

1. Flows between categories (Fig. 3.14)

2. Discouraged workers: people who have become so discouraged by lack of success at finding a job that they stop searching

C) How long are people unemployed?

1. Most unemployment spells are of short duration

a. Unemployment spell = period of time an individual is continuously unemployed

b. Duration = length of unemployment spell

2. Most unemployed people on a given date are experiencing unemployment spells of long duration

3. Reconciling 1 and 2—numerical example:

a. Labor force = 100; on the first day of every month, 2 workers become unemployed for 1 month each; on the first day of every year, 4 workers become unemployed for 1 year each

b. Result: 28 spells of unemployment during year; 24 short (one month), 4 long (one year); so most spells are short

c. At any date, unemployment = six; four have long spells (one year), two have short spells (one month); so most unemployed people on a given date have long spells

D) Why there are always unemployed people

1. Frictional unemployment

a. Search activity of firms and workers due to heterogeneity

b. Matching process takes time

2. Structural unemployment

a. Chronically unemployed: workers who are unemployed a large part of the time

b. Structural unemployment: the long-term and chronic unemployment that exists even when the economy is not in a recession

c. One cause: Lack of skills prevents some workers from finding long-term employment

d. Another cause: Reallocation of workers out of shrinking industries or depressed regions; matching takes a long time

      3. The natural rate of unemployment

        a. $\bar{u}$ = natural rate of unemployment; when output and employment are at full-employment levels

        b. $\bar{u}$ = frictional + structural unemployment

        c. Cyclical unemployment: difference between actual unemployment rate and natural rate of unemployment $(u - \bar{u})$

      4. In touch with the macroeconomy: labor market data

        a. BLS employment report

          (1) Household survey: unemployment, employment

          (2) Establishment survey: jobs

VI. Relating Output and Unemployment: Okun's Law (Sec. 3.6)

  A) Relationship between output (relative to full-employment output) and cyclical unemployment

  B) $(\bar{Y} - Y)/\bar{Y} = 2(u - \bar{u})$ (3.5)

  C) Why is the Okun's Law coefficient 2, and not 1?

      1. Other things happen when cyclical unemployment rises: Labor force falls, hours of work per worker decline, average productivity of labor declines

      2. Result is 2% reduction in output associated with 1 percentage point increase in unemployment rate

  D) Alternative formulation if average growth rate of full-employment output is 3%:

      1. $\Delta Y/Y = 3 - 2\,\Delta u$ (3.6)

      2. Fig. 3.15 shows U.S. data

■ Multiple Choice Questions

1. Equilibrium in the labor market determines

  (a) inflation and employment.

  (b) inflation and the real wage.

  (c) the real wage and employment.

  (d) productivity and employment.

2. Suppose the economy's production function is $Y = AK^{0.3}N^{0.7}$. If $K = 2000$, $N = 100$, and $A = 1$, then $Y = 246$. If A rises by 10%, and K and N are unchanged, by how much does Y increase?

  (a) 5%

  (b) 10%

  (c) 15%

  (d) 20%

3. Suppose the economy's production function is $Y = AK^{0.3}N^{0.7}$. If $K = 2,000$, $N = 100$, and $A = 1$, then $Y = 246$. If K and N each increase by 5%, and A is unchanged, by how much does Y increase?
    (a) 5%
    (b) 10%
    (c) 15%
    (d) 20%

4. Suppose the economy's production function is $Y = AK^{0.3}N^{0.7}$. If $K = 2,000$, $N = 100$, and $A = 1$, then $Y = 246$. If K increases by 10%, and A and N are unchanged, by how much does Y increase?
    (a) 30%
    (b) 10%
    (c) 6%
    (d) 3%

5. An increase in total factor productivity will
    (a) increase the unemployment rate.
    (b) increase the full-employment level of output.
    (c) lower the rate of return to capital.
    (d) shift the production function down.

6. In the production function $Y = AF(K, N)$, A is
    (a) labor productivity.
    (b) total factor productivity.
    (c) capital productivity.
    (d) the marginal productivity of capital.

7. In a graph of the production function relating output to capital, it is *not* true that
    (a) labor supply increases as capital increases.
    (b) the marginal product of capital can be measured as the slope of the production function.
    (c) the marginal product of capital falls as the capital stock increases.
    (d) the shape of the production function reflects diminishing marginal productivity.

8. Because of diminishing marginal productivity
    (a) the labor supply curve is not vertical.
    (b) nominal wages are sticky in a downward direction.
    (c) the labor demand curve is negatively sloped.
    (d) households save only a small share of their income.

9. The marginal product of labor
    (a) equals the output produced per unit of labor employed.
    (b) decreases as more capital is added to the production process.
    (c) depends on the product price.
    (d) declines as more labor is added to the production process.

10. In the diagram of the production function, a beneficial supply shock is shown by
    (a) an upward shift in the production function.
    (b) a movement up along the production function.
    (c) a downward shift in the production function.
    (d) an increase in the convexity of the curve.

11. The real wage
    (a) is the nominal wage divided by the price level.
    (b) automatically increases with the cost of living.
    (c) is the price level divided by the nominal wage.
    (d) is the nominal wage multiplied by the price level.

12. Which of the following statements is true?
    (a) Changes in the total capital stock of the economy and in the amount of labor that firms employ occur quickly.
    (b) Changes in the total capital stock of the economy and in the amount of labor that firms employ occur slowly.
    (c) Changes in the total capital stock of the economy occur slowly, while changes in the amount of labor that firms employ occur quickly.
    (d) Changes in the total capital stock of the economy occur quickly, while changes in the amount of labor that firms employ occur slowly.

13. A favorable supply shock would
    (a) shift the production function up and decrease marginal products at every level of employment.
    (b) shift the production function down and decrease marginal products at every level of employment.
    (c) shift the production function down and increase marginal products at every level of employment.
    (d) shift the production function up and increase marginal products at every level of employment.

14. The Disk-o Company has the following production function:

Number of Workers	Number of Disk-os Produced
0	0
1	10
2	19
3	26
4	31
5	34

If the company hires 3 workers, which of the following could be the real wage rate?
    (a) 2
    (b) 4
    (c) 6
    (d) 8

15. The marginal product of labor (measured in units of output) for New Age Nirvana is given by

$$MPN = A(200 - N)$$

where A measures productivity and N is the number of labor hours used in production. Suppose the price of output is $3 per unit and $A = 2.0$. What will be the demand for labor if the nominal wage is $30?

(a) 170
(b) 185
(c) 190
(d) 195

16. If a country's working-age population declines and its wealth increases, then the labor supply curve
(a) shifts to the left if the effect of the change in wealth is bigger than the effect of the change in the working-age population.
(b) shifts to the right if the effect of the change in wealth is bigger than the effect of the change in the working-age population.
(c) shifts to the left.
(d) shifts to the right.

17. If Jeff's wage rate rises, he decides to work more hours. From this we can infer that
(a) for Jeff, the substitution effect is greater than the income effect.
(b) for Jeff, the substitution effect is equal to the income effect.
(c) for Jeff, the substitution effect is less than the income effect.
(d) Jeff is a nitwit.

18. Suppose the banking industry were to fail, leaving the federal government (through its deposit guarantee programs) to pay for trillions of dollars in losses; they do so by imposing a tax of 50% on all individuals' wealth. What happens to current employment and the real wage rate?
(a) Both employment and the real wage rate would increase.
(b) Both employment and the real wage rate would decrease.
(c) Employment would increase and the real wage would decrease.
(d) Employment would decrease and the real wage would increase.

19. Suppose the marginal product of labor for unskilled labor is given by

$$MPN = 200 - 0.5N$$

The supply of unskilled labor is given by $100 + 4w$. The government imposes a minimum wage of 60. How much unemployment will this create among unskilled labor?
(a) 0
(b) 60
(c) 80
(d) 100

20. A beneficial supply shock increases labor demand. What happens to current employment and the real wage rate?
    (a) Both employment and the real wage rate would increase.
    (b) Both employment and the real wage rate would decrease.
    (c) Employment would increase and the real wage would decrease.
    (d) Employment would decrease and the real wage would increase.

21. Suppose the marginal product of labor is given by

$$MPN = 200 - 0.5N$$

The supply of labor is originally given by $100 + 4w$. If an increase in wealth causes the supply of labor to shift to $70 + 4w$, by how much does the real wage change?
    (a) decreases by 5
    (b) decreases by 10
    (c) increases by 10
    (d) increases by 5

22. Discouraged workers are discouraged because
    (a) their employers continue to underpay them.
    (b) they are working part-time, but they want full-time work.
    (c) they don't have jobs and are pessimistic about their chances of finding a suitable job.
    (d) their employers are too demanding.

23. In the United States, the duration of most unemployment spells is
    (a) less than two weeks.
    (b) about two months or less.
    (c) approximately one year.
    (d) two or three years.

24. The type of unemployment for which the net economic costs are most likely to be small is
    (a) structural unemployment.
    (b) frictional unemployment.
    (c) chronic unemployment.
    (d) cyclical unemployment.

25. Most of the chronically unemployed workers in the U.S. economy are unemployed because
    (a) they are too old or too young to work.
    (b) they are too sick or too disabled to work.
    (c) they do not want to work; they would rather live on welfare.
    (d) they do not have the job skills and personal attributes that employers demand.

26. The kind of unemployment created by technological progress and by changes in competition is called
    (a) progressive unemployment.
    (b) competitive unemployment.
    (c) frictional unemployment.
    (d) structural unemployment.

27. What is the unemployment rate if there are 170 million people employed, 25 million people unemployed, and 35 million not in the labor force?
   (a) 14.7%
   (b) 13.7%
   (c) 12.8%
   (d) 10.9%

28. According to Okun's Law, if the natural rate of unemployment is 5% and the actual unemployment rate is 4%, what is the level of full employment output if output equals $10,125 billion?
   (a) $10,328 billion
   (b) $10,226 billion
   (c) $10,025 billion
   (d) $9,926 billion

29. Assuming that the growth rate of full-employment output is 3%, and that the actual unemployment rate fell 2 percentage points in the last year, Okun's Law predicts that output growth rate over the past year was
   (a) −1%.
   (b) 3%.
   (c) 5%.
   (d) 7%.

30. According to Okun's law, if output grew 7% and full-employment output rose 3%, what would be the change in the unemployment rate?
   (a) −4%
   (b) −2%
   (c) 2%
   (d) 4%

■ Review Questions

1. Why does the labor demand curve slope downward?

2. Identify two variables that shift the labor demand curve and state whether labor demand is positively related or negatively related to each of these variables.

3. Why does the labor supply curve slope upward?

4. Identify four variables that shift the labor supply curve and state whether labor supply is positively related or negatively related to each of these variables.

5. What are structural unemployment and frictional unemployment, and how do they differ? Does the duration of a typical unemployment spell depend on the type of unemployment? How does the natural rate of unemployment relate to structural and frictional unemployment?

6. State the growth rate form of Okun's Law and define the variables in the equation.

■ Numerical Problems

1. Using $Y = AK^{0.5}N^{0.5}$ as the production function for the national economy, calculate total factor productivity (A), where:

    (a) Y = \$4,878 billion, K = \$4,773 billion, and N = 117.9 million workers.

    (b) Y = \$4,821 billion, K = \$4,824 billion, and N = 116.9 million workers.

2. Suppose the production function is $Y = AK^{0.3}N^{0.7}$. Suppose in 1990, K = 1,000, N = 100, and A = 1. In 2000, capital and labor have doubled (so K = 2,000 and N = 200), while A has remained constant.

    (a) By what percentage did output grow from 1990 to 2000?

    (b) If total factor productivity had risen 10% instead of remaining, constant, and capital and labor doubled, by what percentage would output have grown from 1990 to 2000?

3. Suppose the natural rate of unemployment is 5%, with full-employment output of \$7,000 billion. Use Okun's Law to calculate the level of national output if the unemployment rate is:

    (a) 11%.

    (b) 4%.

4. In December 1996, the United States had a labor force of 135,022,000, employment of 127,855,000, and there were 66,614,000 people not in the labor force (all numbers rounded to the nearest 1,000).

    (a) Calculate the unemployment rate.

    (b) Calculate the participation rate.

    (c) Calculate the employment ratio.

■ Analytical Questions

1. What are the real effects on the labor market of a temporary beneficial supply shock that arises because of an increase in productivity?

2. Would a decrease in the capital stock create an increase in the level of employment? Why or why not?

■ Answers

Multiple Choice

1. c	7. a	13. d	19. b	25. d
2. b	8. c	14. c	20. a	26. d
3. a	9. d	15. d	21. d	27. c
4. d	10. a	16. c	22. c	28. d
5. b	11. a	17. a	23. b	29. d
6. b	12. c	18. c	24. b	30. b

Review Questions

1. The labor demand curve is the same as the marginal product of labor curve, because firms are willing to employ the amount of labor needed to equate the real wage and the marginal product of labor. The marginal product of labor declines as labor increases because of diminishing returns.

2. Two variables that shift labor demand are total factor productivity and the capital stock.

   (1) Labor demand is positively related to total factor productivity. A beneficial productivity shock will shift the labor demand curve to the right because it increases the marginal product of labor. An adverse productivity shock will decrease labor demand, shifting the curve to the left.

   (2) Labor demand is positively related to the capital stock. Increasing the capital stock will increase the demand for labor because it raises the marginal product of labor. A decline in the level of the capital stock will decrease labor demand, shifting the labor demand curve to the left.

3. The labor supply curve is positively sloped, indicating that more labor time will be supplied at a higher real wage. Along a given labor supply curve, an increase in the real wage increases the reward to working, which causes workers to increase the amount of labor time they are willing to work; as the real wage increases, workers substitute away from leisure and toward work.

4. Variables that shift the labor supply curve include wealth, the expected future real wage, the size of the working-age population, and the labor force participation rate.

   (1) Labor supply is negatively related to wealth. People who are wealthy don't want to work as much, so an increase in workers' wealth will reduce labor supply, shifting the labor supply curve to the left.

   (2) Labor supply is negatively related to workers' expected future real wage. An increase in the expected future real wage will reduce labor supply because people will want to work less today and work more in the future, so the labor supply curve shifts to the left.

   (3) Labor supply is positively related to the working-age population. An increase in the number of working-age people in the economy will increase labor supply, shifting the labor supply curve to the right.

   (4) Labor supply is positively related to the participation rate. An increase in the participation rate will increase labor supply, shifting the labor supply curve to the right.

5. Structural unemployment is caused by changes in the economy that create a mismatch in the job skills of unemployed workers and those skills required by firms looking for workers to fill vacancies. Examples of structural changes that create structural unemployment include technological advances and changes in foreign competition. Structurally unemployed labor must often relocate or acquire further education or technical training to gain employment.

   Frictional unemployment is created by people entering the labor force to search for a job and by people quitting one job to search for a better one. Unemployment spells for the frictionally unemployed are usually of short duration, because these people have the job skills and personal attributes needed to fill available vacancies.

   The duration of a typical unemployment spell for frictional unemployment is relatively short; the duration of a typical unemployment spell for structural unemployment is relatively long.

   The natural rate of unemployment equals the amount of frictional unemployment plus structural unemployment as a fraction of the labor force.

6. The growth rate form of Okun's law is $\Delta Y/Y = 3 - 2\Delta u$, where $\Delta Y/Y$ is the growth rate of output, 3 is the growth rate of full-employment output, and Δu is the change in the unemployment rate.

Numerical Problems

1. Given that $Y = AK^{0.5}N^{0.5}$, then $A = Y / K^{0.5}N^{0.5}$.

    (a) $A = 4{,}878/[(4{,}773)^{0.5}(117.9)^{0.5}] = 4{,}878/[(69.09)(10.86)] = 6.50.$

    (b) $A = 4{,}821/[(4{,}824)^{0.5}(116.9)^{0.5}] = 4{,}821/[(69.46)(10.81)] = 6.42.$

2. (a) Output doubles (increases 100%), because the inputs doubled and the production function has constant returns to scale. You can calculate output in 1990 equal to 199.5 and output in 2000 is 399.

    (b) Because output doubles in the absence of a change in A, the 10% increase in A increases output by a total of 120%. Calculating output gives 439, which is 120% higher than the output of 199.5 in 1990.

3. The output level form of Okun's law tells us that $(\overline{Y} - Y)/\overline{Y} = 2(u - \overline{u})$. By plugging in the given values into these equations, we can calculate the level of output as follows:

    (a) $(7{,}000 - Y)/7{,}000 = 2\,(0.11 - 0.05) = 2 \times 0.06 = 0.12$, so output is 12% below its full-employment level. Solving for Y, we have $(7{,}000 - Y)/7{,}000 = 0.12$; multiplying both sides of the equation by 7,000 gives $7{,}000 - Y = 840$; solving for Y gives $Y = 6{,}160.$

    (b) $(7{,}000 - Y)/7{,}000 = 2\,(0.04 - 0.05) = 2 \times -0.01 = -0.02$, so output is 2% above its full-employment level. Solving for Y, we have $(7{,}000 - Y)/7{,}000 = -0.02$; multiplying both sides of the equation by 7,000 gives $7{,}000 - Y = -140$; solving for Y gives $Y = 7{,}140.$

4. (a) Unemployment = labor force – employment = 135,022,000 – 127,855,000 = 7,167,000, so the unemployment rate is 7,167,000/135,022,000 = 5.3%.

    (b) The participation rate is the fraction of the adult population in the labor force. The adult population is the labor force + the number not in the labor force = 135,022,000 + 66,614,000 = 201,636,000. The participation rate is then 135,022,000/201,636,000 = 67.0%.

    (c) The employment ratio is the employed fraction of the adult population, which is 127,855,000/201,636,000 = 63.4%.

Analytical Questions

1. A temporary beneficial supply (productivity) shock causes the slope of the production function (the marginal product of labor) to increase at every level of employment, as Figure 3.8 shows. Because the labor demand curve is the marginal product of labor schedule, the labor demand curve also shifts upward, as shown in Figure 3.9. As a result, the real wage rises and employment increases.

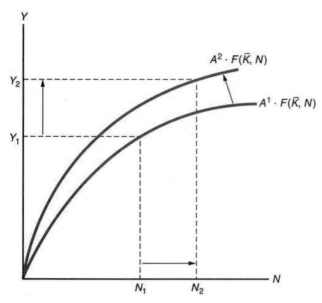

Figure 3.8

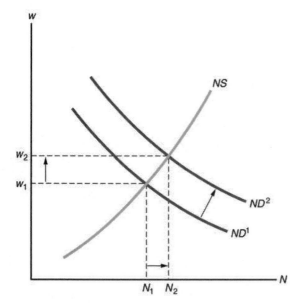

Figure 3.9

2. A decrease in the capital stock decreases the slope of the production function at every level of employment, as shown in Figure 3.10. This decreases the marginal product of labor and causes the labor demand curve to shift down, as shown in Figure 3.11. As a result, the equilibrium level of employment decreases, as does the real wage.

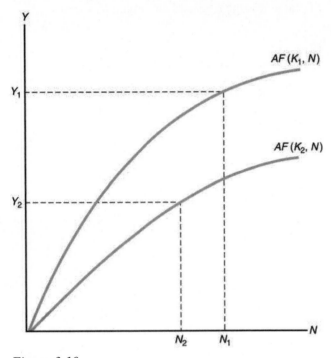

Figure 3.10

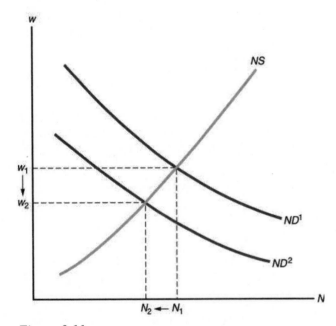

Figure 3.11

Chapter 4
Consumption, Saving, and Investment

■ Introduction

In this chapter, we examine equilibrium in the goods market by looking carefully at the two most important sectors of the economy—consumption and investment. Section 4.1 begins by giving you a detailed description of how people choose to spend and save. It also discusses how the government's budget deficit plays a major role in affecting national saving. Next, Section 4.2 talks about investment, showing how firms decide how much to invest, depending on the user cost of capital and the interest rate. Saving and investment together determine equilibrium in the goods market, as Section 4.3 discusses. Appendix 4.A presents an interesting two-period economic model that's worth your time to learn—it will really help you understand the important economic theory presented in the chapter.

In this chapter, there are two key analytical ideas that you need to understand. The first is how firms decide on their capital stock, as shown in Figure 4.2 in the textbook (reproduced below as Figure 4.1 in this study guide). It's important for you to understand why each curve in the figure looks the way it does, what shifts each curve, and why equilibrium occurs where it does. The other important idea is that of equilibrium in the goods market, shown in textbook Figure 4.6 and textbook Key Diagram 3 (reproduced below as Figure 4.2 in this study guide). You need to understand how saving and investment depend on the real interest rate and what other factors affect each curve. This chapter also introduces the Ricardian equivalence proposition; be sure that you understand what it means, because you'll see it again later in the textbook.

■ Outline

I. **Consumption and Saving (Sec. 4.1)**

    A) The importance of consumption and saving

        1. Desired consumption: consumption amount desired by households

        2. Desired national saving: level of national saving when consumption is at its desired level

$$S^d = Y - C^d - G \tag{4.1}$$

    B) The consumption and saving decision of an individual

        1. A person can consume less than current income (saving is positive)

        2. A person can consume more than current income (saving is negative)

        3. Trade-off between current consumption and future consumption

            a. The price of 1 unit of current consumption is $1 + r$ units of future consumption, where r is the real interest rate

            b. Consumption-smoothing motive: the desire to have a relatively even pattern of consumption over time

C) Effect of changes in current income
  1. Increase in current income: both consumption and saving increase (vice versa for decrease in current income)
  2. Marginal propensity to consume (*MPC*) = fraction of additional current income consumed in current period; between 0 and 1
  3. Aggregate level: When current income (*Y*) rises, C^d rises, but not by as much as *Y*, so S^d rises

D) Effect of changes in expected future income
  1. Higher expected future income leads to more consumption today, so saving falls
  2. Application: consumer sentiment and forecasts of consumer spending
    a. Do consumer sentiment indexes help economists forecast consumer spending?
    b. Data do not seem to give much warning before recessions
    c. Data on consumer spending are correlated with data on consumer confidence
    d. But formal statistical analysis shows that data on consumer confidence do not improve forecasts of consumer spending based on other macro data

E) Effect of changes in wealth
  1. Increase in wealth raises current consumption, so lowers current saving

F) Effect of changes in real interest rate
  1. Increased real interest rate has two opposing effects
    a. Substitution effect: Positive effect on saving, because rate of return is higher; greater reward for saving elicits more saving
    b. Income effect
      (1) For a saver: Negative effect on saving, because it takes less saving to obtain a given amount in the future (target saving)
      (2) For a borrower: Positive effect on saving, because the higher real interest rate means a loss of wealth
    c. Empirical studies have mixed results; probably a slight increase in aggregate saving
  2. Taxes and the real return to saving
    a. Expected after-tax real interest rate:

$$r_{a-t} = (1 - t)i - \pi^e \tag{4.2}$$

    b. Simple examples: $i = 5\%$, $\pi^e = 2\%$; if $t = 30\%$, $r_{a-t} = 1.5\%$; if $t = 20\%$, $r_{a-t} = 2\%$
  3. In touch with the macroeconomy: interest rates
    a. Discusses different interest rates, default risk, term structure (yield curve), and tax status
    b. Because interest rates often move together, we frequently refer to "the" interest rate

G) Fiscal policy
  1. Affects desired consumption through changes in current and expected future income
  2. Directly affects desired national saving, $S^d = Y - C^d - G$
  3. Government purchases (temporary increase)
    a. Higher *G* financed by higher current taxes reduces after-tax income, lowering desired consumption
    b. Even true if financed by higher future taxes, if people realize how future incomes are affected
    c. Because C^d declines less than *G* rises, national saving ($S^d = Y - C^d - G$) declines
    d. So government purchases reduce both desired consumption and desired national saving

4. Taxes
   a. Lump-sum tax cut today, financed by higher future taxes
   b. Decline in future income may offset increase in current income; desired consumption could rise or fall
   c. Ricardian equivalence proposition
      (1) If future income loss exactly offsets current income gain, no change in consumption
      (2) Tax change affects only the timing of taxes, not their ultimate amount (present value)
      (3) In practice, people may not see that future taxes will rise if taxes are cut today; then a tax cut leads to increased desired consumption and reduced desired national saving

H) Application: A Ricardian tax cut?
   1. The Economic Growth and Tax Relief Reconstruction Act (EGTRRA) of 2001 gave rebate checks to taxpayers and cut tax rates substantially
   2. From the first quarter to the third quarter, government saving fell $277 billion (at an annual rate) but private saving increased $180 billion, so national saving declined only $97 billion, so about 2/3 of the tax cut was saved
   3. Most consumers saved their tax rebates and did not spend them
   4. As a result, the tax rebate and tax cut did not stimulate much additional spending by households

II. Investment (Sec. 4.2)

A) Why is investment important?
   1. Investment fluctuates sharply over the business cycle, so we need to understand investment to understand the business cycle
   2. Investment plays a crucial role in economic growth

B) The desired capital stock
   1. Desired capital stock is the amount of capital that allows firms to earn the largest expected profit
   2. Desired capital stock depends on costs and benefits of additional capital
   3. Because investment becomes capital stock with a lag, the benefit of investment is the future marginal product of capital (MPK^f)
   4. The user cost of capital
      a. Example of Kyle's Bakery: cost of capital, depreciation rate, and expected real interest rate
      b. User cost of capital = real cost of using a unit of capital for a specified period of time = real interest cost + depreciation
      c. $uc = rp_K + dp_K = (r + d)p_K$ (4.3)

5. Determining the desired capital stock (Figure 4.1; like text Figure 4.3)

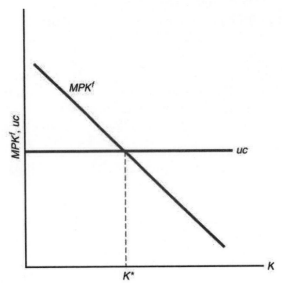

Figure 4.1

   a. Desired capital stock is the level of capital stock at which $MPK^f = uc$

   b. MPK^f falls as K rises due to diminishing marginal productivity

   c. uc doesn't vary with K, so is a horizontal line

   d. If $MPK^f > uc$, profits rise as K is added (marginal benefits > marginal costs)

   e. If $MPK^f < uc$, profits rise as K is reduced (marginal benefits < marginal costs)

   f. Profits are maximized where $MPK^f = uc$

C) Changes in the desired capital stock

   1. Factors that shift the MPK^f curve or change the user cost of capital cause the desired capital stock to change

   2. These factors are changes in the real interest rate, depreciation rate, price of capital, or technological changes that affect the MPK^f (text Figure 4.4 shows effect of change in uc)

   3. Taxes and the desired capital stock

      a. With taxes, the return to capital is only $(1 - \tau)MPK^f$

      b. A firm chooses its desired capital stock so that the return equals the user cost, so

         $(1 - \tau)MPK^f = uc$, which means:

$$MPK^f = uc/(1 - \tau) = (r + d)p_K/(1 - \tau) \qquad (4.4)$$

      c. Tax-adjusted user cost of capital is $uc/(1 - \tau)$

      d. An increase in τ raises the tax-adjusted user cost and reduces the desired capital stock

      e. In reality, there are complications to the tax-adjusted user cost

         (1) We assumed that firm revenues were taxed

            (a) In reality, profits, not revenues, are taxed

            (b) So depreciation allowances reduce the tax paid by firms, because they reduce profits

         (2) Investment tax credits reduce taxes when firms make new investments

(3) Summary measure: the effective tax rate—the tax rate on firm revenue that would have the same effect on the desired capital stock as do the actual provisions of the tax code

(4) Table 4.2 shows effective tax rates for many different countries

f. Application: measuring the effects of taxes on investment

(1) Do changes in the tax rate have a significant effect on investment?

(2) A 1994 study by Cummins, Hubbard, and Hassett found that after major tax reforms, investment responded strongly; elasticity about –0.66 (of investment to user cost of capital)

D) Box 4.1: Investment and the Stock Market

1. Firms change investment in the same direction as the stock market: Tobin's q theory of investment

2. If market value > replacement cost, then firm should invest more

3. Tobin's q = capital's market value divided by its replacement cost

a. If $q < 1$, don't invest

b. If $q > 1$, invest more

4. Stock price times number of shares equals firm's market value, which equals value of firm's capital

a. Formula: $q = V/(p_K K)$, where V is stock market value of firm, K is firm's capital, p_K is price of new capital

b. So $p_K K$ is the replacement cost of firm's capital stock

c. Stock market boom raises V, causing q to rise, increasing investment

5. Data show general tendency of investment to rise when stock market rises; but relationship isn't strong because many other things change at same time

6. This theory is similar to text discussion

a. Higher MPK^f increases future earnings of firm, so V rises

b. A falling real interest rate also raises V as people buy stocks instead of bonds

c. A decrease in the cost of capital, p_K, raises q

E) From the desired capital stock to investment

1. The capital stock changes from two opposing channels

a. New capital increases the capital stock; this is gross investment

b. The capital stock depreciates, which reduces the capital stock

c. Net investment = gross investment (I) minus depreciation:

$$K_{t+1} - K_t = I_t - dK_t \qquad (4.5)$$

where net investment equals the change in the capital stock

d. Text Figure 4.6 shows gross and net investment for the United States

2. Rewriting Eq. (4.5) gives $I_t = K_{t+1} - K_t + dK_t$

a. If firms can change their capital stocks in one period, then the desired capital stock (K^*) = K_{t+1}

b. So $I_t = K^* - K_t + dK_t$ \qquad (4.6)

c. Thus investment has two parts

(1) Desired net increase in the capital stock over the year ($K^* - K_t$)

(2) Investment needed to replace depreciated capital (dK_t)

3. Lags and investment
   a. Some capital can be constructed easily, but other capital may take years to put in place
   b. So investment needed to reach the desired capital stock may be spread out over several years

F) Investment in inventories and housing
   1. Marginal product of capital and user cost also apply, as with equipment and structures

III. Goods Market Equilibrium (Sec. 4.3)

A) The real interest rate adjusts to bring the goods market into equilibrium

   1. $Y = C^d + I^d + G$ (4.7)

      goods market equilibrium condition
   2. Differs from income-expenditure identity, as goods market equilibrium condition need not hold; undesired goods may be produced, so goods market won't be in equilibrium
   3. Alternative representation: because $S^d = Y - C^d - G$,

      $$S^d = I^d$$ (4.8)

B) The saving-investment diagram
   1. Plot S^d vs. I^d (Figure 4.2; Key Diagram 3; like text Figure 4.7)

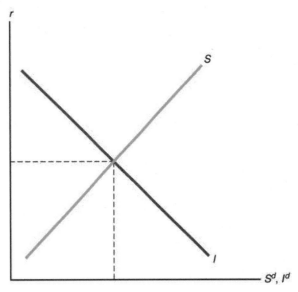

Figure 4.2

   2. Equilibrium where $S^d = I^d$
   3. How to reach equilibrium? Adjustment of r
   4. Shifts of the saving curve
      a. Saving curve shifts right due to a rise in current output, a fall in expected future output, a fall in wealth, a fall in government purchases, a rise in taxes (unless Ricardian equivalence holds, in which case tax changes have no effect)
      b. Example: Temporary increase in government purchases shifts S left
      c. Result of lower savings: higher r, causing crowding out of I

5. Shifts of the investment curve
   a. Investment curve shifts right due to a fall in the effective tax rate or a rise in expected future marginal productivity of capital
   b. Result of increased investment: higher r, higher S and I

C) Application: Macroeconomic consequences of the boom and bust in stock prices
   1. Sharp changes in stock prices affect consumption spending (a wealth effect) and capital investment (via Tobin's q)
   2. Consumption and the 1987 crash
      a. When the stock market crashed in 1987, wealth declined by about $1 trillion
      b. Consumption fell somewhat less than might be expected, and it wasn't enough to cause a recession
      c. There was a temporary decline in confidence about the future, but it was quickly reversed
      d. The small response may have been because there had been a large run-up in stock prices between December 1986 and August 1987, so the crash mostly erased this run-up
   3. Consumption and the rise in stock market wealth in the 1990s
      a. Stock prices more than tripled in real terms
      b. But consumption was not strongly affected by the run-up in stock prices
   4. Consumption and the decline in stock prices in the early 2000s
      a. In the early 2000s, wealth in stocks declined by about $5 trillion
      b. But consumption spending increased as a share of GDP in that period
   5. Investment and Tobin's q
      a. Investment and Tobin's q were not closely correlated following the 1987 crash in stock prices
      b. But the relationship has been tighter in the 1990s and early 2000s, as theory suggests

IV. Appendix 4.A: A Formal Model of Consumption and Saving

A) How much can the consumer afford? The budget constraint
   1. Current income y; future income y^f; initial wealth a
   2. Choice variables: a^f = wealth at beginning of future period; c = current consumption; c^f = future consumption
   3. $a^f = (y + a - c)(1 + r)$, so $c^f = (y + a - c)(1 + r) + y^f$ the budget constraint   (4.A.1)

B) The budget line
   1. Graph budget line in (c, c^f) space (Figure 4.A.1)

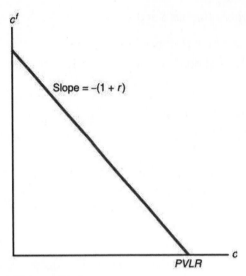

Figure 4.A.1

   2. Slope of line $= -(1 + r)$

C) Present values
   1. Present value is the value of payments to be made in the future in terms of today's dollars or goods
   2. Example: At an interest rate of 10%, $12,000 today invested for one year is worth $13,200 ($12,000 × 1.10); so the present value of $13,200 in one year is $12,000
   3. General formula: Present value = future value/$(1 + i)$, where amounts are in dollar terms and i is the nominal interest rate
   4. Alternatively, if amounts are in real terms, use the real interest rate r instead of the nominal interest rate i

D) Present value and the budget constraint
   1. Present value of lifetime resources:

$$PVLR = y + y^f/(1 + r) + a \qquad\qquad (4.A.2)$$

   2. Present value of lifetime consumption:

$$PVLC = c + c^f/(1 + r)$$

   3. The budget constraint means $PVLC = PVLR$
   4. $c + c^f/(1 + r) = y + y^f/(1 + r) + a \qquad\qquad (4.A.3)$
   5. Horizontal intercept of budget line is $c = PVLR$, $c^f = 0$

E) What does the consumer want? Consumer preferences
   1. Utility = a person's satisfaction or well-being
   2. Graph a person's preference for current versus future consumption using indifference curves

3. An indifference curve shows combinations of c and c^f that give the same utility (Figure 4.A.2)

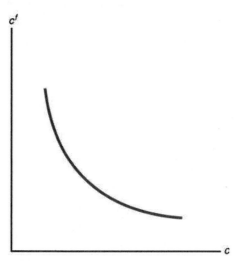

Figure 4.A.2

4. A person is equally happy at any point on an indifference curve
5. Three important properties of indifference curves
    a. Slope downward from left to right: Less consumption in one period requires more consumption in the other period to keep utility unchanged
    b. Indifference curves that are farther up and to the right represent higher levels of utility, because more consumption is preferred to less
    c. Indifference curves are bowed toward the origin, because people have a consumption-smoothing motive, they prefer consuming equal amounts in each period rather than consuming a lot one period and little the other period
F) The optimal level of consumption
    1. Optimal consumption point is where the budget line is tangent to an indifference curve (Figure 4.A.3)

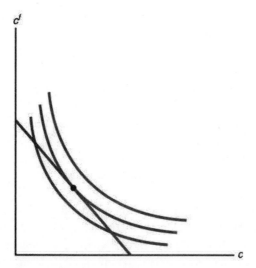

Figure 4.A.3

    2. That's the highest indifference curve that it's possible to reach
    3. All other points on the budget line are on lower indifference curves

G) The effects of changes in income and wealth on consumption and saving

   1. The effect on consumption of a change in income (current or future) or wealth depends only on how the change affects the *PVLR*

     a. An increase in current income (Figure 4.A.4)

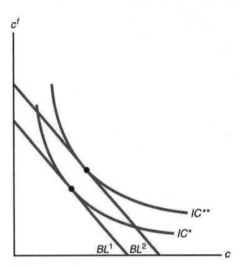

Figure 4.A.4

       (1) Increases *PVLR*, so shifts budget line out parallel to old budget line

       (2) If there is a consumption-smoothing motive, both current and future consumption will increase

       (3) Then both consumption and saving rise because of the rise in current income

     b. An increase in future income

       (1) Same outward shift in budget line as an increase in current income

       (2) Again, with consumption smoothing, both current and future consumption increase

       (3) Now saving declines, because current income is unchanged and current consumption increases

     c. An increase in wealth

       (1) Same parallel shift in budget line, so both current and future consumption rise

       (2) Again, saving declines, because c rises and y is unchanged

     d. The permanent income theory

       (1) Different types of changes in income

          (a) Temporary increase in income: y rises and y^f is unchanged

          (b) Permanent increase in income: Both y and y^f rise

       (2) Permanent income increase causes bigger increase in *PVLR* than a temporary income increase

          (a) So current consumption will rise more with a permanent income increase

          (b) So saving from a permanent increase in income is less than from a temporary increase in income

       (3) This distinction between permanent and temporary income changes was made by Milton Friedman in the 1950s and is known as the permanent income theory

          (a) Permanent changes in income lead to much larger changes in consumption

          (b) Thus permanent income changes are mostly consumed, while temporary income changes are mostly saved

H) Consumption and saving over many periods: The life-cycle model
   1. Life-cycle model was developed by Franco Modigliani and associates in the 1950s
      a. Looks at patterns of income, consumption, and saving over an individual's lifetime
      b. Typical consumer's income and saving pattern shown in Figure 4.A.5

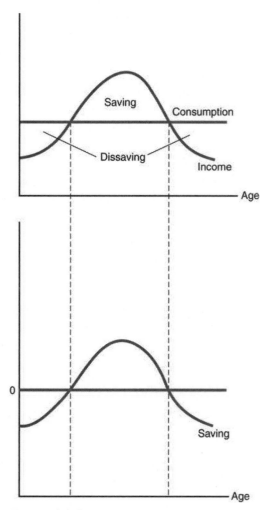

Figure 4.A.5

   c. Real income steadily rises over time until near retirement; at retirement, income drops sharply
   d. Lifetime pattern of consumption is much smoother than the income pattern
      (1) In reality, consumption varies somewhat by age
      (2) For example, when raising children, household consumption is higher than average
      (3) The model can easily be modified to handle this and other variations
   e. Saving has the following lifetime pattern
      (1) Saving is low or negative early in working life
      (2) Maximum saving occurs when income is highest (ages 50 to 60)
      (3) Dissaving occurs in retirement
   2. Bequests and saving
      a. What effect does a bequest motive (a desire to leave an inheritance) have on saving?
      b. Simply consume less and save more than without a bequest motive

3. Ricardian equivalence
   a. We can use the two-period model to examine Ricardian equivalence
   b. The two-period model shows that consumption is changed only if the *PVLR* changes
   c. Suppose the government reduces taxes by 100 in the current period, the interest rate is 10%, and taxes will be increased by 110 in the future period
   d. Then the *PVLR* is unchanged, and thus there is no change in consumption
4. Excess sensitivity and borrowing constraints
   a. Generally, theories about consumption, including the permanent income theory, have been supported by looking at real-world data
   b. But some researchers have found that the data show that the impact of an income or wealth change is different than that implied by a change in the *PVLR*
   c. There seems to be excess sensitivity of consumption to changes in current income
      (1) This could be due to short-sighted behavior
      (2) Or it could be due to borrowing constraints
   d. Borrowing constraints mean people can't borrow as much as they want
      Lenders may worry that a consumer won't pay back the loan, so they won't lend
   e. If a person wouldn't borrow anyway, the borrowing constraint is said to be nonbinding
   f. But if a person wants to borrow and can't, the borrowing constraint is binding
   g. A consumer with a binding borrowing constraint spends all income and wealth on consumption
      (1) So an increase in income or wealth will be entirely spent on consumption as well
      (2) This causes consumption to be excessively sensitive to current income changes
   h. How prevalent are borrowing constraints? Perhaps 20% to 50% of the U.S. population faces binding borrowing constraints

I) The real interest rate and the consumption-saving decision
   1. The real interest rate and the budget line (Figure 4.A.6)

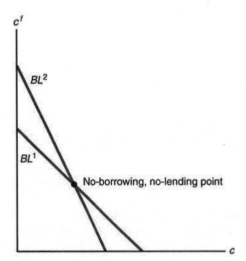

Figure 4.A.6

   a. When the real interest rate rises, one point on the old budget line is also on the new budget line: the no-borrowing, no-lending point
   b. Slope of new budget line is steeper

2. The substitution effect
   a. A higher real interest rate makes future consumption cheaper relative to current consumption
   b. Increasing future consumption and reducing current consumption increases saving
   c. Suppose a person is at the no-borrowing, no-lending point when the real interest rate rises (Figure 4.A.7)

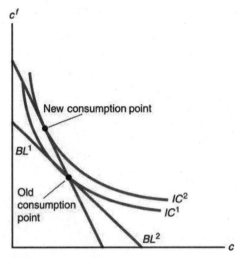

Figure 4.A.7

   (1) An increase in the real interest rate unambiguously leads the person to increase future consumption and decrease current consumption
   (2) The increase in saving, equal to the decrease in current consumption, represents the substitution effect
3. The income effect
   a. If a person is planning to consume at the no-borrowing, no-lending point, then a rise in the real interest rate leads just to a substitution effect
   b. But if a person is planning to consume at a different point than the no-borrowing, no-lending point, there is also an income effect
   c. The intuition of the income effect
   (1) If the person originally planned to be a lender, the rise in the real interest rate gives the person more income in the future period; the income effect works in the opposite direction of the substitution effect, because more future income increases current consumption
   (2) If the person originally planned to be a borrower, the rise in the real interest rate gives the person less income in the future period; the income effect works in the same direction as the substitution effect, because less future income reduces current consumption further

4. The income and substitution effects together
   a. Split the change in the budget line into two parts (Figure 4.A.8)

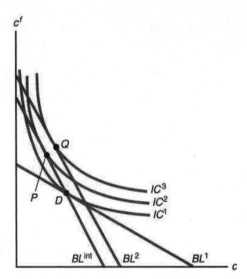

Figure 4.A.8

   (1) A budget line with the same slope as the new budget line, but going through the
       original consumption point (BL^{int})
   (2) The substitution effect is shown by the change from budget line BL^{1} to budget line
       BL^{int}, with the consumption point changing from point D to point P
   (3) The income effect is shown by the change from budget line BL^{int} to budget line BL^{2},
       with consumption point changing from point P to point Q
   b. The substitution effect decreases current consumption, but the income effect increases
      current consumption; so saving may increase or decrease
   c. Both effects increase future consumption
   d. For a borrower, both effects decrease current consumption, so saving definitely increases
      but the effect on future consumption is ambiguous
   e. The effect on aggregate saving of a rise in the real interest rate is ambiguous theoretically
      (1) Empirical research suggests that saving increases
      (2) But the effect is small

■ Multiple Choice Questions

1. In forecasting consumer spending using surveys of consumer confidence, research suggests that
    (a) the forecasts are improved when using consumer confidence measures.
    (b) the forecasts are not improved when using consumer confidence measures.
    (c) the forecasts are improved when using consumer confidence measures for forecasts made during
        recessions, but not expansions.
    (d) the forecasts are not improved when using consumer confidence measures for forecasts made
        during expansions, but not recessions.

2. Rosencrantz's base pay last year was $50,000 and he spent $48,000, thus saving $2,000. At the end of the year, he received a bonus of $2,000 and he spent $1,000 of it, saving the other $1,000. What is his marginal propensity to consume?
   (a) .96
   (b) .50
   (c) .04
   (d) .02

3. A small increase in the real interest rate will most likely
   (a) increase desired saving, but the effect will be relatively small.
   (b) increase desired saving substantially.
   (c) decrease desired saving substantially.
   (d) decrease desired saving, but the effect will be relatively small.

4. An increase in the personal income tax rate on interest income will
   (a) increase desired saving because the expected after-tax real interest rate rises.
   (b) decrease desired saving because the expected after-tax real interest rate rises.
   (c) decrease desired saving because the expected after-tax real interest rate falls.
   (d) increase desired saving because the expected after-tax real interest rate falls.

5. With a nominal interest rate of 4%, an expected inflation rate of 3%, and interest income taxed at a 25% rate, what is the expected after-tax real interest rate?
   (a) 3%
   (b) 2%
   (c) 1%
   (d) 0%

6. If an investor has a tax rate on interest income of 30% and the inflation rate is 4%, which bond has the highest expected after-tax real interest rate?
   (a) A Treasury bond paying 8%
   (b) A corporate bond paying 7%
   (c) A Treasury bond paying 7%
   (d) A municipal bond paying 6%

7. The relationship between a bond's maturity and the interest rate it pays is called the
   (a) yield curve.
   (b) amortization schedule.
   (c) federal funds rate.
   (d) desired investment curve.

8. According to the Ricardian equivalence proposition, a temporary government budget deficit created by cutting taxes
   (a) will cause desired consumption to increase.
   (b) will cause future taxes to increase but will have no real economic effects.
   (c) will have the same real economic effects as a budget deficit created by raising government spending.
   (d) would have the same real effects whether or not consumers expect future taxes to change.

9. The desired level of the capital stock will increase if the
   (a) user cost of capital increases.
   (b) expected future marginal product of capital increases.
   (c) effective tax rate increases.
   (d) price of capital increases.

10. An increase in the price of capital goods will
    (a) increase the expected future marginal product of capital.
    (b) reduce the expected future marginal product of capital.
    (c) increase the interest cost and the depreciation cost of capital.
    (d) increase the interest cost but not affect the depreciation cost of capital.

11. You have just purchased a new VCR to show videos to your customers. The VCR cost $500, and you depreciate the machine at a rate of 25% each year. You can borrow money from the bank at 10%, or receive 6% for depositing money at the bank. The expected inflation rate in the coming year is 5%. You used the company's own funds to purchase the VCR. The firm's user cost of capital for the first year is
    (a) $130.
    (b) $150.
    (c) $155.
    (d) $175.

12. Calculate the user cost of capital of a machine that costs $10,000 and depreciates at a 10% rate, when the nominal interest rate is 6% and the expected inflation rate is 3%.
    (a) $300
    (b) $600
    (c) $1,000
    (d) $1,300

13. Calculate the user cost of capital of a machine that costs $5,000 and depreciates at a 25% rate, when the nominal interest rate is 5% and the expected inflation rate is 10%.
    (a) $100
    (b) $1,000
    (c) $1,500
    (d) $5,000

14. If a firm's expected marginal product of capital exceeds its tax-adjusted user cost of capital, the firm will
    (a) increase its investment spending on capital goods.
    (b) reduce its investment spending on capital goods.
    (c) not change its investment spending on capital goods.
    (d) increase the tax-adjusted user cost of capital.

15. Calculate the after-tax user cost of capital of a machine that costs $5,000 and depreciates at a 25% rate, when the real interest rate is 5% and the tax rate on revenue is 25%.

    (a) $200
    (b) $275
    (c) $2,000
    (d) $2,750

16. A decrease in the expected real interest rate will

    (a) increase the desired capital stock.
    (b) decrease the desired capital stock.
    (c) have no effect on the desired capital stock.
    (d) have the same effect on the desired capital stock as an increase in corporate taxes.

17. If the stock market value of a firm is $8 million and the firm owns $12 million of capital, then Tobin's q equals

    (a) 2/3.
    (b) 1.
    (c) 3/2.
    (d) 4.

18. According to the q theory of investment, a firm should invest more whenever

    (a) q exceeds one.
    (b) q is less than one.
    (c) q is positive.
    (d) q is negative.

19. At the start of the year, your firm's capital stock equaled $10 million, and at the end of the year it equaled $15 million. The average depreciation rate on your capital stock is 20%. Gross investment in the year equaled

    (a) $3 million.
    (b) $4 million.
    (c) $5 million.
    (d) $7 million.

20. In the goods market equilibrium condition for a closed economy, the total demand for goods equals

    (a) $C^d + I^d$.
    (b) $C^d + I^d + G$.
    (c) $C + I + G$.
    (d) $C + I + G^d$.

21. One way of writing the goods market equilibrium condition for a closed economy is

    (a) $Y + C + G = S$.
    (b) $Y + C^d + G^d = S$.
    (c) $S^d = I^d$.
    (d) $Y - C^d - G - S^d = I^d$.

22. An economy has government purchases of 2,000. Desired national saving and desired investment are given by

$$S^d = 200 + 5,000r + .10Y - .20G$$

$$I^d = 1,000 - 4,000r$$

When the full-employment level of output equals 5,000, then the real interest rate that clears the goods market will be

(a) 7.78%.
(b) 10.00%.
(c) 14.44%.
(d) 23.33%.

23. An economy has government purchases of 2,000. Desired national saving and desired investment are given by

$$S^d = 200 + 5,000r + .10Y - .20G$$

$$I^d = 1,000 - 4,000r$$

When the full-employment level of output equals 5,000, then the level of investment when the goods market is in equilibrium will be

(a) 66.8.
(b) 422.4.
(c) 600.0.
(d) 688.8.

24. A higher expected real interest rate will
(a) increase the profitability of new investment.
(b) decrease lending of funds from firms to other economic agents.
(c) reduce the desired investment of all firms.
(d) reduce the desired investment of only those firms that have to borrow.

25. In the saving-investment diagram, an increase in current output would
(a) shift the saving curve to the left.
(b) shift the investment demand curve to the left.
(c) not shift the curves.
(d) shift the saving curve to the right.

26. Any change in the economy that reduces desired national saving for a given value of the real interest rate will shift the desired national saving curve to
(a) the right and increase the real interest rate.
(b) the right and decrease the real interest rate.
(c) the left and increase the real interest rate.
(d) the left and decrease the real interest rate.

27. A temporary increase in government purchases would cause
    (a) a leftward shift in the saving curve and a leftward shift in the investment curve.
    (b) a leftward shift in the saving curve and a rightward shift in the investment curve.
    (c) a leftward shift in the saving curve, but no shift in the investment curve.
    (d) no shift in the saving curve, but a rightward shift in the investment curve.

28. A temporary supply shock, such as a one-month decrease in oil prices, would
    (a) increase the marginal product of capital and increase desired investment.
    (b) decrease the marginal product of capital and decrease desired investment.
    (c) have little or no effect on desired investment.
    (d) increase both the marginal product of capital and the marginal product of labor in the long-term future.

29. David consumes 140 in the current period and 210 in the future period. The real interest rate is 5% per period. David's present value of lifetime consumption is
    (a) 210.
    (b) 340.
    (c) 350.
    (d) 400.

30. David consumes 140 in the current period and 220 in the future period. David's present value of lifetime consumption is 340. The real interest rate is
    (a) 0%.
    (b) 5%.
    (c) 10%.
    (d) 20%.

■ Review Questions

1. What is the marginal propensity to consume, and why is it always less than one?

2. At a given output level, how are desired saving and desired consumption related? Briefly explain. What role do expectations have in determining desired consumption and saving? Briefly explain.

3. Does an increase in the tax rate on interest earnings reduce desired saving? Briefly explain.

4. How would the expected real after-tax rate of return be affected by each of the following events?
   (1) the tax rate on interest income increases
   (2) expected inflation declines

5. What is the effect on the real interest rate of a government budget deficit caused by a temporary increase in government purchases? What does the Ricardian equivalence proposition tell us about the expected real economic effects of a temporary government budget deficit caused by a temporary tax cut? Briefly explain.

6. Identify two variables that shift the desired saving curve. Is desired saving negatively related or positively related to each of these variables?

7. Identify two variables that shift the desired investment curve. Is desired investment negatively related or positively related to each of these variables?

■ Numerical Problems

1. The one-year T-bill rate was 8% on 1/1/01, 7% on 1/1/02, and 6% on 1/1/03. The GDP deflator (1982 = 100) was 150 on 1/1/01, 159 on 1/1/02, 165.4 on 1/1/03, and 173.6 on 1/1/04. The tax rate on interest income is 30%.
    (a) Calculate the after-tax nominal rate of return for 2001, 2002, and 2003.
    (b) If you began with $1,000 on 1/1/01 and invested in T-bills each year (paying taxes at the end of each year), how much would you have in nominal terms on 1/1/04? How much would you have in real terms (1982 dollars)?
    (c) How much was your nominal after-tax interest earned in part (b) over the three years? How much did you earn in real after-tax dollars?

2. Suppose the nominal interest rate is 6%, the tax rate on interest income is 30%, and expected inflation is 3%.
    (a) Calculate the expected after-tax real interest rate.
    (b) Calculate the expected after-tax real interest rate if the nominal interest rate falls to 4%.
    (c) Calculate the expected after-tax real interest rate if the tax rate increases to 50% (with the nominal interest rate at its original value of 6%).
    (d) Calculate the expected after-tax real interest rate if expected inflation increases to 5% (with the nominal interest rate at its original value of 6% and the tax rate at its original value of 30%).

3. Calculate the value of net investment for each of the following values for gross investment (I_t) and depreciation (d), assuming that $K_t = \$5,000$ billion.
    (a) $I_t = \$1,250$ billion and $d = 10\%$
    (b) $I_t = \$750$ billion and $d = 5\%$

4. Suppose desired consumption equals $0.9Y$, where Y is income. Government purchases are $1,000, net exports are zero, and desired investment varies with the real interest rate according to the following schedule:

r	I^d
5%	$3,000
4%	3,500
3%	4,000
2%	4,500

Assume the interest rate adjusts so that the economy gets to equilibrium. Equilibrium output at full employment is $50,000. Find the values of consumption, investment, and the real interest rate at full-employment equilibrium.

■ Analytical Questions

1. How would each of the following changes affect the user cost of capital?
   (1) An increase in the price of capital goods
   (2) A decrease in the real interest rate

2. How would the desired capital stock be affected by a decline in the user cost of capital?

3. What would be the effect on a firm's desired capital stock of a technological advance?

4. How would each of the following changes affect the level of desired capital stock?
   (1) An increase in the effective tax rate on capital
   (2) A decrease in the depreciation rate

5. What are the economic consequences of reductions in defense spending by the government? What happens to national saving, the interest rate, and investment?

■ Answers

Multiple Choice

1. b	7. a	13. b	19. d	25. d
2. b	8. b	14. a	20. b	26. c
3. a	9. b	15. c	21. c	27. c
4. c	10. c	16. a	22. a	28. c
5. d	11. a	17. a	23. d	29. b
6. d	12. d	18. a	24. c	30. c

Review Questions

1. The marginal propensity to consume (*MPC*) is the amount by which desired consumption rises when current income rises by one unit. The marginal propensity to consume is less than one because a part of any increase in current income is saved.

2. At a given output level, desired consumption is negatively related to desired saving. Any increase in desired consumption is a decrease in desired saving, and vice versa. Expectations play a major role in determining desired consumption and desired saving. Expected future income and expected inflation are two examples of expectations variables that partly determine desired consumption and desired saving.

3. An increase in the tax rate on interest earnings has the same effect on desired saving as a decline in the interest rate, because both reduce the after-tax real interest rate. But empirical researchers have not been able to agree on the strength of the effect of a change in the real interest rate on desired saving. Most researchers believe that desired saving is positively related to the interest rate, but that the interest rate is a relatively weak determinant of saving. This is because there's an incentive to save more at a higher rate of return on saving because of the higher payoff, but there's also an incentive to save less, because a saver doesn't need to save as much to reach a target level of accumulated wealth, because the interest rate is higher.

4.   The expected real after-tax rate of return is

$$r_{a-t} = (1-t)\, i - \pi^e.$$

(1) Clearly r_{a-t} would decline if the tax rate on interest income increases.

(2) From the formula, r_{a-t} would increase if expected inflation declines.

5.   A government budget deficit created by a temporary increase in government purchases causes the saving curve to shift to the left. With no shift in the desired investment curve, the result is an increase in the real interest rate, as Figure 4.3 shows.

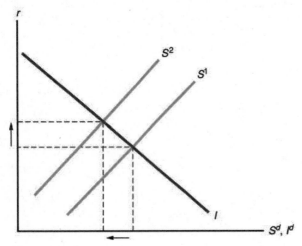

Figure 4.3

According to the Ricardian equivalence proposition, a temporary government budget deficit created by a tax cut will not have any real economic effect, because it will not change national saving, so it will not shift the saving curve. The proposition assumes that households realize they will have to save all the income received from the tax cut in order to pay off the future tax increase needed to pay off the government debt created by the temporary tax cut.

6.   Variables that shift the desired saving curve are current output, expected future output, wealth, the expected real interest rate, government purchases, and taxes. Of these, current output, the expected real interest rate (probably), and taxes (possibly) are positively related to saving; the rest are negatively related.

7.   Variables that shift the desired investment curve are the real interest rate, the expected future marginal product of capital, and the effective tax rate. Desired investment is positively related to the future marginal product of capital, but negatively related to the real interest rate and the effective tax rate.

Numerical Problems

1.   (a) 2001:5.6% = .08 × .7; 2002:4.9% = .07 × .7; 2003:4.2% = .06 × .7

(b) Nominal: $1,154.27 = $1,000 × 1.056 × 1.049 × 1.042; Real: $664.90 = $1,154.27/(173.6/100)

(c) Nominal: $154.27 = $1,154.27 − $1,000; Real: −$1.77 = $664.90 − $1,000/(150/100) = $664.90 − $666.67

2. The expected after-tax real interest rate is $r_{a-t} = (1 - t)i - \pi^e$.

(a) Given the initial values, $r_{a-t} = (1 - .30).06 - .03 = 0.012 = 1.2\%$.

(b) When $i = 4\%$, $r_{a-t} = (1 - .30).04 - .03 = -0.002 = -0.2\%$.

(c) When $t = 50\%$, $r_{a-t} = (1 - .50).06 - .03 = 0.0 = 0.0\%$.

(d) When $\pi^e = 5\%$, $r_{a-t} = (1 - .30).06 - .05 = -0.008 = -0.8\%$.

3. Net investment $= I_t - dK_t$.

(a) Net investment $= \$1,250$ billion $- (.10 \times \$5,000$ billion$) = \$750$ billion.

(b) Net investment $= \$750$ billion $- (.05 \times \$5,000$ billion$) = \$500$ billion.

4. Because $Y = C^d + I^d + G$, $Y = 0.9Y + I^d + G$, so $0.1Y = I^d + G$. Then you can calculate the following table:

r	I^d	G	Y	C^d
5%	$3,000	$1,000	$40,000	$36,000
4%	3,500	1,000	45,000	40,500
3%	4,000	1,000	50,000	45,000
2%	4,500	1,000	55,000	49,500

At equilibrium, $Y = \$50,000$, so $r = 3\%$, $I^d = \$4,000$, and $C = \$45,000$.

Analytical Questions

1. The user cost of capital is $uc = rp_K + dp_K = (r + d)p_K$, where $r =$ the expected real interest rate, $d =$ the depreciation rate for capital, and $p_k =$ the real price of capital goods.

(1) From the equation, the user cost of capital increases if the price of capital goods increases.

(2) From the equation, the user cost of capital decreases if the real interest rate decreases.

2. A firm sets its capital stock such that the future marginal product of capital equals the user cost, where the future marginal product of capital declines as the amount of capital increases. A decline in the user cost requires that the future marginal product of capital also decline to maintain the equality. So the desired capital stock increases.

3. A technological advance causes the future marginal product of capital to increase. This increases the equilibrium level of the capital stock, as Figure 4.4 shows.

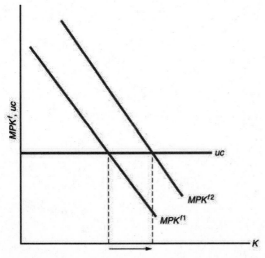

Figure 4.4

4. A firm's desired capital stock is the level at which $MPK^f = uc/(1 - \tau) = (r + d)p_K/(1 - \tau)$.

    (1) An increase in the effective tax rate on capital reduces the desired capital stock, because it increases the tax-adjusted user cost of capital.

    (2) A decrease in the depreciation rate reduces the user cost of capital, thus increasing the desired capital stock.

5. The reduction in defense spending increases national saving, so that the desired saving curve shifts to the right. As a result, the real interest rate declines, and investment increases, as shown in Figure 4.5.

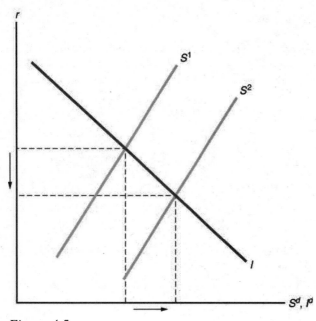

Figure 4.5

Chapter 5
Saving and Investment in the Open Economy

■ Introduction

Chapter 4 introduced equilibrium in the goods market, but to keep things simple it assumed that the economy was closed. In this chapter, we allow for the economy to trade with other countries to see how that changes things. In such an open economy, we find that a country's spending need not equal its production every period—it can borrow or lend to other countries. As in a closed economy, though, what's most important are the country's decisions about how much to save and invest. The chapter begins with some basic balance of payments accounting in Section 5.1, explaining the trade balance and current-account balance, among other things. Then Section 5.2 shows how the condition for equilibrium in the goods market is changed by allowing for international trade. When an open economy is small, it has no effect on the world real interest rate, as discussed in Section 5.3. But when an open economy is large enough to affect the world real interest rate, the analysis is different, as Section 5.4 shows. Finally, Section 5.5 looks at the relationship between government budget deficits and current account deficits.

This is a pretty tough chapter. First, the nuances of balance of payments accounting are a bit difficult to understand. You need to be sure to figure out what's a debit and what's a credit. Then, there are two different models to follow—one for a small economy and the other for a large economy. So the first thing to ask yourself in analyzing any economy is: is the economy small or large? If it's small, then the world real interest rate isn't affected by shifts in saving or investment in the economy. But if the economy is large, then it affects the rest of the world whenever there's a shift in its saving or investment.

■ Outline

I. Balance of Payments Accounting (Sec. 5.1)

    A) Balance of payments accounts

        1. The record of a country's international transactions

        2. Text Table 5.1 shows recent U.S. data

        3. Any transaction that involves a flow of money into the United States is a credit (+) item (enters with a plus sign); for example, exports

        4. Any transaction involving a flow of money out of the United States is a debit (–) item (enters with a minus sign); for example, imports

        5. In touch with the macroeconomy: the balance of payments accounts
           Data released quarterly in *Survey of Current Business*

B) The current account
1. Net exports of goods and services
2. Net income from abroad
    a. Income received from abroad is a credit item, because it causes funds to flow into the United States
    b. Payment of income to foreigners is a debit item
    c. Net income from abroad is part of the current account, and is about equal to *NFP*, net factor payments
3. Net unilateral transfers
    a. Payments made from one country to another
    b. Negative net unilateral transfers for United States, because United States is a net donor to other countries
4. Sum of net exports of goods and services, net income from abroad, and net unilateral transfers is the current account balance
    a. Positive current account balance implies current account surplus
    b. Negative current account balance implies current account deficit

C) The capital and financial account
1. The capital and financial account records trades in existing assets, either real (for example, houses) or financial (for example, stocks and bonds)
2. The capital account records the net flow of unilateral transfers of assets into the country
3. Most transactions appear in the financial account part of the capital and financial account
    a. When home country sells assets to foreign country, that is a capital inflow for the home country and a credit (+) item in the capital and financial account
    b. When assets are purchased from a foreign country, there is a capital outflow from the home country and a debit (–) item in the capital and financial account
4. The official settlements balance
    a. Transactions in official reserve assets are conducted by central banks of countries
    b. Official reserve assets are assets (foreign government securities, bank deposits, and SDRs of the IMF, gold) used in making international payments
    c. Central banks buy (or sell) official reserve assets with (or to obtain) their own currencies
    d. Official settlements balance
        (1) Also called the balance of payments, it equals the net increase in a country's official reserve assets
        (2) For the United States, the net increase in official reserve assets is the rise in U.S. government reserve assets minus foreign central bank holdings of U.S. dollar assets
    e. Having a balance of payments surplus means a country is increasing its official reserve assets; a balance of payments deficit is a reduction in official reserve assets

D) The relationship between the current account and the capital account
1. Current account balance (*CA*) + capital and financial account balance (*KFA*) = 0   (5.1)
2. *CA* + *KFA* = 0 by accounting; every transaction involves offsetting effects
3. Examples given of offsetting transactions (text Table 5.2)
4. In practice, measurement problems, recorded as a statistical discrepancy, prevent *CA* + *KFA* = 0 from holding exactly

E) Net foreign assets and the balance of payments accounts
  1. Net foreign assets are a country's foreign assets minus its foreign liabilities
    a. Net foreign assets may change in value (example: change in stock prices)
    b. Net foreign assets may change through acquisition of new assets or liabilities
  2. The net increase in foreign assets equals a country's current account surplus
  3. A current account surplus implies a capital and financial account deficit, and thus a net increase in holdings of foreign assets (a financial outflow)
  4. A current account deficit implies a capital and financial account surplus, and thus a net decline in holdings of foreign assets (a financial inflow)
  5. Foreign direct investment: a foreign firm buys or builds capital goods
    a. Causes an increase in capital and financial account balance
    b. Portfolio investment: foreigners acquire U.S. securities; also increases capital and financial account balance
  6. Summary: Equivalent measures of a country's international trade and lending
    Current account surplus = capital and financial account deficit = net acquisition of foreign assets = net foreign lending = (if *NFP* and net unilateral transfers are zero) net exports

F) Box 5.1: Does Mars have a current account surplus?
  1. Adding together all countries' current account balances gives a current account deficit for the world
  2. The statistical problem is primarily a misreporting of income from assets held abroad

G) Application: The United States as international debtor
  1. The rise in foreign liabilities by the United States since the early 1980s has been very large
  2. The United States has become the world's largest international debtor
  3. But the net foreign debt of the United States relative to U.S. GDP is relatively small (18%) compared to other countries (some of whom have net foreign debt of over 100% of GDP)
  4. Despite the large net foreign debt, the United States has direct foreign investment (companies, land) in other countries about equal in size to other countries' foreign direct investment in the United States
  5. What really matters is not size of net foreign debt, but country's wealth (physical and human capital)
    a. If net foreign debt rises but wealth rises, there's no problem
    b. But U.S. wealth isn't rising as much as net foreign debt, which is worrisome

II. Goods Market Equilibrium in an Open Economy (Sec. 5.2)

A) From Chapter 2,

$$S = I + CA = I + (NX + NFP) \tag{5.2}$$

  1. So national saving has two uses:
    a. Increase the capital stock by domestic investment
    b. Increase the stock of net foreign assets by lending to foreigners
  2. To get goods market equilibrium, national saving and investment must equal their desired levels:
    a. $S^d = I^d + CA = I^d + (NX + NFP)$ \hfill (5.3)
    b. Goods market equilibrium in an open economy

c. Assuming net factor payments are zero, then

$$S^d = I^d + NX \tag{5.4}$$

3. Alternative method:

a. $Y = C^d + I^d + G + NX$ \hfill (5.5)

b. $NX = Y - (C^d + I^d + G)$ \hfill (5.6)

Net exports equal output (Y) minus absorption ($C^d + I^d + G$)

III. Saving and Investment in a Small Open Economy (Sec. 5.3)

A) Small open economy: an economy too small to affect the world real interest rate

1. World real interest rate (r^w): the real interest rate in the international capital market

2. Key assumption: Residents of the small open economy can borrow or lend at the expected world real interest rate (Figure 5.1; Key diagram 4; like text Figures 5.1 and 5.2)

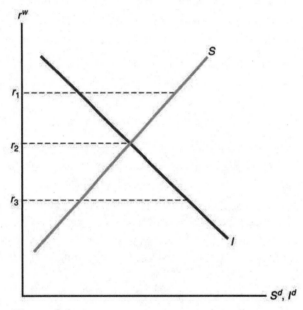

Figure 5.1

3. Result: r^w may be such that $S^d > I^d$, $S^d = I^d$, or $S^d < I^d$

a. If $r^w = r_1$, then $S^d > I^d$, so the excess of desired saving over desired investment is lent internationally (net foreign lending is positive) and $NX > 0$

b. If $r^w = r_2$, then $S^d = I^d$, so there is no net foreign lending and $NX = 0$

c. If $r^w = r_3$, then $S^d < I^d$, so the excess of desired investment over desired saving is financed by borrowing internationally (net foreign lending is negative) and $NX < 0$

4. Alternative interpretation: in terms of output and absorption

5. Net exports equals net foreign lending equals the current account balance (assuming net factor payments and net unilateral transfers are zero)

B) The effects of economic shocks in a small open economy

1. Anything that increases desired national saving (Y rises, future output falls, or G falls) relative to desired investment (MPK^f falls, τ rises) at a given world interest rate increases net foreign lending, and vice versa

2. A temporary adverse supply shock
    Temporary drop in income leads to a drop in saving, so net foreign lending declines; shown in text Figure 5.3
3. An increase in the expected future marginal product of capital
    Desired investment rises, so net foreign lending falls; shown in text Figure 5.4

C) Application: The impact of globalization on the U.S. economy
    1. World's economies are increasingly interdependent—more international trade and investment
        a. Should the U.S. reign in globalization?
    2. Historical data on trends in trade from 1929 to 2005
        a. Figure 5.5
        b. Note large gains in both exports and imports over past 50 years (as % of GDP)
    3. Historical data on trends in investment from 1982 to 2004
        a. Note large gains in both our investments abroad and foreigners' investments in U.S. over past 20 years (as % of GDP)
        b. Worrisome issue: U.S. is now world's largest international debtor (Fig. 5.6)
    4. Costs of globalization: U.S. jobs lost in particular sectors
    5. Benefits of globalization: U.S. jobs gained in particular sectors
        a. U.S. exports increase
        b. Cheaper imported goods means more goods and services at lower prices—gains from trade
    6. But loss for jobs from foreign trade is a small fraction of total job loss in U.S.
    7. Recent years: big changes in business services industry—call centers, etc.
        a. Critics: moving jobs abroad
        b. Reality: U.S. is world leader in exporting business services—far more is done in U.S. and sold abroad than vice versa (Fig. 5.7)
        c. So U.S. benefits from such activity far more than it "loses"

IV. Saving and Investment in Large Open Economies (Sec. 5.4)

A) Large open economy: an economy large enough to affect the world real interest rate
    1. Suppose there are just two economies in the world
        a. The home or domestic economy (saving S, investment I)
        b. The foreign economy, representing the rest of the world (saving S_{For}, investment I_{For})
    2. The world real interest rate moves to equilibrate desired international lending by one country with desired international borrowing by the other (Figure 5.2; Key diagram 5; text Figure 5.8)
    3. Equivalent statement: The equilibrium world real interest rate is determined such that a current account surplus in one country is equal in magnitude to the current account deficit in the other
    4. Changes in the equilibrium world real interest rate: Any factor that increases desired international lending of a country relative to desired international borrowing causes the world real interest rate to fall

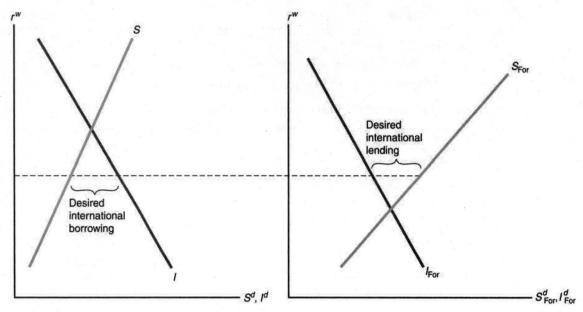

Figure 5.2

B) Application: Recent trends in the U.S. current account deficit
  1. Is the large U.S. current account deficit sustainable?
     a. Will adjustment occur, and if so, how?
     b. Data on U.S. current account deficit—it is getting worse, not better (Fig. 5.9)
  2. Why is the U.S. current account deficit continuing to increase?
     a. Lower foreign demand
     b. Better international investment opportunities
     c. Higher oil prices
     d. Increased saving by developing countries
  3. Lower foreign demand
     a. Slower economic growth in Japan and Europe in early 2000s
     b. People there are saving more and investing in U.S. more, but buying fewer U.S. goods
  4. Better international investment opportunities (Fig. 5.10)
     a. U.S. investors are diversifying investments internationally
     b. Foreign investors are investing more in U.S.
  5. Higher oil prices
     a. U.S. imports much more oil than it exports
     b. Doubling of oil prices recently led to decline in current account balance of over 1% of GDP (Fig. 5.11)
  6. Increased saving by developing countries
     a. Many developing nations want to invest in safe places like U.S., rather than borrowing and getting into financial crises
     b. They changed from being international borrowers to being international lenders
  7. Some people also blame U.S. government deficit—twin deficits argument
     a. But in late 1990s, U.S. government ran surpluses, and current account deficit got larger
     b. Other countries with current account surpluses also run larger government budget deficits than U.S.

8. What does the future hold?
   a. Probably rising import prices and falling export prices, caused by a fall in value of dollar
   b. Leading to lower imports and higher exports, reducing current account deficit

V. **Fiscal Policy and the Current Account (Sec. 5.5)**

Are government budget deficits necessarily accompanied by current account deficits? That is, are there "twin deficits"?

A) The critical factor: the response of national saving
   1. An increase in the government budget deficit raises the current account deficit only if the increase in the budget deficit reduces desired national saving
   2. In a small open economy, if an increase in the government budget deficit reduces desired national saving, the saving curve shifts left, thus reducing the current account balance (Fig. 5.12)

B) The government budget deficit and national saving
   1. A deficit caused by increased government purchases
      a. No question here: The deficit definitely reduces national saving
      b. Result: The current account balance declines
   2. A deficit resulting from a tax cut
      a. S^d falls only if C^d rises
      b. So S^d won't change if Ricardian equivalence holds, because then a tax cut won't affect consumption
      c. But if people don't foresee the future taxes implied by a tax cut today, they will consume more, desired saving will decline, and so will the current account balance

C) Application: the twin deficits
   1. Relationship between the U.S. government budget deficit and U.S. current account deficit
   2. Text Figure 5.8 shows data from 1960 to 1998
   3. The deficits appear to be twins in the 1980s and early 1990s, moving closely together
   4. But at other times (during World Wars I and II, and during 1975) government budget deficits grew, yet the current account balance increased
   5. The evidence is also mixed for foreign countries

■ Multiple Choice Questions

1. Which of the following transactions would not be included in the current account of the home country?
   (a) A consumer good is imported into the home country.
   (b) A home country resident makes a deposit in a foreign bank.
   (c) A foreign student pays tuition to a university in the home country.
   (d) A home country resident receives income on his or her foreign assets.

2. If a U.S. firm buys stereos from a Japanese firm and the Japanese firm uses the dollars it gets to buy U.S. Treasury bonds, what items are recorded in the U.S. balance of payments accounts?
   (a) credit the trade account; credit the capital and financial account
   (b) credit the trade account; debit the capital and financial account
   (c) debit the trade account; debit the capital and financial account
   (d) debit the trade account; credit the capital and financial account

3. If a French company sells 1,000 gallons of Perrier to a U.S. company at 5 euros per gallon, and uses the money to buy stock in a Spanish cork company, how does this affect the French balance of payments accounts?
    (a) debit: capital and financial account; credit: merchandise trade
    (b) debit: merchandise trade; credit: capital and financial account
    (c) debit: net investment income from abroad; credit: capital and financial account
    (d) debit: merchandise trade; credit: net investment income from abroad

4. The difference between the current account balance and net exports is
    (a) the capital account.
    (b) net unilateral transfers plus net factor payments from abroad.
    (c) adjustments in net foreign assets.
    (d) income receipts from foreign assets.

5. If the Federal Reserve buys $3 billion worth of Japanese yen, $6 billion of euros, and sells $5 billion of British pounds, how does this affect the official settlements balance?
    (a) Falls by $4 billion
    (b) Rises by $4 billion
    (c) Rises by $9 billion
    (d) Falls by $5 billion

6. An economic benefit of capital outflows is that they
    (a) reduce domestic unemployment.
    (b) reduce domestic saving.
    (c) increase domestic investment.
    (d) create future income payment inflows.

7. The official settlements balance
    (a) is always negative when there is a current account deficit.
    (b) always equals zero.
    (c) declines when U.S. official reserves increase.
    (d) is also called the balance of payments.

8. Suppose the current account shows debits of $4.7 billion and credits of $5.3 billion. The current account balance is _____, and the capital and financial account balance is _____.
    (a) +$0.6 billion; –$0.6 billion
    (b) +$0.6 billion; +$0.6 billion
    (c) –$0.6 billion; –$0.6 billion
    (d) –$0.6 billion; +$0.6 billion

9. Suppose output is $35 billion, government purchases are $10 billion, desired consumption is $15 billion, and desired investment is $6 billion. Net foreign lending would be equal to
    (a) –$4 billion.
    (b) –$2 billion.
    (c) $2 billion.
    (d) $4 billion.

10. You just read that forecasters predict the United States will run a current account deficit next year. From this you would infer that the United States will also
    (a) run a capital and financial account deficit next year.
    (b) decrease its official reserve assets next year.
    (c) run a balance of payments surplus next year.
    (d) decrease its holding of net foreign assets next year.

11. Absorption refers to
    (a) the total amount of imports purchased by a country.
    (b) the net amount of imports purchased by a country.
    (c) total spending by domestic residents, businesses, and governments.
    (d) GDP less desired consumption, desired investment, and government purchases.

12. The goods market equilibrium condition in an open economy shows that
    (a) $NX = S^d - I^d$
    (b) $S^d + NX = I^d$
    (c) $S^d + I^d = NX$
    (d) $S^d = I^d$

13. In a saving-investment diagram for a small open economy
    (a) the saving curve is vertical at some fixed level of output.
    (b) the saving curve is horizontal at some fixed interest rate.
    (c) the interest rate is fixed at the world real interest rate.
    (d) equilibrium requires that $S^d = I^d$.

14. Suppose output is $35 billion, government purchases are $10 billion, desired consumption is $15 billion, and desired investment is $6 billion. Desired savings is equal to
    (a) $2 billion.
    (b) $10 billion.
    (c) $14 billion.
    (d) $16 billion.

15. You have just read in the newspaper that a hurricane has destroyed Guatemala's coffee crop for this year. Guatemala is a small open economy. Based on this information alone, you would expect that
    (a) desired investment would fall in Guatemala.
    (b) desired investment would increase in Guatemala.
    (c) net foreign lending by Guatemala would increase.
    (d) net foreign lending by Guatemala would decrease.

16. A small open economy increases its desired saving. This causes the world real interest rate to _____ and the country's current account balance to _____.
    (a) fall; fall
    (b) remain unchanged; rise
    (c) fall; rise
    (d) remain unchanged; fall

17. If there is an increase in taxes on business firms in a small open economy, it causes the current account to _____ and saving to _____.
    (a) fall; fall
    (b) rise; remain unchanged
    (c) fall; remain unchanged
    (d) rise; fall

18. In a small open economy, $S^d = 200 + 500\ r^w$ and $I^d = 300 - 200\ r^w$. If $r^w = 0.1$, then net exports =
    (a) –50.
    (b) –30.
    (c) 30.
    (d) 50.

19. In a small open economy, $S^d = 200 + 500\ r^w$ and $I^d = 300 - 200\ r^w$. If $r^w = 0.2$, then net exports =
    (a) –60.
    (b) –40.
    (c) 40.
    (d) 60.

20. In a small open economy, $S^d = 200 + 500\ r^w$ and $I^d = 300 - 200\ r^w$. If $r^w = 0.2$, and output = 1,000, then absorption =
    (a) 40.
    (b) 60.
    (c) 940.
    (d) 960.

21. In a small open economy, $S^d = 200 + 500\ r^w$ and $I^d = 300 - 200\ r^w$. If $r^w = 0.2$, and absorption = 1,000, then output =
    (a) 940.
    (b) 960.
    (c) 1,000.
    (d) 1,040.

22. A country's real interest rate would increase if
    (a) the government imposed capital controls in a large open economy and the capital and financial account had been in surplus.
    (b) the government imposed capital controls in a large open economy and the capital and financial account had been in deficit.
    (c) there were a temporary positive supply shock in a small open economy.
    (d) there were a temporary negative supply shock in a small open economy.

23. A large open economy
    (a) dominates world trade in one or more products.
    (b) is physically larger than all small open economies.
    (c) has a larger population than all small open economies.
    (d) lends or borrows enough in the international capital market to influence the world real interest rate.

24. In a two-economy model of the United States and another large economy made up of the rest of the world, if desired saving by the rest of the world declined,
    (a) U.S. investment would increase.
    (b) U.S. saving would decrease.
    (c) the world real interest rate would increase.
    (d) the world real interest rate would decrease.

25. When future labor income rises in a large open economy, it causes the current account to _____ and investment to _____.
    (a) fall; rise
    (b) rise; remain unchanged
    (c) fall; fall
    (d) rise; rise

26. In a large open economy, the home country's saving and investment equations are: $S^d = 200 + 700 \ r^w$ and $I^d = 300 - 200 \ r^w$. The foreign country's saving and investment equations are: $S^d = 50 + 300 \ r^w$ and $I^d = 75 - 50 \ r^w$. In equilibrium, the world real interest rate =
    (a) 0.10.
    (b) 0.20.
    (c) 0.25.
    (d) 0.40.

27. In a large open economy, the home country's saving and investment equations are: $S^d = 200 + 700 \ r^w$ and $I^d = 300 - 200 \ r^w$. The foreign country's saving and investment equations are: $S^d = 50 + 300 \ r^w$ and $I^d = 75 - 50 \ r^w$. In equilibrium, the home country's net exports =
    (a) –10.
    (b) –5.
    (c)   5.
    (d) 10.

28. Assuming no change in the effective tax rate on capital, an increase in the government budget deficit will raise the current account deficit if and only if the increase in the budget deficit
    (a) reduces desired national saving.
    (b) increases desired national saving.
    (c) reduces desired national investment.
    (d) increases desired national investment.

29. Suppose the government of a small open economy reduces its spending, so that national saving increases. The result is
    (a) an increase in the real interest rate.
    (b) an increase in net exports.
    (c) a decrease in the real interest rate.
    (d) an increase in investment.

30. Suppose the government of a large open economy reduces its spending, so that national saving increases. The result is
    (a) a decrease in the foreign country's net exports.
    (b) an increase in the real interest rate.
    (c) a increase in the foreign country's net exports.
    (d) a decrease in investment.

■ Review Questions

1. Briefly define the current account and the capital and financial account. Why is the sum of these two accounts equal to zero?

2. What determines the interest rate in a small open economy?

3. What determines the interest rate in a large open economy?

4. Is the United States a large open economy? Briefly explain.

5. What were the principal causes of the U.S. government budget deficits of the 1980s? How did these budget deficits lead to the twin deficits? According to the Ricardian equivalence proposition, should twin deficits arise as a result of tax cuts?

■ Numerical Problems

1. Show where each of the following transactions belongs on the U.S. balance of payments table, using an exchange rate of 100 Japanese yen per U.S. dollar.
    (a) A Japanese firm spends 5 billion yen to buy personal computers from IBM (a U.S. firm).
    (b) A wealthy Japanese businessman gives $100,000 to the San Diego Zoo.
    (c) A U.S. firm buys 1 million Sony Walkmans at 6,000 yen each (Sony is a Japanese firm).
    (d) A Japanese investment banking firm buys 500 million dollars worth of newly issued U.S. government Treasury bills.
    (e) U.S. steel firms send 2,000 executives to Japan to take courses in the Japanese method of steel production and Japanese management techniques, paying 2 million yen per executive.
    (f) Repeat parts (a)–(e) for the balance of payments table of Japan.

2. Use the following data to calculate net exports (*NX*), the current account balance (*CA*), and the capital and financial account balance (*KFA*): Exports = $800 billion, imports = $900 billion, net income from foreign assets = $25 billion, net unilateral transfers = –$25 billion, net increase in U.S.-owned assets abroad other than official reserve assets = $90 billion, and official settlements balance = –$10 billion.

3. Suppose an economy has output of 2,000, government spending of 40, consumption of 1,600, and absorption of 1,940. Calculate the equilibrium values of investment and net exports.

4. In a small open economy,
    $S^d = \$20$ billion + ($\$100$ billion) r^w,
    $I^d = \$30$ billion − ($\$100$ billion) r^w,
    $Y = \$70$ billion,
    $G = \$20$ billion,
    $r^w = .04$.

    (a) Calculate the current account balance.
    (b) Calculate net exports.
    (c) Calculate desired consumption.
    (d) Calculate absorption.

5.   Assume that net exports equal the current account balance ($NX = CA$), and that initially $NX =$ $50 billion. Use the goods market equilibrium condition for a small open economy to calculate the effect of a temporary tax cut of $200 billion on net exports under each of the following conditions:
    (a) S^d and I^d remain unchanged
    (b) S^d declines by $50 billion and I^d declines by $50 billion
    (c) S^d declines by $200 billion and I^d remains unchanged

6.   In a large open economy, the home country's saving and investment equations are: $S^d = 200 + 1,400\ r^w$ and $I^d = 300 - 400\ r^w$. The foreign country's saving and investment equations are: $S^d = 50 + 600\ r^w$ and $I^d = 75 - 100\ r^w$. Calculate the equilibrium world real interest rate, saving and investment in each country, and the current account balance in each country.

■ Analytical Questions

1.   In a small open economy, describe what happens when an increase in wealth causes national saving to decline. Explain the impact on the real interest rate, saving, investment, net exports, and absorption in equilibrium.

2.   Suppose the government of a large open economy announces a major expansion of government spending to dig a tunnel to the Earth's core, to be financed entirely by borrowing. What effect does this have on the world real interest rate, national saving, investment, and the current account balance in equilibrium?

■ Answers

Multiple Choice

1. b	7. d	13. c	19. c	25. c
2. d	8. a	14. b	20. d	26. a
3. a	9. d	15. d	21. d	27. a
4. b	10. d	16. b	22. a	28. a
5. b	11. c	17. b	23. d	29. b
6. d	12. a	18. b	24. c	30. a

Review Questions

1.   The current account measures the value of net exports of currently produced goods and services, plus net factor payments from abroad, and net unilateral transfers into a country. The capital and financial account measures the value of net capital inflows into a country from trade in existing real and financial assets.

    The current account plus the capital and financial account equals zero because every international transaction is a trade of goods, services, or assets, and the two sides to any transaction always have offsetting effects on the current account and the capital and financial account.

2. The world real interest rate is determined by the aggregate supply of saving and demand for investment in the international capital market. Changes in domestic saving or investment in a small open economy do not affect the interest rate.

3. The world real interest rate is determined so that the world's saving equals the world's investment. This means that if one large country has a current account surplus, the rest of the world must have a current account deficit, and vice versa. Changes in domestic saving or investment affect the world real interest rate.

4. Yes, the United States is a large open economy. It is an open economy because it engages in international transactions; it is a large economy because it lends and borrows enough in international capital markets to affect the world real interest rate.

5. The principal causes of the U.S. federal government budget deficits of the 1980s were a reduction in government revenue (in part because of the Economic Recovery Tax Act of 1981) and increased military spending. The twin deficits arose because the increased government budget deficit reduced national saving, leading to a current account deficit. According to the Ricardian equivalence proposition, a government budget deficit created by a tax cut will have no real economic effects because it will not affect saving. According to this theory the government budget deficit and the trade deficit are independent events.

Numerical Problems

1. (a) Credit: $50 million exports of merchandise
    (b) Credit: $100,000 net unilateral transfers
    (c) Debit: $60 million imports of merchandise
    (d) Credit: $500 million increase in foreign-owned assets in United States
    (e) Debit: $40 million imports of services
    (f) Debit: 5 billion yen imports of merchandise
    (g) Debit: 10 million yen net unilateral transfers
    (h) Credit: 6 billion yen exports of merchandise
    (i) Debit: 50 billion yen increase in Japanese-owned assets abroad
    (j) Credit: 4 billion yen exports of services

2. NX = exports – imports
    $$= \$800 \text{ billion} - \$900 \text{ billion}$$
    $$= -\$100 \text{ billion.}$$

    $CA = NX +$ net income from foreign assets + net unilateral transfers
    $$= -\$100 \text{ billion} + \$25 \text{ billion} - \$25 \text{ billion}$$
    $$= -\$100 \text{ billion.}$$

    KFA = net increase in U.S.-owned assets abroad – official settlements balance
    $$= \$90 \text{ billion} + \$10 \text{ billion}$$
    $$= \$100 \text{ billion.}$$

3. Because absorption $= C + I + G$, then $1,940 = 1,600 + I + 40$, so $I = 1,940 - 1,640 = 300$. Net exports $= Y -$ absorption $= 2,000 - 1,940 = 60$.

4. (a) –$2 billion
    (b) –$2 billion
    (c) $26 billion
    (d) $72 billion

5. Use the formula $NX = S^d - I^d$.

    (a) With no change in S^d and I^d, NX remains unchanged.

    (b) When S^d declines by $50 billion and I^d declines by $50 billion, then NX remains unchanged.

    (c) When S^d declines by $200 billion and I^d remains unchanged, NX declines by $200 billion.

6. Worldwide savings equals $200 + 1,400\ r^w + 50 + 600\ r^w = 250 + 2,000\ r^w$. Worldwide investment equals $300 - 400\ r^w + 75 - 100\ r^w = 375 - 500\ r^w$. Setting worldwide saving equal to worldwide investment gives: $250 + 2,000\ r^w = 375 - 500\ r^w$, so $2,500\ r^w = 125$, so $r^w = 125/2,500 = 0.05$. Plugging into the original equations gives $S^d = 200 + 1,400\ r^w = 200 + (1,400 \times 0.05) = 270$, $I^d = 300 - 400\ r^w = 300 - (400 \times 0.05) = 280$, $CA = S - I = 270 - 280 = -10$. In the foreign country, $S^d = 50 + 600\ r^w = 50 + (600 \times 0.05) = 80$, $I^d = 75 - 100\ r^w = 75 - (100 \times 0.05) = 70$, $CA = S - I = 80 - 70 = 10$.

Analytical Questions

1. With the saving curve shifting to the left in a small open economy, in equilibrium, saving declines, but investment and the real interest rate are unchanged. Because $NX = S - I$, NX declines. Because absorption equals output minus net exports, and net exports decline, then absorption increases.

2. Desired national saving shifts left as shown in Figure 5.3, causing the equilibrium world real interest rate to rise, investment to fall, desired national saving to fall, and the current account balance to fall.

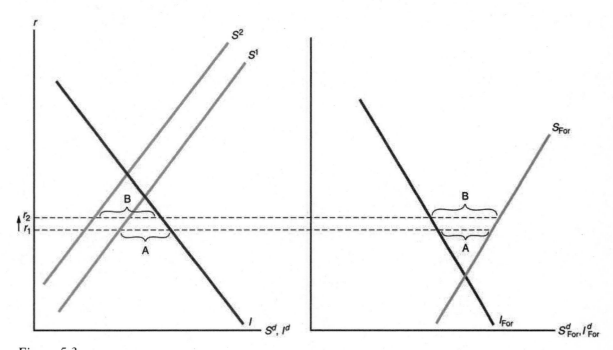

Figure 5.3

Chapter 6
Long-Run Economic Growth

■ Introduction

The purpose of this chapter is to identify forces that determine the growth rate of an economy. You'll see that changes in productivity are the key element in determining growth, but that saving and investment decisions are also important. You'll also see the types of policies that governments may use to influence the rate of growth.

Section 6.1 begins by examining the sources of economic growth, starting with a production function for the economy and breaking it down to account for growth in each element. Then, Section 6.2 covers growth dynamics in the Solow model, and looks at how in the long run, equilibrium is reached when the economy is at a steady state. This leads to a discussion of what determines long-run living standards. Then, there's a description of endogenous growth theory and how human capital and technological innovation can lead to growth. Finally, Section 6.3 discusses government policies that can be used (potentially) to raise long-run living standards, including policies that increase saving and policies that increase productivity.

Many students find the Solow model of Section 6.2 quite challenging. There are both equations [especially Equations (6.7) and (6.10)] and figures (Figures 6.2 and 6.3) that you must comprehend well to fully understand how the model works. You should work on a lot of problems that relate to the Solow model in both this study guide and in the textbook to ensure that you understand the model completely.

■ Outline

I. **The Sources of Economic Growth (Sec. 6.1)**
    A) Production function

$$Y = AF(K, N) \tag{6.1}$$

   1. Decompose into growth rate form: the growth accounting equation

$$\Delta Y/Y = \Delta A/A + a_K \, \Delta K/K + a_N \, \Delta N/N \tag{6.2}$$

   2. The a terms are the elasticities of output with respect to the inputs (capital and labor)
   3. Interpretation
        a. A rise of 10% in A raises output by 10%
        b. A rise of 10% in K raises output by a_K times 10%
        c. A rise of 10% in N raises output by a_N times 10%
   4. Both a_K and a_N are less than 1 due to diminishing marginal productivity

B) Growth accounting

1. Four steps in breaking output growth into its causes (productivity growth, capital input growth, labor input growth)

    a. Get data on $\Delta Y/Y$, $\Delta K/K$, and $\Delta N/N$, adjusting for quality changes

    b. Estimate a_K and a_N from historical data

    c. Calculate the contributions of K and N as $a_K \Delta K/K$ and $a_N \Delta N/N$, respectively

    d. Calculate productivity growth as the residual: $\Delta A/A = \Delta Y/Y - a_K \Delta K/K - a_N \Delta N/N$

2. Growth accounting and the productivity slowdown

    a. Denison's results for 1929–1982 (text Table 6.3)

        (1) Entire period output growth 2.92%; due to labor 1.34%; due to capital 0.56%; due to productivity 1.02%

        (2) Pre-1948 capital growth was much slower than post-1948

        (3) Post-1973 labor growth slightly slower than pre-1973

        (4) Productivity growth is major difference

            (a) Entire period: 1.02%

            (b) 1929–1948: 1.01%

            (c) 1948–1973: 1.53%

            (d) 1973–1982: –0.27%

    b. Productivity growth slowdown occurred in all major developed countries

3. Application: the post-1973 slowdown in productivity growth
    What caused the decline in productivity?

    a. Measurement—inadequate accounting for quality improvements

    b. The legal and human environment—regulations for pollution control and worker safety, crime, and declines in educational quality

    c. Oil prices—huge increase in oil prices reduced productivity of capital and labor, especially in basic industries

    d. New industrial revolution—learning process for information technology from 1973 to 1990 meant slower growth

4. Application: the recent surge in U.S. productivity growth

    a. Labor productivity growth increased sharply in the second half of the 1990s

    b. Labor productivity and TFP have grown steadily over the past 20 years, with only labor productivity showing evidence of a pickup in the late 1990s (Fig. 6.1)

    c. Labor productivity growth has generally exceeded TFP growth since 1995 (Fig. 6.2)

    d. The gap between labor productivity growth and TFP growth can be seen in the equation

$$\frac{\Delta Y}{Y} - \frac{\Delta N}{N} = \frac{\Delta A}{A} + a_K \left(\frac{\Delta K}{K} - \frac{\Delta N}{N} \right) \qquad (6.3)$$

        (1) Equation (6.3) suggests that labor productivity growth (the left-side term) exceeds TFP growth (the first right-side term) when capital growth exceeds labor growth

    d. The increase in labor productivity can be traced to the ICT (information and communications technologies) revolution

        (1) But other countries also had an ICT revolution, and their labor productivity did not rise as much as in the United States

        (2) European labor productivity did not rise as much as in the U.S. because of government regulations

e. Why is there such a lag between ICT investment and increases in productivity?

  (1) Because productivity improvements require not just technological advances, but also investment in intangible capital—research and development, reorganization of firms, and worker training

f. Is the recent episode unique in U.S. history?

  (1) Not really: 1873–1890—steam power, trains, telegraph; 1917–1927—electrification in factories; 1948–1973—transistor

II.   Growth Dynamics: The Solow Model (Sec. 6.2)

A) Three basic questions about growth

  1. What's the relationship between the long-run standard of living and the saving rate, population growth rate, and rate of technical progress?

  2. How does economic growth change over time? Will it speed up, slow down, or stabilize?

  3. Are there economic forces that will allow poorer countries to catch up to richer countries?

B) Setup of the Solow model

  1. Basic assumptions and variables

    a. Population and work force grow at same rate n

    b. Economy is closed and $G = 0$

    c. $C_t = Y_t - I_t$ (6.4)

    d. Rewrite everything in per-worker terms: $y_t = Y/N_t$; $c_t = C_t/N_t$; $k_t = K/N_t$

    e. k_t is also called the capital-labor ratio

  2. The per-worker production function

    a. $y_t = f(k_t)$ (6.5)

    b. Assume no productivity growth for now (add it later)

    c. Plot of per-worker production function—text Figure 6.3

    d. Same shape as aggregate production function

  3. Steady states

    a. Steady state: y_t, c_t, and k_t are constant over time

    b. Gross investment must

      (1) Replace worn-out capital, dK_t

      (2) Expand so the capital stock grows as the economy grows, nK_t

    c. $I_t = (n + d)K_t$ (6.6)

    d. From Eq. (6.4),

$$C_t = Y_t - I_t = Y_t - (n + d)K_t$$ (6.7)

    e. In per-worker terms, in steady state

$$c = f(k) - (n + d)k$$ (6.8)

f. Plot of c, $f(k)$, and $(n + d)k$ (Figure 6.1; identical to text Figure 6.4)

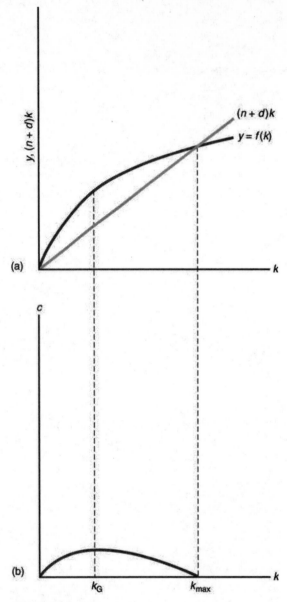

Figure 6.1

g. Increasing k will increase c up to a point
   (1) This is k_G in the figure, the Golden Rule capital-labor ratio
   (2) For k beyond this point, c will decline
   (3) But we assume henceforth that k is less than k_G, so c always rises as k rises
4. Reaching the steady state
   a. Suppose saving is proportional to current income:

$$S_t = sY_t,$$

(6.9)

   where s is the saving rate, which is between 0 and 1

b. Equating saving to investment gives

$$sY_t = (n + d)K_t \qquad (6.10)$$

c. Putting this in per-worker terms gives

$$sf(k) = (n + d)k \qquad (6.11)$$

d. Plot of $sf(k)$ and $(n + d)k$ (Figure 6.2; identical to text Figure 6.5)

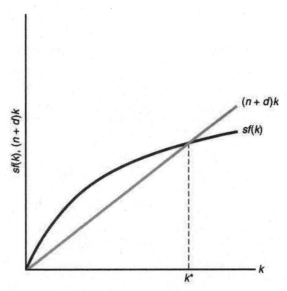

Figure 6.2

e. The only possible steady-state capital-labor ratio is k^*
f. Output at that point is $y^* = f(k^*)$; consumption is $c^* = f(k^*) - (n + d)k^*$
g. If k begins at some level other than k^*, it will move toward k^*
    (1) For k below k^*, saving > the amount of investment needed to keep k constant, so k rises
    (2) For k above k^*, saving < the amount of investment needed to keep k constant, so k falls
h. To summarize, with no productivity growth, the economy reaches a steady state, with constant capital-labor ratio, output per worker, and consumption per worker

C) The fundamental determinants of long-run living standards
    1. The saving rate
        a. Higher saving rate means higher capital-labor ratio, higher output per worker, and higher consumption per worker (shown in text Figure 6.6)
        b. Should a policy goal be to raise the saving rate?
            (1) Not necessarily, because the cost is lower consumption in the short run
            (2) There is a trade-off between present and future consumption
    2. Population growth
        a. Higher population growth means a lower capital-labor ratio, lower output per worker, and lower consumption per worker (shown in text Figure 6.7)
        b. Should a policy goal be to reduce population growth?
            (1) Doing so will raise consumption per worker
            (2) But it will reduce total output and consumption, affecting a nation's ability to defend itself or influence world events

   c. The Solow model also assumes that the proportion of the population of working age is fixed
     (1) But when population growth changes dramatically this may not be true
     (2) Changes in cohort sizes may cause problems for social security systems and areas like health care

3. Productivity growth
   a. The key factor in economic growth is productivity improvement
   b. Productivity improvement raises output per worker for a given level of the capital-labor ratio
   c. In equilibrium, productivity improvement increases the capital-labor ratio, output per worker, and consumption per worker
     (1) Productivity improvement directly improves the amount that can be produced at any capital-labor ratio
     (2) The increase in output per worker increases the supply of saving, causing the long-run capital-labor ratio to rise
   d. Can consumption per worker grow indefinitely?
     (1) The saving rate can't rise forever (it peaks at 100%) and the population growth rate can't fall forever
     (2) But productivity and innovation can always occur, so living standards can rise continuously
   e. Summary: The rate of productivity improvement is the dominant factor determining how quickly living standards rise

4. Application: The growth of China
   a. China is an economic juggernaut
     (1) Population 1.3 billion people
     (2) Starting with low level of GDP, but growing rapidly
       (a) About 1/9 of U.S. GDP per capita in 1998
       (b) Growth in recent years is very rapid (Fig. 6.10)
   b. Fast output growth attributable to
     (1) Huge increase in capital investment
     (2) Fast productivity growth (in part from changing to a market economy)
     (3) Increased trade
   c. Investment is huge in China; at the cost of current consumption, so saving is high
   d. Labor
     (1) China has a huge labor force; comparative advantage in labor-intensive industries (and wages are low)
     (2) As China grows, wages and standard of living will rise
   e. Problems China faces
     (1) Weak banking system
     (2) Increasing income inequality
     (3) Much unemployment in rural areas

D) Endogenous growth theory—explaining the sources of productivity growth
  1. Aggregate production function

$$Y = AK \qquad (6.12)$$

   a. Constant MPK
     (1) Human capital
       (a) Knowledge, skills, and training of individuals
       (b) Human capital tends to increase in same proportion as physical capital
     (2) Research and development programs
     (3) Increases in capital and output generate increased technical knowledge, which offsets decline in MPK from having more capital
  2. Implications of endogenous growth
   a. Suppose saving is a constant fraction of output: $S = sAK$
   b. Because investment = net investment + depreciation, $I = \Delta K + dK$
   c. Setting investment equal to saving implies:

$$\Delta K + dK = sAK \qquad (6.13)$$

   d. Rearrange (6.13):

$$\Delta K / K = sA - d \qquad (6.14)$$

   e. Because output is proportional to capital, $\Delta Y / Y = \Delta K / K$, so

$$\Delta Y / Y = sA - d \qquad (6.15)$$

   f. Thus the saving rate affects the long-run growth rate (not true in Solow model)
  3. Summary
   a. Endogenous growth theory attempts to explain, rather than assume, the economy's growth rate
   b. The growth rate depends on many things, such as the saving rate, that can be affected by government policies

III. Government Policies to Raise Long-Run Living Standards (Sec. 6.3)

A) Policies to affect the saving rate
  1. If the private market is efficient, the government shouldn't try to change the saving rate
   a. The private market's saving rate represents its trade-off of present for future consumption
   b. But if tax laws or myopia cause an inefficiently low level of saving, government policy to raise the saving rate may be justified
  2. How can saving be increased?
   a. One way is to raise the real interest rate to encourage saving; but the response of saving to changes in the real interest rate seems to be small
   b. Another way is to increase government saving
     (1) The government could reduce the deficit or run a surplus
     (2) But under Ricardian equivalence, tax increases to reduce the deficit won't affect national saving

    B) Policies to raise the rate of productivity growth
        1. Improving infrastructure
            a. Infrastructure: highways, bridges, utilities, dams, airports
            b. Empirical studies suggest a link between infrastructure and productivity
            c. U.S. infrastructure spending has declined in the last two decades
            d. Would increased infrastructure spending increase productivity?
                (1) There might be reverse causation: Richer countries with higher productivity spend more on infrastructure, rather than vice versa
                (2) Infrastructure investments by government may be inefficient, because politics, not economic efficiency, is often the main determinant
        2. Building human capital
            a. There's a strong connection between productivity and human capital
            b. Government can encourage human capital formation through educational policies, worker training and relocation programs, and health programs
            c. Another form of human capital is entrepreneurial skill
               Government could help by removing barriers like red tape
        3. Encouraging research and development
            Government can encourage R and D through direct aid to research

■ Multiple Choice Questions

1. From 1980 to 1990 North Samaria's economy grew at an annual rate of 3.5%, but from 1990 to 2000 it grew by only 1% per year. In 1990 per capita income was $8,000. How much higher would per capita income have been in 2000 if growth from 1990 to 2000 had been 3.5% rather than 1%?

    (a) $2,241
    (b) $2,448
    (c) $2,508
    (d) $3,285

2. Suppose the current level of output is 10,000 and the elasticity of output with respect to labor is 0.8. A 10% increase in labor would increase the current level of output to

    (a) 10,008.
    (b) 10,080.
    (c) 10,800.
    (d) 18,000.

3. Suppose the current level of output is 5,000. A 10% increase in productivity would increase the current level of output to

    (a) 5,050.
    (b) 5,100.
    (c) 5,500.
    (d) 6,000.

4. Over the past year, productivity grew 1.8%, capital grew 2%, and labor grew 1%. If the elasticities of output with respect to capital and labor are 0.2 and 0.8, respectively, how much did output grow?
    (a) 1%
    (b) 2%
    (c) 3%
    (d) 4%

5. The equation:

$$\Delta Y/Y = \Delta A/A + a_K \Delta K/K + a_N \Delta N/N$$

    is known as
    (a) the production function.
    (b) the Solow model.
    (c) the productivity formula.
    (d) the growth accounting equation.

6. In the growth accounting equation, productivity growth is
    (a) the difference between output growth and labor growth.
    (b) the difference between output per worker growth and labor per worker growth.
    (c) the difference between labor growth and capital growth.
    (d) output growth minus the sum of labor growth and capital growth, weighted by the elasticities of output with respect to labor and capital.

7. Over the past year, output grew 4%, capital grew 2%, and labor grew 1%. If the elasticities of output with respect to capital and labor are 0.3 and 0.7, respectively, how much did productivity grow?
    (a) 2.0%
    (b) 2.7%
    (c) 3.0%
    (d) 3.3%

8. Over the past year, output grew 4%, capital grew 2%, and labor grew 1%. If the elasticities of output with respect to capital and labor are 0.5 and 0.5, respectively, how much did productivity grow?
    (a) 1.0%
    (b) 1.5%
    (c) 2.0%
    (d) 2.5%

9. Edward Denison's analysis of the American economy found that
    (a) total factor productivity was the largest source of economic growth since 1948.
    (b) the contribution of labor growth has been more variable than the contribution of capital growth.
    (c) productivity growth has been positive over any period of more than five years since World War II.
    (d) the contribution of labor growth has been greater than the contribution of capital growth.

10. The computerization of police departments throughout the country has greatly reduced the crime rate. What macroeconomic variable is likely to be directly affected by this change?
    (a) Productivity
    (b) Inflation
    (c) The real interest rate
    (d) The trade deficit

11. The oil price explanation of the slowdown in economic growth after 1973 is inconsistent with which of the following facts?
    (a) Productivity growth did not increase sharply when oil prices declined (in real terms) in the 1980s.
    (b) The productivity slowdown began just as oil prices were quadrupled in 1973.
    (c) The productivity slowdown occurred in all industrial countries.
    (d) Industry-by-industry analysis of the impact on oil prices bears out the damage done by the oil price increases.

12. A striking conclusion of the Solow model is that in the absence of productivity growth, in the long run
    (a) the economy reaches a steady state.
    (b) consumption per worker equals the capital stock per worker.
    (c) consumption per worker equals output per worker.
    (d) consumption per worker equals investment per worker.

13. Which of the following best describes a steady state?
    (a) Political stability is maintained by the state.
    (b) People's standard of living is increasing at a stable rate.
    (c) Each firm in the economy receives a steady stream of income.
    (d) Output per worker, consumption per worker, and capital per worker are constant.

14. Steady state consumption per worker is
    (a) larger in the short run than in the long run.
    (b) less than steady state investment per worker.
    (c) less than steady state saving per worker.
    (d) steady state production per worker minus steady state investment per worker.

15. According to the Solow model, a decrease in the capital-labor ratio will
    (a) always reduce steady state consumption per worker.
    (b) always increase steady state consumption per worker.
    (c) reduce steady state consumption per worker if the capital-labor ratio is below the Golden rule capital-labor ratio.
    (d) increase steady state consumption per worker if the capital-labor ratio is below the Golden rule capital-labor ratio.

16. If the steady-state capital-labor ratio is equal to the Golden Rule capital-labor ratio, then in the steady state
    (a) output per worker equals investment per worker.
    (b) output per worker equals depreciation per worker.
    (c) investment per worker is as large as possible.
    (d) consumption per worker is as large as possible.

17. In the Solow model, if $f(k) = 2k^{0.5}$, $s = 0.25$, $n = 0.1$, and $d = 0.4$, what is the value of k at equilibrium?
    (a) 1
    (b) 2
    (c) 3
    (d) 4

18. In the Solow model, if $f(k) = 2k^{0.5}$, $s = 0.25$, $n = 0.05$, and $d = 0.2$, what is the value of $f(k)$ at equilibrium?
    (a) 2
    (b) 4
    (c) 6
    (d) 8

19. In the Solow model, if $k = 8$, $y = 25$, and $s = 0.2$, what is c?
    (a) 24
    (b) 20
    (c) 18
    (d) 12

20. According to the Solow model
    (a) there are constant returns to capital in the long run.
    (b) there are increasing returns to labor in the long run.
    (c) an increase in saving per worker will produce continuing increases in a country's standard of living in the long run.
    (d) the steady-state capital-labor ratio will be such that steady-state saving per worker equals steady-state investment per worker.

21. In the Solow model, if saving per worker initially exceeds investment per worker
    (a) the economy will experience inflation.
    (b) the capital-labor ratio will increase.
    (c) investment per worker will decline.
    (d) saving per worker will decline.

22. In the Solow model, the steady-state capital-labor ratio will decline if
    (a) the saving rate per worker increases.
    (b) the consumption rate per worker declines.
    (c) population growth increases.
    (d) productivity increases.

23. In the steady state diagram of the Solow model, an increase in saving per worker is shown by
    (a) shifting the saving-per-worker curve down, resulting in a lower steady-state capital-labor ratio.
    (b) shifting the saving-per-worker curve up, resulting in a higher steady-state capital-labor ratio.
    (c) shifting the saving-per-worker curve up, resulting in a lower steady-state capital-labor ratio.
    (d) shifting the saving-per-worker curve down, resulting in a higher steady-state capital-labor ratio.

24. New technology increases the useful life of computers, causing a permanent decrease in the rate of capital depreciation. This would cause
    (a) steady-state capital per worker to increase.
    (b) steady-state output per worker to fall.
    (c) steady-state consumption per worker to decrease.
    (d) the steady-state total capital stock to be unaffected.

25. A decline in population growth will lead to a _____ in the steady-state capital-labor ratio and a _____ in output per worker.
    (a) fall; fall
    (b) fall; rise
    (c) rise; rise
    (d) rise; fall

26. In the long run, a productivity improvement will cause
    (a) an increase in the capital-labor ratio and an increase in consumption per worker.
    (b) an increase in the capital-labor ratio and a decrease in consumption per worker.
    (c) a decrease in the capital-labor ratio and a decrease in consumption per worker.
    (d) a decrease in the capital-labor ratio and an increase in consumption per worker.

27. In the textbook model of endogenous growth, long-run output growth would rise if there were either a _____ in the saving rate or a _____ in the depreciation rate.
    (a) rise; rise
    (b) rise; fall
    (c) fall; rise
    (d) fall; fall

28. Which of the following is *not* an example of human capital formation?
    (a) Increases in the educational achievements of the population
    (b) Increases in job skills of the labor force
    (c) Improvements in the nutrition and health of the labor force
    (d) Increases in the birth rate of the population

29. Government policies that could raise the rate of productivity growth include all of the following except
    (a) improving infrastructure.
    (b) improving forecasts of unemployment.
    (c) helping build human capital by worker training programs.
    (d) encouraging research and development.

30. Which of the following would be a useful way to increase the saving rate?
    (a) tax breaks to increase the real return that savers receive
    (b) increasing taxes if Ricardian equivalence holds
    (c) increasing government spending
    (d) increasing taxes on capital goods

■ Review Questions

1. Identify and briefly describe the three principal sources of economic growth. Identify and briefly describe one cause of a change in each of these three variables that would increase economic growth.

2. Identify and briefly explain five potential causes of the post-1973 growth slowdown in the United States.

3. Briefly explain the shape of the per-worker production curve in the Solow model. If investment per worker initially exceeds saving per worker, how is the steady-state capital-labor ratio achieved?

4. How would each of the following changes affect the capital-labor ratio?
   (a) A decline in saving per worker
   (b) A decline in population
   (c) A decline in productivity

5. Why does the Solow growth model predict convergence in the standards of living of people in rich and poor countries, and why does the empirical evidence appear to reject the theory?

6. Describe the main ideas of endogenous growth theory. What does it have to say about the role of government in economic growth?

■ Numerical Problems

1. Use the growth accounting equation to calculate productivity growth, given output growth of 3.5%, capital stock growth of 5%, labor employment growth of 2%, the output elasticity of capital of 0.3, and the output elasticity of labor of 0.7.

2. In the past ten years, Patagonia's total output has increased from 2,000 to 3,000, the capital stock has risen from 4,000 to 5,200, and the labor force has increased from 400 to 580. Suppose $a_K = 0.4$ and $a_N = 0.6$.
   (a) How much did capital contribute to economic growth over the decade?
   (b) How much did labor contribute to economic growth over the decade?
   (c) How much did productivity contribute to economic growth over the decade?

3. A country has the per-worker production function

$$y_t = 3k_t^{2/3},$$

where y_t is output per worker and k_t is the capital-labor ratio. The depreciation rate is 0.1 and the population growth rate is 0.05. The saving function is

$$S_t = 0.2Y_t,$$

where S_t is total national saving and Y_t is total output.

(a) What is the steady-state value of capital-labor ratio?

(b) What is the steady-state value of output per worker?

(c) What is the steady-state value of consumption per worker?

4. Calculate the real GDP per capita after four years of 10% annual economic growth for a country starting with a real GDP per capita of $15,000. Compare this to the real GDP per capita after four years of 1% annual economic growth for a country starting with a real GDP per capita of $20,000. Assume there is no population growth in either country.

■ Analytical Questions

1. (a) Draw figures showing the relationship in the Solow model between the capital-labor ratio and (1) output per worker and steady-state investment per worker, (2) consumption per worker, and (3) steady-state investment per worker and saving per worker.

    (b) Suppose the steady-state capital stock is less than the Golden Rule capital stock. Show what happens to each of your figures in part (a) when each of the following changes occur, and explain what happens to the capital-labor ratio, output per worker, and consumption per worker.

    (1) Population growth rises.

    (2) The depreciation rate falls.

    (3) The saving rate rises.

    (4) Productivity declines.

■ Answers

Multiple Choice

1. b	7. b	13. d	19. b	25. c
2. c	8. d	14. d	20. d	26. a
3. c	9. d	15. c	21. b	27. b
4. c	10. a	16. d	22. c	28. d
5. d	11. a	17. a	23. b	29. b
6. d	12. a	18. b	24. a	30. a

Review Questions

1. The three principal sources of economic growth are: (1) labor growth—increases in the work force; (2) capital growth—increases in the amount of capital employed in the economy; and (3) productivity growth—increases in output for given amounts of labor and capital.

    Causes of positive changes in the sources of economic growth are: (1) labor growth—an increase in the size of the population through immigration or birth and an increase in the share of the population that works (e.g., more women) will increase labor growth; (2) capital growth—an increase in the rate of saving will increase capital growth; and (3) productivity growth—an increase in human capital and a technological advance will increase productivity.

2. Five of the significant causes of the post-1973 growth slowdown in the United States are:

    (1) Measurement problems. Actual growth may have exceeded measured economic growth during this period; the slowdown may be, at least in part, an illusion. Production of services now dominates production of goods, but increases in the quality and quantity of services (e.g., haircuts and financial consultant services) are harder to measure than increases in the quality and quantity of goods.

    (2) Legal and human environment. New legislated regulations to reduce pollution and improve worker safety and health caused some workers and capital to be allocated to meeting these new regulatory requirements, which reduced the amount of labor and capital available to produce goods and services. Increased use of labor and capital to fight crimes and a decline in educational quality (e.g., human capital) also reduced overall productivity.

    (3) Technological depletion. The technological depletion hypothesis suggests that there were relatively few valuable technological innovations after 1973 and that earlier innovations are no longer producing significant productivity gains. Although significant breakthroughs in electronics (e.g., computers) and in biogenetic engineering (e.g., gene-splicing) have been achieved, they have not as yet produced significant productivity increases.

    (4) Commercial adaptation. American firms have been slow during this period to make commercially profitable use of recent scientific and technological breakthroughs, whereas some foreign firms, including Japanese firms, have benefited greatly from these breakthroughs.

    (5) Oil price increases. The substantial oil price increases in the post-1973 period lowered the amount of output that could be produced from a given amount of capital and labor, thus lowering productivity. Oil price increases caused the prices of all sources of energy and the prices of all intermediate products to increase, thereby significantly increasing final production costs.

3. The per-worker production curve is positively sloped because adding capital to each unit of labor increases output per worker. The curve is concave (i.e., increasing at a decreasing rate) because of diminishing marginal productivity of capital; output increases at a slower rate than capital when capital is added to production.

    The steady-state capital-labor ratio is the capital-labor ratio at which saving per worker $[sf(k)]$ equals investment per worker $[(n + d)k]$. If investment per worker initially exceeds saving per worker, then the initial capital-labor ratio exceeds the steady-state capital-labor ratio. The capital-labor ratio will decline because saving is insufficient to provide enough capital to maintain the initial capital-labor ratio. The capital-labor ratio will continue to decline until it reaches the steady-state capital-labor ratio.

4. (a) A decline in saving per worker causes the steady-state capital-labor ratio to decline.

    (b) A decline in population causes the steady-state capital-labor ratio to increase.

    (c) A decline in productivity causes the steady-state capital-labor ratio to decline.

5. The Solow model predicts that the standards of living of two closed economies with different capital-labor ratios will eventually converge if they have the same production function, saving rate, and population growth rate. This is because they will have the same steady-state capital-labor ratio toward which both economies move, and the steady-state capital-labor ratio determines their long-run standard of living. If the two countries are open economies, convergence will be faster and will occur even if the two countries have different saving-per-worker functions; in this case, saving will flow out of the rich, high-saving-rate country into the poor country until the investment per worker is the same in each country. The lack of strong empirical support for unconditional convergence may be explained by inefficiencies in the international capital market and by variables that are missing from the model, including differences in human capital, political stability, and the availability of natural resources.

6. Endogenous growth theory explains the main sources of productivity growth: human capital (the knowledge, skills, and training of individuals) and technological innovation (caused by research and development programs and learning by doing). Government may play a positive role, because policies that increase the capital-labor ratio may lead to a virtuous circle of growth, raising living standards. Also, the government may foster education and research and development.

Numerical Problems

1. The growth accounting equation is $\Delta Y/Y = \Delta A/A + a_K \Delta K/K + a_N \Delta N/N$.

    Therefore, productivity growth is $\Delta A/A = \Delta Y/Y - a_K \Delta K/K - a_N \Delta N/N$.

    For the given values, productivity growth $= 3.5\% - (0.3)(5\%) - (0.7)(2\%) = 0.6\%$.

2. (a) $a_K \Delta K/K = 0.4(1200/4000) = 12\%$.

    (b) $a_N \Delta N/N = 0.6(180/400) = 27\%$.

    (c) $\Delta Y/Y = 50\%$.

    $$\Delta A/A = \Delta Y/Y - a_K \Delta K/K - a_N \Delta N/N$$
    $$= 50\% - 12\% - 27\% = 11\%.$$

3. (a) $sf(k) = (n + d)k$, so $0.2 \times 3k^{2/3} = 0.15k$; or $k^{1/3} = 4$, so $k = 64$.

    (b) $y = 3k^{2/3} = 48$.

    (c) $c = (1 - s)y = 0.8y = 38.4$.

4. One country starts with real GDP per capita = $15,000 and achieves 10% economic growth each year, with no population growth. Its real GDP per capita at the end of the first year is $15,000 × 1.1 = $16,500; at the end of the second year it is $16,500 × 1.1 = $18,150; at the end of the third year it is $18,150 × 1.1 = $19,965; and at the end of the fourth year it is $19,965 × 1.1 = $21,962. Note that the same calculation can be done in one step as $15,000 × 1.1^4 = $21,962.

    The other country starts with real GDP per capita = $20,000 and achieves 1% economic growth each year, with no population growth. Its real GDP per capita at the end of the first year is $20,000 × 1.01 = $20,200; at the end of the second year it is $20,200 × 1.01 = $20,402; at the end of the third year it is $20,402 × 1.01 = $20,606; and at the end of the fourth year it is $20,606 × 1.01 = $20,812. The $20,812 real GDP per capita for this country is now $1,150 lower than the real GDP per capita of the first country, even though it started with real GDP per capita that was $5,000 lower. So a country that grows rapidly can catch up quickly to a richer country that grows more slowly.

Analytical Questions

1.   (a) See Figures 6.3 and 6.4.

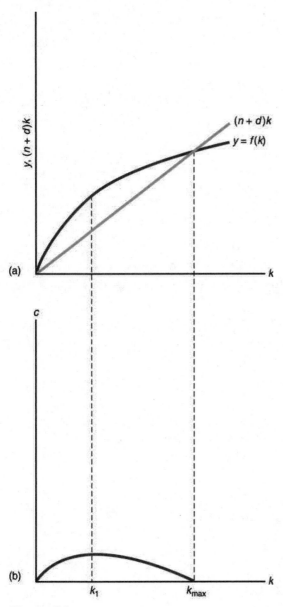

Figure 6.3

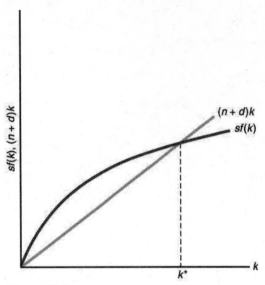

Figure 6.4

(b) With the steady-state capital stock less than the Golden Rule capital stock, if a change occurs that raises the steady-state capital stock, steady-state output and consumption will both rise, and vice versa.

   (1) The rise in population growth shifts the line representing $(n + d)k$ up, as Figure 6.5 shows, so k, y, and c all fall.

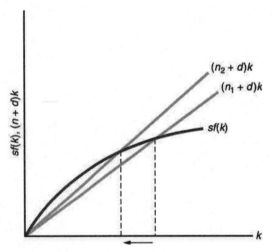

Figure 6.5

(2) The fall in the depreciation rate shifts the line representing $(n + d)k$ down, as Figure 6.6 shows, so k, y, and c all rise.

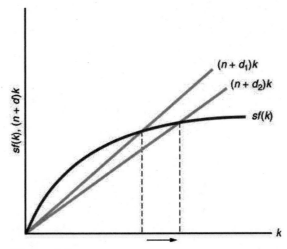

Figure 6.6

(3) The rise in the saving rate shifts the line representing $sf(k)$ up, as Figure 6.7 shows, so k, y, and c all rise.

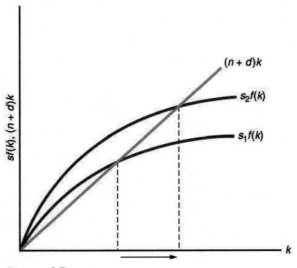

Figure 6.7

(4) The decline in productivity shifts the line representing $sf(k)$ down, as Figure 6.8 shows, so k, y, and c all fall.

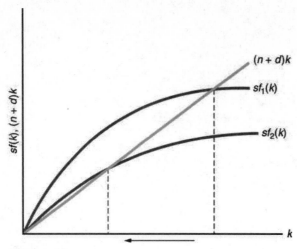

Figure 6.8

Chapter 7
The Asset Market, Money, and Prices

■ Introduction

This chapter examines money and prices in great detail. The chapter begins by discussing what money is and why people hold it in Section 7.1. It also discusses the main measures of the money supply. Then, Section 7.2 shows that the decision about money demand is part of a broader portfolio decision, in which people decide on what assets to hold based on expected return, risk, liquidity, and other factors. Section 7.3 covers the demand for money itself, deriving a function that explains money demand and introducing the quantity theory of money. In Section 7.4, equilibrium in the asset market is shown to occur when money supply equals money demand. Finally, Section 7.5 shows how money growth is related to inflation.

■ Outline

I.   **What is Money? (Sec. 7.1)**

A)   Money: assets that are widely used and accepted as payment

B)   The functions of money

1.   Medium of exchange

a.   Barter is inefficient—it requires a double coincidence of wants

b.   Money allows people to trade their labor for money, then use the money to buy goods and services in separate transactions

c.   Money thus permits people to trade with less cost in time and effort

d.   Money also allows specialization, because trading is much easier, so people don't have to produce their own food, clothing, and shelter

2.   Unit of account

a.   Money is the basic unit for measuring economic value

b.   This simplifies comparisons of prices, wages, and incomes

c.   The unit-of-account function is closely linked with the medium-of-exchange function

d.   But countries with very high inflation may use a different unit of account, so they don't have to constantly change prices

3.   Store of value

a.   Money can be used to hold wealth

b.   Most people use money only as a store of value for a short period and for small amounts, because it earns less interest than money in the bank

    4. Box 7.1: money in a prisoner-of-war camp

       a. Radford article on the use of cigarettes as money

       b. Cigarette use as money developed because barter was inefficient

       c. Even nonsmokers used cigarettes as money

       d. Characteristics of cigarettes as money: standardized (so value was easy to ascertain), low in value (so "change" could be made), portable, fairly sturdy

       e. Problem with having a commodity money like cigarettes: can't smoke them and use them as money at the same time

C) Measuring money—the monetary aggregates

    1. Distinguishing what is money from what isn't money is sometimes difficult

       a. For example, MMMFs allow checkwriting, but give a higher return than bank checking accounts: Are they money?

       b. There's no single best measure of the money stock

    2. The M1 monetary aggregate

       a. Consists of currency and traveler's checks held by the public, demand deposits (which pay no interest), and other checkable deposits (which may pay interest)

       b. All components of M1 are used in making payments, so M1 is the closest money measure to our theoretical description of money

    3. The M2 monetary aggregate

       a. M2 = M1 + less moneylike assets

       b. Additional assets in M2 include savings deposits, small (< $100,000) time deposits, noninstitutional MMMF balances, money-market deposit accounts (MMDAs)

          (1) Savings deposits include passbook savings accounts

          (2) Time deposits bear interest and have a fixed term (substantial penalty for early withdrawal)

          (3) MMMFs invest in very short-term securities and allow checkwriting

          (4) MMDAs are offered by banks as a competitor to MMMFs

    4. Table 7.1 shows recent data

D) Box 7.2: Where have all the dollars gone?

    1. In 2006, U.S. currency averaged about $2,500 per person, but surveys show people only hold about $100

    2. Some is held by businesses and the underground economy, but most is held abroad

    3. Foreigners hold dollars because of inflation in their local currency and political instability

    4. Because currency is 1/2 of M1 and over 1/2 of currency is held abroad, foreigners hold over 1/4 of M1

       a. The data show large fluctuations in M1 when major events occur abroad, like military conflicts

    5. The United States benefits from foreign holdings of our currency, because we essentially get an interest-free loan

E) The money supply

    1. Money supply = money stock = amount of money available in the economy

    2. How does the central bank of a country increase the money supply?

       a. Use newly printed money to buy financial assets from the public—an open-market purchase

       b. To reduce the money supply, sell financial assets to the public to remove money from circulation—an open-market sale

       c. Open-market purchases and sales are called open-market operations

       d. Could also buy newly issued government bonds directly from the government (i.e., the Treasury)

         (1) This is the same as the government financing its expenditures directly by printing money

         (2) This happens frequently in some countries (though is forbidden by law in the United States)

    3. Throughout text, use the variable M to represent money supply; this might be M1, M2, or some other aggregate

II.   Portfolio Allocation and the Demand for Assets (Sec. 7.2)

How do people allocate their wealth among various assets? The portfolio allocation decision

A) Expected return

    1. Rate of return = an asset's increase in value per unit of time

       a. Bank account: Rate of return = interest rate

       b. Corporate stock: Rate of return = dividend yield + percent increase in stock price

    2. Investors want assets with the highest expected return (other things being equal)

    3. Returns aren't always known in advance (for example, stock prices fluctuate unexpectedly), so people must estimate their *expected return*

B) Risk

    1. Risk is the degree of uncertainty in an asset's return

    2. People don't like risk, so prefer assets with low risk (other things being equal)

C) Liquidity

    1. Liquidity is the ease and quickness with which an asset can be traded

    2. Money is very liquid

    3. Assets like automobiles and houses are very illiquid—it may take a long time and large transaction costs to trade them

    4. Stocks and bonds are fairly liquid, some more so than others

    5. Investors prefer liquid assets (other things being equal)

D) Time to maturity

    1. Time to maturity: the amount of time until an asset matures and the investor is repaid the principal

    2. Expectations theory of the term structure of interest rates: the idea that investors compare returns on bonds with differing times to maturity; in equilibrium, holding different types of bonds over the same period yields the same expected return

    3. Because long-term interest rates usually exceed short-term interest rates, a risk premium exists: the compensation to an investor for bearing the risk of holding a long-term bond

E) Asset demands

   1. Trade-off among expected return, risk, liquidity, and time to maturity

   2. Assets with low risk and high liquidity, like checking accounts, have low expected returns

   3. Investors consider diversification: spreading out investments in different assets to reduce risk

   4. The amount a wealth holder wants of an asset is his or her demand for that asset

   5. The sum of asset demands equals total wealth

III. The Demand for Money (Sec. 7.3)

A) The demand for money is the quantity of monetary assets people want to hold in their portfolios

   1. Money demand depends on expected return, risk, and liquidity

   2. Money is the most liquid asset

   3. Money pays a low return

   4. People's money-holding decisions depend on how much they value liquidity against the low return on money

B) Key macroeconomic variables that affect money demand

   1. Price level

      a. The higher the price level, the more money you need for transactions

      b. Prices are ten times as high today as in 1935, so it takes ten times as much money for equivalent transactions

      c. Nominal money demand is thus proportional to the price level

   2. Real income

      a. The more transactions you conduct, the more money you need

      b. Real income is a prime determinant of the number of transactions you conduct

      c. So money demand rises as real income rises

      d. But money demand isn't proportional to real income, because higher-income individuals use money more efficiently, and because a country's financial sophistication grows as its income rises (use of credit and more sophisticated assets)

      e. Result: Money demand rises less than 1-to-1 with a rise in real income

   3. Interest rates

      a. An increase in the interest rate or return on nonmonetary assets decreases the demand for money

      b. An increase in the interest rate on money increases money demand

      c. This occurs as people trade off liquidity for return

      d. Though there are many nonmonetary assets with many different interest rates, because they often move together we assume that for nonmonetary assets there's just one nominal interest rate, i

      e. The real interest rate, which affects saving and investment decisions, is $r = i - \pi^e$

      f. The nominal interest paid on money is i^m

C) The money demand function

   1. $M^d = P \times L(Y, i)$ (7.1)

      a. M^d is nominal money demand (aggregate)

      b. P is the price level

      c. L is the money demand function

      d. Y is real income or output

      e. i is the nominal interest rate on nonmonetary assets

2. As discussed above, nominal money demand is proportional to the price level

3. A rise in Y increases money demand; a rise in i reduces money demand

4. We exclude i^m from Eq. (7.1) because it doesn't vary much

5. Alternative expression:

$$M^d = P \times L(Y, r + \pi^e) \qquad (7.2)$$

A rise in r or π^e reduces money demand

6. Alternative expression:

$$M^d/P = L(Y, r + \pi^e) \qquad (7.3)$$

7. The left side of Eq. (7.3) is the demand for real balances, or real money demand

D) Other factors affecting money demand

1. Wealth: A rise in wealth may increase money demand, but not by much

2. Risk

   a. Increased riskiness in the economy may increase money demand

   b. Times of erratic inflation bring increased risk to money, so money demand declines

3. Liquidity of alternative assets: Deregulation, competition, and innovation have given other assets more liquidity, reducing the demand for money

4. Payment technologies: Credit cards, ATMs, and other financial innovations reduce money demand

E) Elasticities of money demand

1. How strong are the various effects on money demand?

2. Statistical studies on the money demand function show results in elasticities

3. Elasticity: The percent change in money demand caused by a one percent change in some factor

4. Income elasticity of money demand

   a. Positive: Higher income increases money demand

   b. Less than one: Higher income increases money demand less than proportionately

   c. Goldfeld's results: income elasticity = 2/3

5. Interest elasticity of money demand
   Small and negative: Higher interest rate on nonmonetary assets reduces money demand slightly

6. Price elasticity of money demand is unitary, so money demand is proportional to the price level

F) Velocity and the quantity theory of money

1. Velocity (V) measures how much money "turns over" each period

2. V = nominal GDP/nominal money stock = PY/M $\qquad (7.4)$

3. Plot of velocities for M1 and M2 (text Figure 7.1) shows fairly stable velocity for M2, erratic velocity for M1 beginning in early 1980s

4. Quantity theory of money: Real money demand is proportional to real income
   a. If so,

$$M^d/P = kY \qquad (7.5)$$

   b. Assumes constant velocity, where velocity isn't affected by income or interest rates

c. But velocity of M1 is not constant; it rose steadily from 1960 to 1980 and has been erratic since then

(1) Part of the change in velocity is due to changes in interest rates in the 1980s

(2) Financial innovations also played a role in velocity's decline in the early 1980s

d. M2 velocity is closer to being a constant, but not over short periods

G) Application: financial regulation, innovation, and the instability of money demand

1. Goldfeld (1973) found a stable money (M1) demand function

2. But late 1974 to early 1976, M1 demand fell relative to that predicted by the model

3. And in the early 1980s, M1 demand rose relative to that predicted by the model

4. Why did money demand shift erratically?
Increased innovation and changes in the financial system (see text Figure 7.2)

a. New assets were invented in the 1970s, liquid assets that paid interest
People switched wealth from M1 to these assets, reducing M1 demand

(1) MMMFs

(2) Overnight repurchase agreements

b. New assets in the 1980s, interest-bearing checking accounts; their use brought wealth into M1, raising money demand

5. Developments in the 1990s

a. Sweep programs reduce demand for reserves and M1

b. M2 erratic because of increased use of mutual funds

IV. Asset Market Equilibrium (Sec. 7.4)

A) Asset market equilibrium—an aggregation assumption

1. Assume that all assets can be grouped into two categories, money and nonmonetary assets

a. Money includes currency and checking accounts

(1) Pays interest rate i^m

(2) Supply is fixed at M

b. Nonmonetary assets include stocks, bonds, land, etc.

(1) Pays interest rate $i = r + \pi^e$

(2) Supply is fixed at NM

2. Asset market equilibrium occurs when quantity of money supplied equals quantity of money demanded

a. $m^d + nm^d$ = total nominal wealth of an individual

b. $M^d + NM^d$ = aggregate nominal wealth (from adding up individual wealth)   (7.6)

c. $M + NM$ = aggregate nominal wealth (supply of assets)   (7.7)

d. Subtracting Eq. (7.7) from Eq. (7.6) gives

$$(M^d - M) + (NM^d - NM) = 0 \qquad (7.8)$$

e. So the excess demand for money ($M^d - M$) plus the excess demand for nonmonetary assets ($NM^d - NM$) equals 0

f. So if money supply equals money demand, nonmonetary asset supply must equal nonmonetary asset demand; then the entire asset market is in equilibrium

B) The asset market equilibrium condition

1. $M/P = L(Y, r + \pi^e)$ (7.9)

real money supply = real money demand

a. M is determined by the central bank

b. π^e is fixed (for now)

c. The labor market determines the level of employment; using employment in the production function determines Y

d. Given Y, the goods market equilibrium condition determines r

2. With all the other variables in Eq. (7.9) determined, the asset market equilibrium condition determines the price level

a. $P = M/L(Y, r + \pi^e)$ (7.10)

b. The price level is the ratio of nominal money supply to real money demand

c. For example, doubling the money supply would double the price level

V. Money Growth and Inflation (Sec. 7.5)

A) The inflation rate is closely related to the growth rate of the money supply

1. Rewrite Eq. (7.10) in growth-rate terms:

$$\Delta P/P = \Delta M/M - \Delta L(Y, r + \pi^e)/L(Y, r + \pi^e)$$ (7.11)

2. If the asset market is in equilibrium, the inflation rate equals the growth rate of the nominal money supply minus the growth rate of real money demand

3. To predict inflation we must forecast both money supply growth and real money demand growth

a. In long-run equilibrium, we will have i constant, so let's look just at growth in Y

b. Let η_Y be the elasticity of money demand with respect to income

c. Then from Eq. (7.11),

$$\pi = \Delta M/M - \eta_Y \Delta Y/Y$$ (7.12)

d. Example: If output grows 3% per year, the income elasticity of money demand is 2/3, and the money supply is growing at a 10% rate, then the inflation rate will be 8%

B) Application: money growth and inflation in the European countries in transition

1. Though the countries of Eastern Europe are becoming more market-oriented, Russia and some others have high inflation because of rapid money growth

2. Both the growth rates of money demand and money supply affect inflation, but (in cases of high inflation) usually growth of nominal money supply is the most important factor

a. For example, if the income elasticity of money demand were 2/3 and real output grew 15%, real money demand would grow 10% (= 2/3 × 15%); or if income fell 15%, real money demand would fall 10%

b. So money demand doesn't vary much, no matter how well or poorly an economy is doing, but nominal money supply growth differs across countries by hundreds of percentage points, so large inflation differences must be due to money supply, not money demand

3. Text Figure 7.3 shows the link between money growth and inflation in these countries; inflation is clearly positively associated with money growth

   4. So why do countries allow money supplies to grow quickly, if they know it will cause inflation?
      a. They sometimes find that printing money is the only way to finance government expenditures
      b. This is especially true for very poor countries, or countries in political crisis
C) The expected inflation rate and the nominal interest rate
   1. For a given real interest rate (r), expected inflation (π^e) determines the nominal interest rate $(i = r + \pi^e)$
   2. What factors determine expected inflation?
      a. People could use Eq. (7.12), relating inflation to the growth rates of the nominal money supply and real income
         (1) If people expect an increase in money growth, they would then expect a commensurate increase in the inflation rate
         (2) The expected inflation rate would equal the current inflation rate if money growth and income growth were stable
      b. Expectations can't be observed directly
         (1) They can be measured roughly by surveys
         (2) If real interest rates are stable, expected inflation can be inferred from nominal interest rates
         (3) Policy actions that cause expected inflation to rise should cause nominal interest rates to rise
   3. Text Figure 7.4 plots U.S. inflation and nominal interest rates
      a. Inflation and nominal interest rates have tended to move together
      b. But the real interest rate is clearly not constant
      c. The real interest rate was negative in the mid 1970s, then became much higher and positive in the late 1970s to early 1980s
D) Application: measuring inflation expectations
   1. How do we find out people's expectations of inflation?
      a. We could look at surveys
      b. But a better way is to observe implicit expectations from bond interest rates
   2. The U.S. government issues nominal bonds and Treasury Inflation Indexed Securities (TIIS)
      a. TIIS bonds make real interest payments by adjusting interest and principal for inflation
      b. Compare nominal interest rate with real interest rate (Figure 7.5)
   3. The interest rate differential: interest rate on nominal bonds minus real interest rate on TIIS bonds
      a. The interest rate differential is a rough measure of expected inflation
      b. TIIS bonds have lower inflation risk, so the measure of expected inflation may be too high
      c. TIIS bonds do not have as liquid a market, so the measure of expected inflation may be too low
      d. The net effect of the two effects is likely to be small, so the measure of expected inflation may be about right

4. The data show fluctuations in the expected inflation rate based on the interest rate differential (Figure 7.6)

    a. In contrast, the rate of expected inflation measured in surveys has been fairly constant

    b. Either bond market participants have very different inflation expectations than forecasters, or else the degree of inflation risk and liquidity on TIIS bonds varied substantially from 1998 to 2006

■ Multiple Choice Questions

1. A system in which people trade goods they don't want to consume for goods they do want to consume is called

    (a) an indirect exchange economy.

    (b) a commodity money system.

    (c) a barter system.

    (d) a fiat money system.

2. The following are all functions of money EXCEPT

    (a) medium of exchange.

    (b) store of value.

    (c) source of anxiety.

    (d) unit of account.

3. Which of the following best illustrates the medium of exchange function of money?

    (a) The price of a new car is $25,000.

    (b) A penny saved is a penny earned.

    (c) A person owes $10,000 on his or her credit card.

    (d) You pay $3 to purchase a bag of apples.

4. In some countries the U.S. dollar is used as a unit of account rather than the local currency. The primary reason for this is that

    (a) the nation has been running a trade surplus.

    (b) the nation has been running a trade deficit.

    (c) the U.S. inflation rate is higher than the local inflation rate.

    (d) U.S. dollars reduce the need to change prices frequently.

5. M1 includes

    (a) demand deposits.

    (b) savings deposits.

    (c) time deposits.

    (d) money market mutual funds.

6. Which of the following statements about M1 and M2 is *not* true?

    (a) Demand deposits are part of M1.

    (b) M2 is more liquid than M1.

    (c) M2 is larger than M1.

    (d) Savings accounts are part of M2.

7. Which of the following is *not* included in M2?
   (a) Money market mutual funds held by individuals
   (b) Money market deposit accounts
   (c) Money market mutual funds held by institutions
   (d) Small-denomination time deposits

8. Suppose your bank lowers its minimum-balance requirement on NOW accounts by $500. You take $500 out of your NOW account and put it in your passbook savings account. What is the overall effect on M1 and M2?
   (a) M1 falls by $500, M2 rises by $500.
   (b) M1 is unchanged, M2 is unchanged.
   (c) M1 falls by $500, M2 is unchanged.
   (d) M1 is unchanged, M2 rises by $500.

9. The stock of U.S. currency per U.S. resident (calculated as the total U.S. currency divided by the U.S. population) in 2005 was about
   (a) $100.
   (b) $500.
   (c) $1,000.
   (d) $2,500.

10. Suppose you read in the paper that the central bank of the United States plans to expand the money supply. The central bank is most likely to do this by
    (a) printing more currency and distributing it.
    (b) purchasing government bonds from the public.
    (c) selling government bonds to the public.
    (d) buying newly issued government bonds directly from the government itself.

11. You are putting together a portfolio of assets. The four most important characteristics of the assets you will choose are expected return, time to maturity,
    (a) risk, and liquidity.
    (b) risk, and collateral.
    (c) risk, and reward.
    (d) liquidity, and standard issue size.

12. The existence of a _____ means that the interest rate on a two-year bond will exceed the average interest rate on two successive one-year bonds.
    (a) risky asset
    (b) non-collateralized obligation
    (c) term structure
    (d) risk premium

13. Which of the following portfolio allocation decisions represents the best individual response to an increase in the interest rate on nonmonetary assets?
    (a) Sell some stocks and use the money to buy bonds.
    (b) Sell some bonds and use the money to buy stocks.
    (c) Trade some money for nonmonetary assets.
    (d) Sell some land and use the money to buy nonmonetary assets.

14. A 1% increase in real income usually leads to _____ in money demand.
    (a) a decrease
    (b) no change
    (c) an increase of less than 1%
    (d) an increase of 1%

15. During the past year, there was an increase in the price level and an increase in interest rates on financial assets, but a fall in personal incomes. The overall demand for money fell. Which of the following factors was most likely to have contributed to this fall in the demand for money?
    (a) Changes in the price level and in interest rates
    (b) Changes in interest rates and personal incomes
    (c) Changes in the price level and personal incomes
    (d) Changes in personal incomes only

16. Money demand is given by

    $$M^d/P = 1,000 + .2Y - 1,000i.$$

    Given that $P = 200$, $Y = 2,000$, and $i = .10$, nominal money demand is equal to
    (a) 1,300.
    (b) 1,500.
    (c) 260,000.
    (d) 300,000.

17. If the interest elasticity of money demand is $-1/4$, by what percent does money demand rise if the nominal interest rate rises from 4% to 5%?
    (a) 6.25%
    (b) 0.25%
    (c) -0.25%
    (d) -6.25%

18. If real income rises 5%, prices rise 2%, and nominal money demand rises 6%, what is the income elasticity of real money demand?
    (a) 3/4
    (b) 4/5
    (c) 5/6
    (d) 6/7

19. Instability in M1 money demand in the mid-1970s and since the early 1980s is most closely related to changes in
    (a) Federal Reserve chairmen.
    (b) the risks of nonmonetary assets.
    (c) real GNP.
    (d) deregulation, financial innovations, and payment technologies.

20. According to the quantity theory of money, velocity
    (a) increases with nominal income.
    (b) is positively related to the real interest rate.
    (c) is constant.
    (d) is proportional to the price level.

21. If nominal GDP is $7 trillion, the price level is 200, and the nominal money stock is $1 trillion, then velocity is
    (a) 1/7.
    (b) 2.
    (c) 3.5.
    (d) 7.

22. Suppose velocity is 6, real output is 6,000, and the price level is 200. What is the level of real money demand in this economy?
    (a) 1,000
    (b) 2,000
    (c) 20,000
    (d) 200,000

23. Suppose velocity is constant at 3, real output is 6,000, and the price level is 20. From this initial situation, the government increases the nominal money supply to 50,000. If velocity and output remain unchanged, by how much will the price level increase?
    (a) 10%
    (b) 20%
    (c) 25%
    (d) 50%

24. Suppose the real money demand function is

    $$M^d/P = 2400 + 0.2Y - 10,000\,(r + \pi^e).$$

    Assume $M = 5,000$, $\pi^e = .03$, and $Y = 5,000$. If the price level were to increase from 2.0 to 2.5, then the real interest rate would increase by how many percentage points (assuming M^d, π^e, and Y are unchanged)?
    (a) 4
    (b) 5
    (c) 9
    (d) 14

25. When the quantity of money supplied equals the quantity of money demanded, then
    (a) the goods market is in equilibrium.
    (b) the money market is in equilibrium.
    (c) the asset market is in equilibrium.
    (d) the money market is not in equilibrium.

26. Which of these variables is not directly involved in the asset market equilibrium condition?
    (a) investment
    (b) nominal money supply
    (c) real interest rate
    (d) expected inflation rate

27. If the asset market is to remain in equilibrium, then if the money supply increases, output is unchanged, the price level is unchanged, and the expected inflation rate is unchanged, then
    (a) the real interest rate must rise.
    (b) the real interest rate must decline.
    (c) the nominal interest rate must rise.
    (d) the inflation rate must rise.

28. If the asset market is in equilibrium, the growth rate of the nominal money supply minus the growth rate of real money demand equals
    (a) the real interest rate.
    (b) the inflation rate.
    (c) the price level.
    (d) the growth rate of real output.

29. If the asset market is in equilibrium, the money supply increases 5%, the income elasticity of money demand equals 2/3, and real income grows 3%, and all other factors affecting real money demand are unchanged, then the inflation rate equals
    (a) 3%.
    (b) 5%.
    (c) 7%.
    (d) 8%.

30. Bonds sold by the U.S. government that offer a certain real interest rate are known as
    (a) Treasury Inflation Indexed Securities.
    (b) Real Treasury Notes.
    (c) Special Price Indexed Debt Real Securities.
    (d) Zero Coupon Bonds.

■ Review Questions

1. Identify and briefly describe the three principal functions of money.

2. What are the major components of M1? What are the major components of M2?

3. Identify and briefly define the four principal characteristics of assets that influence portfolio allocation decisions.

4. Identify three possible causes of an increase in money demand.

5. Briefly explain how money demand and velocity are related.

6. Define asset market equilibrium and state the asset market equilibrium condition.

■ Numerical Problems

1. Suppose the income elasticity of money demand is 0.75 and the interest elasticity of money demand is –0.2. By what percentage does real money demand change in each of the following circumstances?
    (a) Income rises 2%.
    (b) The interest rate rises from 4% to 5%.
    (c) Income falls 4%.
    (d) The interest rate falls from 6% to 4%.
    (e) Income rises 3% at the same time that the interest rate rises from 2% to 3%.

2. Calculate the decline in money demand for each of the following changes in the interest rate, given that money demand is $500 billion at an interest rate of 5%.
    (a) The interest rises to 8% and the interest elasticity of money demand is –0.1.
    (b) The interest rate falls to 2% and the interest elasticity of money demand is –0.2.

3. Calculate the inflation rate for each of the following conditions, assuming that the income elasticity of money demand is 2/3 and that the nominal interest rate is constant.
    (a) Nominal money supply growth is 4% and real income growth is 6%.
    (b) Nominal money supply growth is 12% and real income growth is 6%.
    (c) Nominal money supply growth is –2% and real income growth is –3%.

4. Calculate the expected rate of inflation for each of the following conditions.
    (a) The nominal interest rate is 10% and the real interest rate is 4%.
    (b) The nominal interest rate is 6% and the real interest rate is 3%.
    (c) The nominal interest rate is 4% and the real interest rate is –1%.

■ Analytical Questions

1. In each of the following cases, one factor affecting money demand changes. You must tell how the second factor would have to change if real money demand were to remain unchanged overall.

    (a) Expected inflation rises; real income _____.

    (b) Nominal interest rate on money rises; wealth _____.

    (c) Risk on stocks and bonds rises; efficiency of payments technology _____.

    (d) Risk on money rises; real interest rate on nonmoney assets _____.

    (e) Liquidity of nonmonetary assets rises; expected inflation _____.

    (f) Wealth rises; risk on nonmonetary assets _____.

■ Answers

Multiple Choice

1. c	7. c	13. c	19. d	25. c
2. c	8. c	14. c	20. c	26. a
3. d	9. d	15. b	21. d	27. b
4. d	10. b	16. c	22. a	28. b
5. a	11. a	17. d	23. c	29. a
6. b	12. d	18. b	24. b	30. a

[*Note*: Most people miss question 8 because they automatically answer a, forgetting that M1 is part of M2.]

Review Questions

1. The three principal functions of money are the following:

    (1) Medium of exchange. Money is used to pay for the factors of production, goods and services, and nonmonetary assets.

    (2) Unit of account. Money is the standard used to compare the market values of dissimilar resources, goods, and assets. For example, the dollar is the monetary standard for the United States; the value of things is measured in dollar units.

    (3) Store of value. Money is used as a way of holding wealth. For example, keeping money in a checking account represents using money as a store of value.

2. The principal components of M1 are currency, demand deposits, other checkable deposits, and traveler's checks. Currency includes coins and Federal Reserve notes (i.e., paper money). Other checkable deposits are checking accounts at banks and thrifts that earn interest (e.g., NOW accounts).

    The principal components of M2 are M1, savings account deposits including money market deposit accounts (MMDAs), small time deposits, and money market mutual funds (MMMFs). Small time deposits are certificates of deposits (CDs) of less than $100,000 denomination.

3. The four principal characteristics of assets that determine portfolio allocation decisions are the following:

    (1) Expected returns: investor's best guess about the rate of increase in an asset's value over time.

    (2) Risk: the likelihood that the actual return will significantly differ from the expected return.

    (3) Liquidity: the ease and quickness with which an asset can be exchanged for goods, services, or other assets.

    (4) Time to maturity: the time until the principal is repaid.

4. The real quantity of money demanded would increase if real income increased, if the real interest rate on nonmonetary assets declined, if expected inflation declined, if the nominal interest rate declined, if wealth increased, if the risk on nonmoney assets increased, if the risk on money declined, if the liquidity of alternative assets fell, or if payments technologies became less efficient.

5. Velocity is negatively related to real money demand. Velocity = PY/M = nominal income/nominal money supply = the number of times each dollar is spent in buying final goods and services produced in the current time period. In equilibrium, real money supply = real money demand. By replacing M/P with L, we see that velocity equals real output divided by real money demand. Velocity increases when real money demand declines for a given real income. If real demand for money increases relative to real income, velocity declines.

6. Asset market equilibrium exists when the quantity of assets supplied equals the quantity of assets demanded in a national economy in some time period. The aggregate net value of a country's assets is its wealth. The asset market equilibrium equation is $M^d = PL(Y, r + \pi^e)$.

Numerical Problems

1. Use the formula $\%\Delta m^d = \eta_Y \%\Delta Y + \eta_i \%\Delta i$.
    (a) 1.5%
    (b) –5.0%
    (c) –3.0%
    (d) 6.7%
    (e) –7.75%

2. An increase in the interest rate reduces the demand for real money balances. An increase in the interest rate from 5% to 8% is a 60% increase in the interest rate.
    (a) Change in real money demand = –0.1(60%)($500 billion) = (–6%)($500 billion) = –$30 billion.
    (b) Change in real money demand = –0.2(–60%)($500 billion) = (12%)($500 billion) = $60 billion.

3. Use the equation $\pi = \Delta M/M - \eta_Y \Delta Y/Y$.
    (a) Inflation rate = 4% – 2/3(6%) = 4% – 4% = 0%.
    (b) Inflation rate = 12% – 2/3(6%) = 12% – 4% = 8%.
    (c) Inflation rate = –2% – 2/3(–3%) = –2% + 2% = 0%.

4. The expected rate of inflation = the nominal interest rate – the real interest rate.
    (a) Expected inflation = 10% – 4% = 6%.
    (b) Expected inflation = 6% – 3% = 3%.
    (c) Expected inflation = 4% – (–1%) = 5%.

Analytical Questions

1. Money demand is related positively to real income, wealth, the risk on nonmoney assets, and the nominal interest rate on money. Money demand is related negatively to the real interest rate on nonmoney assets, expected inflation, the risk on money, the liquidity of nonmoney assets, and the efficiency of payments technologies.

    (a) The rise in expected inflation reduces money demand, so real income must rise to increase money demand.

    (b) The rise in the nominal interest rate on money rises, so wealth must fall to decrease money demand.

    (c) The increased risk on stocks and bonds raises money demand, so the efficiency of the payments technology must rise to reduce money demand.

    (d) The rise in the risk on money reduces money demand, so the real interest rate on nonmoney assets must fall to increase money demand.

    (e) The rise in the liquidity of nonmonetary assets reduces money demand, so expected inflation must fall to increase money demand.

    (f) The rise in wealth increases money demand, so the risk on nonmonetary assets must fall to decrease money demand.

Chapter 8
Business Cycles

■ Introduction

This chapter is the first of four that discuss the business cycle. It discusses the facts about business cycles, Chapter 9 then develops a basic *IS-LM* model of the economy, Chapter 10 looks at the classical approach to analyzing the business cycle, and Chapter 11 examines the Keynesian model of the business cycle.

This chapter begins by looking at the basic features of the business cycle in Section 8.1. Section 8.2 then provides a brief history of U.S. business cycles. The relationships between major economic variables are discussed in Section 8.3. Finally, Section 8.4 gives a preview of the economic model that will be used to analyze the business cycle.

■ Outline

I.   **What is a Business Cycle? (Sec. 8.1)**

A)   U.S. research on cycles began in 1920 at the National Bureau of Economic Research (NBER)

1.   NBER maintains the business cycle chronology—a detailed history of business cycles

2.   NBER sponsors business cycle studies

B)   Burns and Mitchell (*Measuring Business Cycles*, 1946) make five main points about business cycles:

1.   Business cycles are fluctuations of *aggregate economic activity*, not a specific variable

2.   There are expansions and contractions

a.   Aggregate economic activity declines in a *contraction* or *recession* until it reaches a *trough* (Figure 8.1)

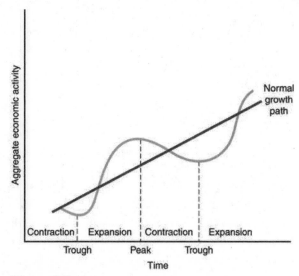

Figure 8.1

    b. Then activity increases in an *expansion* or *boom* until it reaches a *peak*

    c. A particularly severe recession is called a *depression*

    d. The sequence from one peak to the next, or from one trough to the next, is a *business cycle*

    e. Peaks and troughs are *turning points*

    f. Turning points are officially designated by the NBER Business Cycle Dating Committee

  3. Economic variables show *comovement*—they have regular and predictable patterns of behavior over the course of the business cycle

  4. The business cycle is recurrent, but not periodic

    a. Recurrent means the pattern of *contraction–trough–expansion–peak* occurs again and again

    b. Not being periodic means that it doesn't occur at regular, predictable intervals

  5. The business cycle is persistent

    a. Declines are followed by further declines; growth is followed by more growth

    b. Because of persistence, forecasting turning points is quite important

II. The American Business Cycle: The Historical Record (Sec. 8.2)

A) Text Table 8.1 gives the NBER business cycle chronology

B) The pre–World War I period

  1. Recessions were common from 1865 to 1917, with 338 months of contraction and 382 months of expansion (compared to 518 months of expansion and 96 months of contraction from 1945 to 1996)

  2. The longest contraction on record was 65 months, from October 1873 to March 1879

C) The Great Depression and World War II

  1. The worst economic contraction was the Great Depression of the 1930s

    a. Real GDP fell nearly 30% from the peak in August 1929 to the trough in March 1933

    b. The unemployment rate rose from 3% to nearly 25%

    c. Thousands of banks failed, the stock market collapsed, many farmers went bankrupt, and international trade was halted

    d. There were really two business cycles in the Great Depression

      (1) A contraction from August 1929 to March 1933, followed by an expansion that peaked in May 1937

      (2) A contraction from May 1937 to June 1938

    e. By May 1937, output had nearly returned to its 1929 peak, but the unemployment rate was high (14%)

    f. In 1939 the unemployment rate was over 17%

  2. The Great Depression ended with the start of World War II

    a. Wartime production brought the unemployment rate below 2%

    b. Real GDP almost doubled between 1939 and 1944

D) Post–World War II business cycles

  1. From 1945 to 1970 there were five mild contractions

  2. The longest expansion on record was 106 months, from February 1961 to December 1969

  3. Some economists thought the business cycle was dead

  4. But the OPEC oil shock of 1973 caused a sharp recession, with real GDP declining 3%, the unemployment rate rising to 9%, and inflation rising to over 10%

5. The 1981–1982 recession was also severe, with the unemployment rate over 11%, but inflation declining from 11% to less than 4%

6. The 1990–1991 recession was mild and short, but the recovery was slow and erratic

E) The "long boom"

1. From 1982 to the present, only one brief recession, from July 1990 to March 1991

2. Expansion from 1991 to present is longest in U.S. history

F) Have American business cycles become less severe?

1. Economists believed that business cycles weren't as bad after World War II as they were before

2. The average contraction before 1929 lasted 21 months compared to 11 months after 1945

3. The average expansion before 1929 lasted 25 months compared to 50 months after 1945

4. Romer's 1986 article sparked a strong debate, as it argued that pre-1929 data were not measured well, and that business cycles weren't that bad before 1929

5. New research has focused on the reasons for the decline in the volatility of U.S. output

   a. Stock and Watson's research showed that the decline came from a sharp drop in volatility around 1984 for many economic variables; dubbed the Great Moderation

   b. They found that the change from manufacturing to services was not a major cause of the reduction in volatility

   c. Stock and Watson showed that evidence that changes in how firms managed their inventories, which some researchers thought was the main source of the drop in volatility, was sensitive to the empirical method used, and thus not a convincing explanation

   d. Improvements in housing markets may have contributed to the decline in volatility, but cannot explain the sudden drop in volatility, as those changes occurred gradually over time

   e. Reduced volatility in oil prices was also not an important factor in reducing the volatility of output

6. After showing that many theories for the reduced volatility in output were not convincing, Stock and Watson found three factors that were important

   a. Reductions in the volatility of food and other commodity prices account for about 15% of the volatility in output

   b. Reduced fluctuations in productivity were responsible for another 15% of the reduction in output's volatility

   c. Improvements in monetary policy were the most important factor, accounting for 20% to 30% of the reduction in the volatility of output

   d. The remaining reduction in output's volatility remains unexplained—some unknown form of good luck in terms of smaller shocks to the economy

III. Business Cycle Facts (Sec. 8.3)

A) All business cycles have features in common

B) The cyclical behavior of economic variables—direction and timing

1. What *direction* does a variable move relative to aggregate economic activity?

   a. *Procyclical*: in the same direction

   b. *Countercyclical*: in the opposite direction

   c. *Acyclical*: with no clear pattern

2. What is the *timing* of a variable's movements relative to aggregate economic activity?
   a. *Leading*: in advance
   b. *Coincident*: at the same time
   c. *Lagging*: after
3. In touch with the macroeconomy—leading indicators
   a. Leading indicators are designed to help predict peaks and troughs
   b. The first index was developed by Mitchell and Burns of the NBER in 1938, was later produced by the U.S. Commerce Department, and now is run by the Conference Board
   c. A decline in the index for two or three months in a row warns of recession danger
   d. Problems with the leading indicators
      (1) Data are available promptly, but often revised later, so the index may give misleading signals
      (2) The index has given a number of false warnings
      (3) The index provides little information on the timing of the recession or its severity
      (4) Structural changes in the economy necessitate periodic revision of the index
   e. Research by Diebold and Rudebusch showed that the index does not help forecast industrial production in real time
   f. In real time, the index sometimes gave no warning of recessions
      (1) The index gave no advance warning of the recession that began in December 1970
      (2) The index was late in calling the recession that began in November 1973; the index did not turn down two months in a row until September 1974
   g. After the fact, the index of leading indicators is revised and appears to have predicted the recessions well
   h. Stock and Watson attempted to improve the index by creating some new indexes based on newer statistical methods, but the results were disappointing as the new index failed to predict the recessions that began in 1990 and 2001
   i. Because recessions may be caused by sudden shocks, the search for a good index of leading indicators may be fruitless

C) Cyclical behavior of key macroeconomic variables, shown in text Figures 8.4 to 8.10
   1. Procyclical
      a. Coincident: industrial production, consumption, business fixed investment, employment
      b. Leading: residential investment, inventory investment, average labor productivity, money growth, stock prices
      c. Lagging: inflation, nominal interest rates
      d. Timing not designated: government purchases, real wage
   2. Countercyclical: unemployment (timing is unclassified)
   3. Acyclical: real interest rates (timing is not designated)
   4. Volatility: durable goods production is more volatile than nondurable goods and services; investment spending is more volatile than consumption

D) International aspects of the business cycle

1. The cyclical behavior of key economic variables in other countries is similar to that in the United States

2. Major industrial countries frequently have recessions and expansions at about the same time

3. Text Figure 8.11 illustrates common cycles for Japan, Canada, the United States, France, Germany, and the United Kingdom

4. In addition, each economy faces small fluctuations that aren't shared with other countries

E) Box 8.1: The seasonal cycle and the business cycle

1. Output varies over the seasons: highest in the fourth quarter, lowest in the first quarter

2. Most economic data are seasonally adjusted to remove regular seasonal movements

3. Barsky and Miron's 1989 study shows that the movements of variables across the seasons are similar to the movements of variables over the business cycle

4. If the seasonal cycle is like the business cycle, and the seasonal cycle represents desirable responses to various factors (Christmas, the weather) for which government intervention is inappropriate, should government intervention be used to smooth out the business cycle?

IV. Business Cycle Analysis: A Preview (Sec. 8.4)

A) What explains business cycle fluctuations?

1. Two major components of business cycle theories

a. A description of the shocks

b. A model of how the economy responds to shocks

2. Two major business cycle theories

a. classical theory

b. Keynesian theory

3. Study both theories in aggregate demand-aggregate supply (AD-AS) framework

B) Aggregate demand and aggregate supply: A brief introduction

1. The model (along with the building block IS-LM model) will be developed in Chapters 9–11

2. The model has three main components; all plotted in (P, Y) space

a. aggregate demand curve

b. short-run aggregate supply curve

c. long-run aggregate supply curve

3. Aggregate demand curve

a. Shows quantity of goods and services demanded (Y) for any price level (P)

b. Higher P means less aggregate demand (lower Y), so the aggregate demand curve slopes downward; reasons why discussed in Chapter 9

c. An increase in aggregate demand for a given P shifts the aggregate demand curve up and to the right; and vice versa

(1) Example: a rise in the stock market increases consumption, shifting the aggregate demand curve up and to the right

(2) Example: a decline in government purchases shifts the aggregate demand curve down and to the left

4. Aggregate supply curve

a. The aggregate supply curve shows how much output producers are willing to supply at any given price level

b. The short-run aggregate supply curve is horizontal; prices are fixed in the short run

c. The long-run aggregate supply curve is vertical at the full-employment level of output

d. Equilibrium (Figure 8.2; like text Figure 8.10)

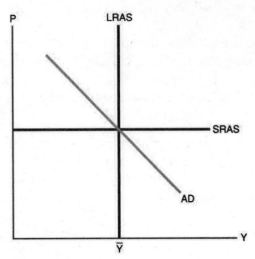

Figure 8.2

(1) Short-run equilibrium: the aggregate demand curve intersects the short-run aggregate supply curve
(2) Long-run equilibrium: the aggregate demand curve intersects the long-run aggregate supply curve

C) Aggregate demand shocks
1. An aggregate demand shock is a change that shifts the aggregate demand curve
2. Example: a negative aggregate demand shock (Figure 8.3; like text Figure 8.11)

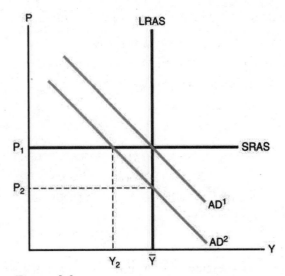

Figure 8.3

a. The aggregate demand curve shifts down and to the left
b. Short-run equilibrium occurs where the aggregate demand curve intersects the short-run aggregate supply curve; output falls, price level is unchanged
c. Long-run equilibrium occurs where the aggregate demand curve intersects the long-run aggregate supply curve; output returns to its original level, price level has fallen

3. How long does it take to get to the long run?
    a. Classical theory: prices adjust rapidly
        (1) So recessions are short-lived
        (2) No need for government intervention
    b. Keynesian theory: prices (and wages) adjust slowly
        (1) Adjustment may take several years
        (2) So the government can fight recessions by taking action to shift the aggregate demand curve

D. Aggregate supply shocks
    1. Classicals view aggregate supply shocks as the main cause of fluctuations in output
        a. An aggregate supply shock is a shift of the long-run aggregate supply curve
        b. Factors that cause aggregate supply shocks are things like changes in productivity or labor supply
    2. Example: a negative aggregate supply shock (Figure 8.4, like text Figure 8.12)

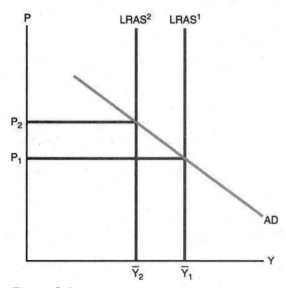

Figure 8.4

    a. Initial long-run equilibrium at intersection of *LRAS^1* and *AD*, with full-employment output level $\overline{Y}_1$
    b. Aggregate supply shock reduces full-employment output from $\overline{Y}_1$ to $\overline{Y}_2$, causing long-run aggregate supply curve to shift left from *LRAS^1* to *LRAS^2*
    c. New equilibrium has lower output and higher price level
    d. So recession is accompanied by higher price level
    3. Keynesians also recognize the importance of supply shocks; their views are discussed further in Chapter 11

■ Multiple Choice Questions

1. A detailed history of business cycles is known as a
   (a) historical decomposition.
   (b) trend analysis.
   (c) Hodrick-Prescott filter.
   (d) business cycle chronology.

2. The high point in the business cycle is referred to as the
   (a) expansion.
   (b) boom.
   (c) peak.
   (d) turning point.

3. The entire sequence of a decline in aggregate economic activity followed by recovery, measured from peak to peak or trough to trough, is a
   (a) long-run trend.
   (b) potential output path.
   (c) business cycle.
   (d) recurrent comovement.

4. The dates of turning points are determined by a committee from the
   (a) FBI.
   (b) BLS.
   (c) BEA.
   (d) NBER.

5. The tendency of many economic variables to move together in a predictable way over the business cycle is called
   (a) recurrence.
   (b) persistence.
   (c) comovement.
   (d) inflation.

6. Business cycles all display the following characteristics EXCEPT
   (a) a period of expansion followed by one of contraction.
   (b) comovement of many economic variables.
   (c) rising prices during an expansion and falling prices during the contraction.
   (d) they last a period of one to twelve years.

7. The fact that business cycles are recurrent but not periodic means that
    (a) business cycles occur at predictable intervals, but do not last a predetermined length of time.
    (b) the business cycle's standard contraction-trough-expansion-peak pattern has been observed to occur over and over again, but not at predictable intervals.
    (c) business cycles occur at predictable intervals, but do not all follow a standard contraction-trough-expansion-peak pattern.
    (d) business cycles last a predetermined length of time, but do not all follow a standard contraction-trough-expansion-peak pattern.

8. Turning points in business cycles occur when
    (a) a new business cycle is initiated at the trough.
    (b) the economy hits the peak or trough in the business cycle.
    (c) the business cycle begins to follow a new pattern that differs from previous business cycles.
    (d) a new business cycle is initiated at the peak.

9. The deepest contraction in American history occurred
    (a) during the 1870s.
    (b) in the years right before World War I.
    (c) during the 1930s.
    (d) during the 1970s.

10. In the Great Depression, the financial sector collapsed as
    (a) banks engaged in ruinous competition.
    (b) the stock market boomed, so people withdrew most of their funds from banks and invested heavily in stocks.
    (c) the bond market boomed, so people withdrew most of their funds from banks and invested heavily in bonds.
    (d) many banks closed.

11. The deep recession of 1973–1975 was mainly caused by
    (a) flawed technology that caused a drop in TFP.
    (b) an unexplained drop in business optimism.
    (c) slower money growth.
    (d) higher oil prices.

12. The long boom began in
    (a) 1947.
    (b) 1975.
    (c) 1982.
    (d) 1991.

13. Christina Romer's estimates of the business cycles prior to World War II showed that the business cycle
    (a) had greater fluctuations before World War II than previous estimates had shown.
    (b) had smaller fluctuations before World War II than previously estimated.
    (c) had smaller fluctuations before World War II than after World War II.
    (d) had larger fluctuations after World War II than had been previously measured.

14. The widespread decline in the volatility of many macroeconomic variables after 1984 led economists to term this period the
    (a) Great Moderation.
    (b) Low Volatility Era.
    (c) Steady State.
    (d) Ironic Inflation.

15. Which of the following macroeconomic variables is procyclical and leads the business cycle?
    (a) Business fixed investment
    (b) The money supply
    (c) Nominal interest rates
    (d) Unemployment

16. Which of the following macroeconomic variables could not be used as a leading economic indicator?
    (a) Residential investment
    (b) Employment
    (c) The money supply
    (d) Stock prices

17. Which of the following is not a procyclical variable?
    (a) Unemployment rate
    (b) Business fixed investment
    (c) Average labor productivity
    (d) Stock prices

18. When the values of coincident variables are declining, aggregate economic activity
    (a) will begin to decline within six months.
    (b) might start to decline in the next year.
    (c) has been declining for at least six months.
    (d) is declining.

19. Lagging variables are aggregate economic variables that
    (a) reach a peak after leading variables but before coincident variables reach a peak.
    (b) reach a peak after coincident variables reach a peak.
    (c) reach a peak two or more years after aggregate economic activity reaches a peak.
    (d) are insensitive to business cycles.

20. Which of the following macroeconomic variables is countercyclical?

    (a) Real interest rates

    (b) Unemployment

    (c) Money growth

    (d) Consumption

21. You want to invest in a firm whose profits show small fluctuations throughout the business cycle. Which of the following would you invest in?

    (a) A corporation that depended heavily on business fixed investment

    (b) A corporation that depended heavily on residential investment

    (c) A corporation that depended heavily on consumer nondurables

    (d) A corporation that depended heavily on consumer durables

22. Using the seasonal business cycle as your guide, during which quarter would you be most likely to expect a drop in your corporation's sales?

    (a) The first quarter of the year (January–March)

    (b) The second quarter of the year (April–June)

    (c) The third quarter of the year (July–September)

    (d) The fourth quarter of the year (October–December)

23. Wars, new inventions, harvest failures, and changes in government policy are examples of what economists refer to as

    (a) the components of GDP.

    (b) propagation mechanisms.

    (c) shocks.

    (d) demand innovations.

24. When plotted with the aggregate price level on the vertical axis and output on the horizontal axis, the aggregate demand curve

    (a) slopes upward.

    (b) slopes downward.

    (c) is vertical.

    (d) is horizontal.

25. An increase in consumer spending would cause

    (a) the aggregate demand curve to shift to the right.

    (b) the aggregate demand curve to shift to the left.

    (c) a movement down and to the right along the aggregate demand curve.

    (d) a movement up and to the left along the aggregate demand curve.

26. When plotted with the aggregate price level on the vertical axis and output on the horizontal axis, the short-run aggregate supply curve (in the absence of misperceptions)

    (a) slopes upward.

    (b) slopes downward.

    (c) is vertical.

    (d) is horizontal.

27. In the short run (before the price level adjusts to restore general equilibrium), a decrease in inventory investment by business firms would cause output to _____ and the price level to _____.
    (a) rise; rise
    (b) rise; stay constant
    (c) fall; stay constant
    (d) fall; rise

28. After a shift in the aggregate demand curve, which variable adjusts to restore general equilibrium?
    (a) price level
    (b) real interest rate
    (c) consumption spending
    (d) investment spending

29. In the long run, an increase in consumer spending would cause output to _____ and the aggregate price level to _____.
    (a) stay constant; rise
    (b) rise; rise
    (c) rise; stay constant
    (d) stay constant; stay constant

30. In the long run, a decrease in inventory investment by business firms would cause the price level to _____ and output to _____.
    (a) rise; fall
    (b) stay constant; stay constant
    (c) fall; stay constant
    (d) fall; fall

■ Review Questions

1. Define the following characteristics of business cycles: recurrence and persistence.

2. Identify the comovements (i.e., direction and timing) of the following variables over a business cycle: (a) industrial production; (b) unemployment; (c) nominal interest rates; (d) nominal money supply growth; and (e) investment.

3. Identify two industries that are particularly sensitive to business cycles.

4. Briefly describe how the Index of Leading Indicators would forecast a contraction.

5. Why do Keynesians see an important role for the government in fighting recessions, while classicals do not?

■ Numerical Problems

1. Use the *NBER* data in Table 8.1 in the textbook on U.S. business cycle turning points to calculate:
   (a) the shortest business cycle from peak to peak; (b) the shortest business cycle from trough to trough; (c) the longest business cycle from peak to peak; and (d) the longest business cycle from trough to trough.

■ Analytical Questions

1. Suppose consumers became more optimistic about the future. How would this likely change consumption? Would this affect the aggregate-demand curve or aggregate-supply curve? In the short run, what would be the effect on output and the price level (assuming the *SRAS* curve is horizontal)?

2. Suppose labor supply declined. Would this affect the aggregate demand curve or the aggregate supply curve? What would be the effect on output and the price level?

■ Answers

Multiple Choice

1. d	7. b	13. b	19. b	25. a
2. c	8. b	14. a	20. b	26. d
3. c	9. c	15. b	21. c	27. c
4. d	10. d	16. b	22. a	28. a
5. c	11. d	17. a	23. c	29. a
6. c	12. c	18. d	24. b	30. c

Review Questions

1. Business cycles exhibit recurrence and persistence:
   (1) Recurrence means that each complete cycle is followed by another complete cycle.
   (2) Persistence means that, once begun, each contraction tends to continue. Likewise, once begun, each expansion tends to continue. For example, the 1981–1982 contraction lasted for 16 months, and the 1982–1990 expansion lasted for 93 months. These are persistent events.

2. (a) Industrial production is a procyclical and coincident variable.
   (b) Unemployment is a countercyclical variable whose timing is unclassified by the Conference Board.
   (c) Nominal interest rates are procyclical and lagging.
   (d) Nominal money supply growth is a procyclical and leading variable.
   (e) Investment includes inventory investment and residential investment, which are procyclical and leading variables; it also includes business fixed investment, which is a procyclical and coincident variable.

3. Consumer durables, capital investment goods, and housing industries are particularly sensitive to business cycle fluctuations. The auto industry is an example of an industry producing a consumer durable. The drill press industry is an example of an industry producing a capital good.

4. A decline in the index for three consecutive months during an expansion forecasts that a contraction will begin in the next three to six months.

5. Keynesians argue that because it takes prices a long time to adjust to restore equilibrium, the government can fight recessions by taking actions like increasing government spending. Classicals, however, think prices adjust quickly, so there's no need for government action.

Numerical Problems

1. (a) The shortest business cycle from peak to peak is 17 months, which extended from August 1918 to December 1919. This includes 7 months of contraction followed by 10 months of expansion.

    (b) The shortest business cycle from trough to trough is 28 months, which extended from July 1980 to October 1982. This includes 12 months of expansion followed by 16 months of contraction.

    (c) The longest business cycle from peak to peak is 128 months, which extended from July 1990 to March 2001. This includes 8 months of contraction followed by 120 months of expansion.

    (d) The longest business cycle from trough to trough is 128 months, which extended from March 1991 to November 2001. This includes 120 months of expansion followed by 8 months of contraction.

Analytical Questions

1. Consumption would increase, so the aggregate demand curve would shift to the right, causing output to rise and no change in the price level, as Figure 8.5 shows.

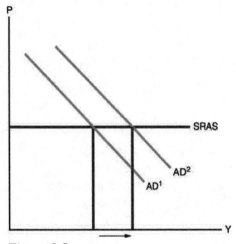

Figure 8.5

2.   The decline in the labor supply shifts the long-run aggregate supply curve to the left, causing the price level to increase and output to decline, as Figure 8.6 shows.

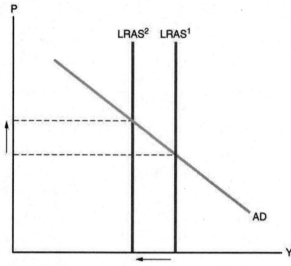

Figure 8.6

Chapter 9
The *IS-LM/AD-AS* Model: A General Framework for Macroeconomic Analysis

■ Introduction

This chapter combines the labor market (Chapter 3), the goods market (Chapter 4), and the asset market (Chapter 7) into a complete macroeconomic model (for a closed economy). Although the *IS-LM* model was originally a Keynesian model because it assumes prices are fixed, by allowing prices to adjust, it's possible to use the *IS-LM* framework to discuss the classical approach. Using one model for both approaches (the classical model in Chapter 10 and the Keynesian model in Chapter 11) avoids the need to learn two different models and helps show clearly both the similarities and the differences of the two approaches.

The chapter is organized along the lines of a section for each piece of the model. Section 9.1 begins by discussing the *FE* line, which represents equilibrium in the labor market. Then, Section 9.2 introduces the *IS* curve, along which there is equilibrium in the goods market. And Section 9.3 covers the *LM* curve, along which the money market is in equilibrium. In all three of these sections, each curve is discussed, followed by an analysis of what shifts each curve. Next, in Section 9.4, the three curves are combined. Their joint intersection is the point of general equilibrium. The way the economy adjusts to reach general equilibrium is by changes in the price level, as Section 9.5 shows. Finally, the *IS, LM,* and *FE* curves are combined in a different way in Section 9.6 to generate the *AD-AS* model.

This chapter is challenging because it introduces the full-blown macro model of the economy. But it really isn't as complicated as it looks. Every time you have to analyze a situation with the model, you just need to think about what curve gets shifted and what direction it shifts. Then look at what happens to the equilibrium point. By working a number of exercises in both the textbook and study guide, you'll find that using the model becomes routine.

■ Outline

I.   **The *FE* Line: Equilibrium in the Labor Market (Sec. 9.1)**

    A) In the discussion of the labor market in Chapter 3, we showed how equilibrium in the labor market leads to employment at its full-employment level $\overline{N}$ and output at $\overline{Y}$

B) If we plot output against the real interest rate, we get a vertical line at $Y = \bar{Y}$, because labor market equilibrium is unaffected by changes in the real interest rate (Figure 9.1)

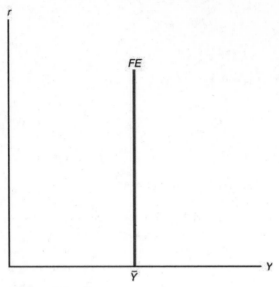

Figure 9.1

C) Factors that shift the *FE* line

1. $\bar{Y}$ is determined by the full-employment level of employment and the current levels of capital and productivity; any change in these variables shifts the *FE* line

2. Summary Table 11 lists the factors that shift the full-employment line

    a. The full-employment line shifts right because of

        (1) a beneficial supply shock
        (2) an increase in labor supply
        (3) an increase in the capital stock

    b. The full-employment line shifts left when the opposite happens to the three factors above

II. The *IS* Curve: Equilibrium in the Goods Market (Sec. 9.2)

A) The goods market clears when desired investment equals desired national saving

1. Adjustments in the real interest rate bring about equilibrium

2. For any level of output *Y*, the *IS* curve shows the real interest rate *r* for which the goods market is in equilibrium

3. Derivation of the *IS* curve from the saving-investment diagram (Figure 9.2)

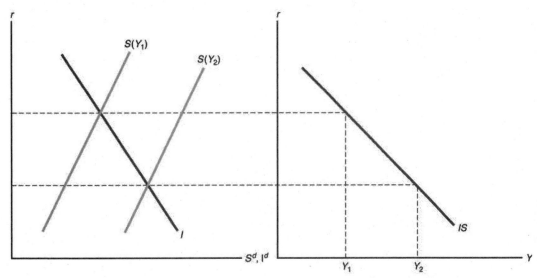

Figure 9.2

a. Key features
   (1) The saving curve slopes upward because a higher real interest rate increases saving
   (2) An increase in output shifts the saving curve to the right, because people save more when their income is higher
   (3) The investment curve slopes downward because a higher real interest rate reduces the desired capital stock, thus reducing investment

b. Consider two different levels of output
   (1) At the higher level of output, the saving curve is shifted to the right compared to the situation at the lower level of output
   (2) Because the investment curve is downward sloping, equilibrium at the higher level of output has a lower real interest rate
   (3) Thus a higher level of output must lead to a lower real interest rate, so the *IS* curve slopes downward
   (4) The *IS* curve shows the relationship between the real interest rate and output for which investment equals saving

c. Alternative interpretation in terms of goods market equilibrium
   (1) Beginning at a point of equilibrium, suppose the real interest rate rises
   (2) The increased real interest rate causes people to increase saving and thus reduce consumption, and causes firms to reduce investment
   (3) So the quantity of goods demanded declines
   (4) To restore equilibrium, the quantity of goods supplied would have to decline
   (5) So higher real interest rates are associated with lower output, that is, the *IS* curve slopes downward

B) Factors that shift the *IS* curve

1. Any change that reduces desired national saving relative to desired investment shifts the *IS* curve up and to the right

   a. Intuitively, imagine constant output, so a reduction in saving means more investment relative to saving; the interest rate must rise to reduce investment and increase saving (Figure 9.3)

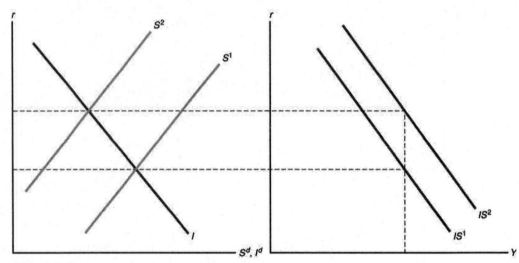

Figure 9.3

2. Similarly, a change that increases desired national saving relative to desired investment shifts the *IS* curve down and to the left

3. An alternative way of stating this is that a change that increases aggregate demand for goods shifts the *IS* curve up and to the right

   a. In this case, the increase in aggregate demand for goods exceeds the supply

   b. The real interest rate must rise to reduce desired consumption and investment and restore equilibrium

4. Summary Table 12 lists the factors that shift the *IS* curve

   a. The *IS* curve shifts up and to the right because of

      (1) an increase in expected future output
      (2) an increase in wealth
      (3) a temporary increase in government purchases
      (4) a decline in taxes (if Ricardian equivalence doesn't hold)
      (5) an increase in the expected future marginal product of capital
      (6) a decrease in the effective tax rate on capital

   b. The *IS* curve shifts down and to the left when the opposite happens to the six factors above

III. The *LM* Curve: Asset Market Equilibrium (Sec. 9.3)

A) The interest rate and the price of a nonmonetary asset

1. The price of a nonmonetary asset is inversely related to its interest rate or yield

   a. Example: A bond pays $10,000 in one year; its current price is $9,615, and its interest rate is 4%, because ($10,000 − $9,615)/$9,615 = .04 = 4%

   b. If the price of the bond in the market were to fall to $9,524, its yield would rise to 5%, because ($10,000 − $9,524)/$9,524 = .05 = 5%

2. For a given level of expected inflation, the price of a nonmonetary asset is inversely related to the real interest rate

B) The equality of money demanded and money supplied

   1. Equilibrium in the asset market requires that the real money supply equal the real quantity of money demanded

   2. Real money supply is determined by the central bank and isn't affected by the real interest rate

   3. Real money demand falls as the real interest rate rises

   4. Real money demand rises as the level of output rises

   5. The *LM* curve (Figure 9.4) is derived by plotting real money demand for different levels of output and looking at the resulting equilibrium

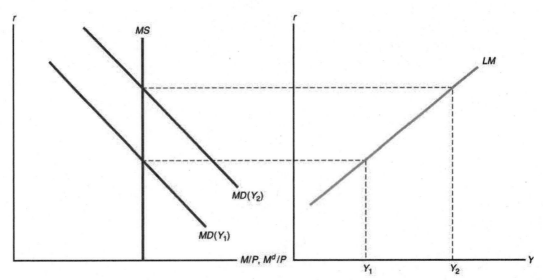

Figure 9.4

   6. By what mechanism is equilibrium restored?

      a. Starting at equilibrium, suppose output rises, so real money demand increases

      b. The rise in people's demand for money makes them sell nonmonetary assets, so the price of those assets falls and the real interest rate rises

      c. As the interest rate rises, the demand for money declines until equilibrium is reached

   7. The *LM* curve shows the combinations of the real interest rate and output that clear the asset market

      a. Intuitively, for any given level of output, the *LM* curve shows the real interest rate necessary to equate real money demand and supply

      b. Thus the *LM* curve slopes upward from left to right

C) Factors that shift the *LM* curve

   1. Any change that reduces real money supply relative to real money demand shifts the *LM* curve up

      a. For a given level of output, the reduction in real money supply relative to real money demand causes the equilibrium real interest rate to rise

      b. The rise in the real interest rate is shown as an upward shift of the *LM* curve

2. Similarly, a change that increases real money supply relative to real money demand shifts the *LM* curve down and to the right

3. Summary Table 13 lists the factors that shift the *LM* curve
   a. The *LM* curve shifts down and to the right because of
      (1) an increase in the nominal money supply
      (2) a decrease in the price level
      (3) an increase in expected inflation
      (4) a decrease in the nominal interest rate on money
      (5) a decrease in wealth
      (6) a decrease in the risk of alternative assets relative to the risk of holding money
      (7) an increase in the liquidity of alternative assets
      (8) an increase in the efficiency of payment technologies
   b. The *LM* curve shifts up and to the left when the opposite happens to the eight factors listed above

4. Changes in the real money supply
   a. An increase in the real money supply shifts the *LM* curve down and to the right (Figure 9.5)

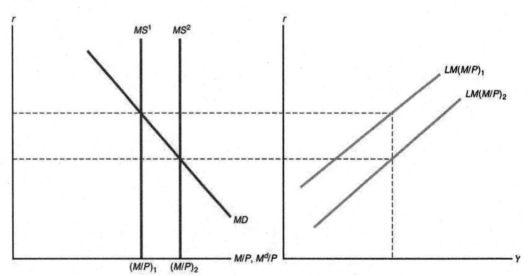

Figure 9.5

   b. Similarly, a drop in real money supply shifts the *LM* curve up and to the left
   c. The real money supply changes when the nominal money supply changes at a different rate than the price level

5. Changes in real money demand
   a. An increase in real money demand shifts the *LM* curve up and to the left (Figure 9.6)

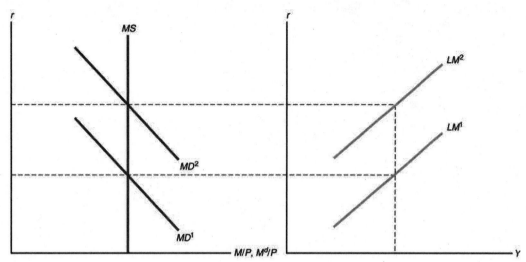

Figure 9.6

   b. Similarly, a drop in real money demand shifts the *LM* curve down and to the right

IV.   General Equilibrium in the Complete *IS-LM* Model (Sec. 9.4)

   A) When all markets are simultaneously in equilibrium there is a *general equilibrium*
   1. This occurs where the *FE*, *IS*, and *LM* curves intersect (Figure 9.7)

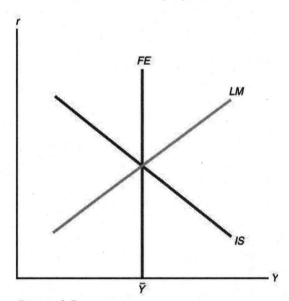

Figure 9.7

   B) Applying the *IS-LM* framework: A temporary adverse supply shock
   1. Suppose the productivity parameter in the production function falls temporarily
   2. The supply shock reduces the marginal productivity of labor, hence labor demand
      a. With lower labor demand, the equilibrium real wage and employment fall
      b. Lower employment and lower productivity both reduce the equilibrium level of output,
         thus shifting the *FE* line to the left

3. There's no effect of a temporary supply shock on the *IS* or *LM* curves
4. Because the *FE*, *IS*, and *LM* curves don't intersect, the price level adjusts, shifting the *LM* curve until a general equilibrium is reached
   a. In this case the price level rises to shift the *LM* curve up and to the left to restore equilibrium (Figure 9.8)

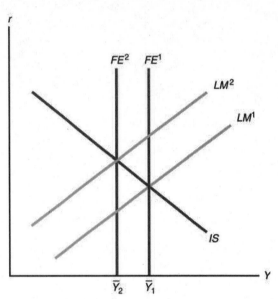

Figure 9.8

5. The inflation rate rises temporarily, not permanently
6. Summary: The real wage, employment, and output decline, while the real interest rate and price level are higher
   a. There is a temporary burst of inflation as the price level moves to a higher level
   b. Because the real interest rate is higher and output is lower, consumption and investment must be lower

C) Application: Oil price shocks revisited
   1. Does the *IS-LM* model correctly predict the results of an adverse supply shock?
   2. The data from the 1973–1974 and 1979–1980 oil price shocks show the following
      a. As discussed in Chapter 3, output, employment, and the real wage declined
      b. Consumption fell slightly and investment fell substantially
      c. Inflation surged temporarily
      d. All the above results are consistent with the theory
      e. But the real interest rate did not rise during the 1973–1974 oil price shock (though it did during the 1979–1980 shock)
         (1) It could be that people expected the 1973–1974 oil price shock to be permanent
         (2) In that case the real interest rate would not necessarily rise
         (3) If so, people's expectations were correct, because the 1973–1974 shock seems to have been permanent, while the 1979–1980 shock was reversed quickly

D) Box 9.1: Econometric models and macroeconomic forecasts

1. Many models that are used for macroeconomic research and analysis are based on the *IS-LM* model

2. There are three major steps in using an economic model for forecasting

   a. An *econometric model* estimates the parameters of the model (slopes, intercepts, elasticities) through statistical analysis of the data

   b. Projections are made of *exogenous variables* (variables outside the model), like oil prices and changes in productivity

   c. The model is solved for the values of *endogenous variables*, such as output, employment, and interest rates

3. The Federal Reserve Board's FRB/US model, introduced in 1996, improves on the old model by better handling of expectations, improved modeling of reactions to shocks, and use of newer statistical techniques

4. The FRB/US model is the workhorse for policy analysis by the Fed's staff economists

5. Board of Governor's staff adjust the FRB/US forecasts with their judgment; the subsequent forecasts reported in the Greenbook have been found to be superior to private-sector forecasts

V. Price Adjustment and the Attainment of General Equilibrium (Sec. 9.5)

A) The effects of a monetary expansion

1. An increase in money supply shifts the *LM* curve down and to the right

2. Because financial markets respond most quickly to changes in economic conditions, the asset market responds to the disequilibrium

   a. The *FE* line is slow to respond, because job matching and wage renegotiation take time

   b. The *IS* curve responds somewhat slowly

   c. We assume that the labor market is temporarily out of equilibrium, so there's a short-run equilibrium at the intersection of the *IS* and *LM* curves

3. The increase in the money supply causes people to try to get rid of excess money balances by buying assets, driving the real interest rate down

   a. The decline in the real interest rate causes consumption and investment to increase temporarily

   b. Output is assumed to increase temporarily to meet the extra demand

4. The adjustment of the price level

   a. Because the demand for goods exceeds firms' desired supply of goods, firms raise prices

   b. The rise in the price level causes the *LM* curve to shift up

c. The price level continues to rise until the *LM* curve intersects with the *FE* line and the *IS* curve at general equilibrium (Figure 9.9)

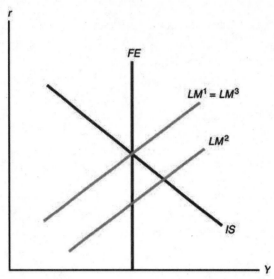

Figure 9.9

d. The result is no change in employment, output, or the real interest rate
e. The price level is higher by the same proportion as the increase in the money supply
f. So all real variables (including the real wage) are unchanged, while nominal values (including the nominal wage) have risen proportionately with the change in the money supply

5. Trend money growth and inflation
   a. This analysis also handles the case in which the money supply is growing continuously
   b. If both the money supply and price level rise by the same proportion, there is no change in the real money supply, and the *LM* curve doesn't shift
   c. If the money supply grew faster than the price level, the *LM* curve would shift down and to the right
   d. Often, then, we'll discuss things in relative terms
      (1) The examples can often be thought of as a change in *M* or *P* relative to the expected or trend growth of money and inflation
      (2) Thus when we talk about "an increase in the money supply," we have in mind an increase in the growth rate relative to the trend
      (3) Similarly, a result that the price level declines can be interpreted as the price level declining relative to a trend; for example, inflation may fall from 7% to 4%

B) Classical versus Keynesian versions of the *IS-LM* model
   1. There are two key questions in the debate between classical and Keynesian approaches
      a. How rapidly does the economy reach general equilibrium?
      b. What are the effects of monetary policy on the economy?

2. Price adjustment and the self-correcting economy
    a. The economy is brought into general equilibrium by adjustment of the price level
    b. The speed at which this adjustment occurs is much debated
    c. Classical economists see rapid adjustment of the price level
        (1) So the economy returns quickly to full employment after a shock
        (2) If firms change prices instead of output in response to a change in demand, the adjustment process is almost immediate
    d. Keynesian economists see slow adjustment of the price level
        (1) It may be several years before prices and wages adjust fully
        (2) When not in general equilibrium, output is determined by aggregate demand at the intersection of the *IS* and *LM* curves, and the labor market is not in equilibrium
3. Monetary neutrality
    a. Money is neutral if a change in the nominal money supply changes the price level proportionately but has no effect on real variables
    b. The classical view is that a monetary expansion affects prices quickly with at most a transitory effect on real variables
    c. Keynesians think the economy may spend a long time in disequilibrium, so a monetary expansion increases output and employment and causes the real interest rate to fall
    d. Keynesians believe in monetary neutrality in the long run but not the short run, while classicals believe it holds even in the relatively short run

VI. Aggregate Demand and Aggregate Supply (Sec. 9.6)

A) Use the *IS-LM* model to develop the *AD-AS* model
    1. The two models are equivalent
    2. Depending on the issue, one model or the other may prove more useful
        a. *IS-LM* relates the real interest rate to output
        b. *AD-AS* relates the price level to output

B) The aggregate demand curve
1. The *AD* curve shows the relationship between the quantity of goods demanded and the price level when the goods market and asset market are in equilibrium
    a. So the *AD* curve represents the price level and output level at which the *IS* and *LM* curves intersect (Figure 9.10)

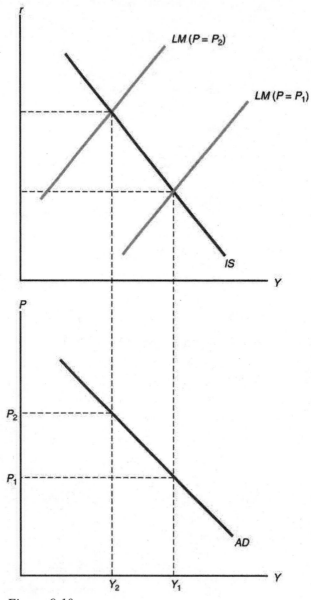

Figure 9.10

b. The *AD* curve is unlike other demand curves, which relate the quantity demanded of a good to its relative price; the *AD* curve relates the total quantity of goods demanded to the general price level, not a relative price
c. The *AD* curve slopes downward because a higher price level is associated with lower real money supply, shifting the *LM* curve up, raising the real interest rate, and decreasing output demanded

2. Factors that shift the *AD* curve
   a. Any factor that causes the intersection of the *IS* and *LM* curves to shift to the left causes the *AD* curve to shift down and to the left; any factor causing the *IS-LM* intersection to shift to the right causes the *AD* curve to shift up and to the right
   b. For example, a temporary increase in government purchases shifts the *IS* curve up and to the right, so it shifts the *AD* curve up and to the right as well (Figure 9.11)

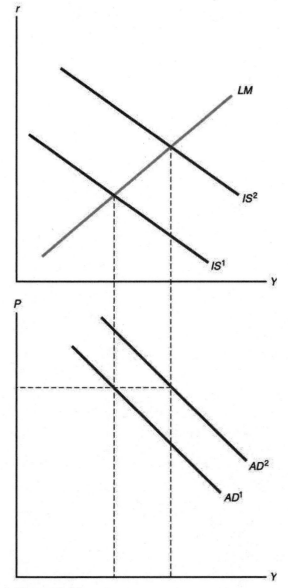

Figure 9.11

   c. Summary Table 14: Factors that shift the *AD* curve
      (1) Factors that shift the *IS* curve up and to the right and thus the *AD* curve up and to the right as well
          (a) Increases in future output (Y^f), wealth, government purchases (G), or the expected future marginal productivity of capital (MPK^f)
          (b) Decreases in taxes (T) if Ricardian equivalence doesn't hold, or the effective tax rate on capital (τ)

(2) Factors that shift the *LM* curve down and to the right and thus the *AD* curve up and to the right as well

(a) Increases in the nominal money supply (*M*) or in expected inflation (π^e)

(b) Decreases in the nominal interest rate on money (i^m) or the real demand for money

C) The aggregate supply curve

1. The aggregate supply curve shows the relationship between the price level and the aggregate amount of output that firms supply

2. In the short run, prices remain fixed, so firms supply whatever output is demanded

a. The short-run aggregate supply curve is horizontal (Figure 9.12)

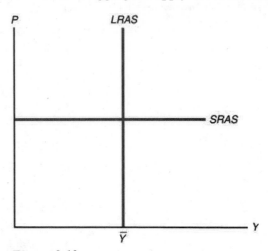

Figure 9.12

3. Full-employment output isn't affected by the price level, so the long-run aggregate supply curve (*LRAS*) is a vertical line at $Y = \bar{Y}$ in Figure 9.12

4. Factors that shift the aggregate supply curves

a. The *SRAS* curve shifts whenever firms change their prices in the short run

(1) Factors like increased costs of producing goods lead firms to increase prices, shifting *SRAS* up

(2) Factors leading to reduced prices shift *SRAS* down

b. Anything that increases $\bar{Y}$ shifts the *LRAS* curve right; anything that decreases $\bar{Y}$ shifts *LRAS* left

c. Examples include changes in the labor force or productivity changes that affect labor demand

D) Equilibrium in the *AD-AS* model
1. Short-run equilibrium: *AD* intersects *SRAS*
2. Long-run equilibrium: *AD* intersects *LRAS*
   a. Also called general equilibrium
   b. *AD*, *LRAS*, and *SRAS* all intersect at same point (Figure 9.13)

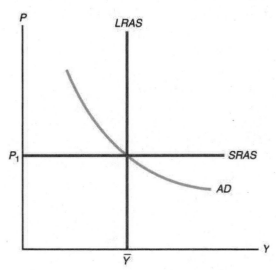

Figure 9.13

   c. If the economy isn't in general equilibrium, economic forces work to restore general
       equilibrium both in *AD-AS* diagram and *IS-LM* diagram
E) Monetary neutrality in the *AD-AS* model (Figure 9.14 and key diagram 7)

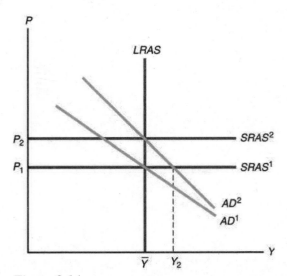

Figure 9.14

1. Suppose the economy begins in general equilibrium, but then the money supply is increased
    by 10%
2. This shifts the *AD* curve upward by 10% (from AD^1 to AD^2) because to maintain the
    aggregate quantity demanded at a given level, the price level would have to rise by 10% so
    that real money supply wouldn't change and would remain equal to real money demand
3. In the short run, with the price level fixed, equilibrium occurs where AD^2 intersects $SRAS^1$,
    with a higher level of output

4. Because output exceeds $\overline{Y}$, over time firms raise prices and the short-run aggregate supply curve shifts up to $SRAS^2$, restoring long-run equilibrium
5. The result is a higher price level—higher by 10%
6. Money is neutral in the long run, as output is unchanged

F) The key question is: How long does it take to get from the short run to the long run?
   1. The answer to this question is what separates classicals from Keynesians

■ Multiple Choice Questions

1. Which of the following curves in the *IS-LM* model is vertical?
   (a) The *IS* curve
   (b) The *LM* curve
   (c) The *FE* line
   (d) The *AD* curve

2. Which of the following would shift the *FE* line to the left?
   (a) A beneficial supply shock
   (b) A decrease in labor supply
   (c) An increase in consumer spending
   (d) An increase in the money supply

3. Which of the following would shift the *FE* line to the right?
   (a) An adverse supply shock
   (b) A decrease in labor supply
   (c) An increase in the capital stock
   (d) An increase in the future marginal productivity of capital

4. A beneficial supply shock would cause the *FE* line to
   (a) shift to the right.
   (b) shift to the left.
   (c) remain unchanged.
   (d) remain unchanged if the shock is temporary; shift to the right if the shock is permanent.

5. An increase in the effective tax rate on capital would cause the *IS* curve to
   (a) shift up and to the right.
   (b) shift down and to the left.
   (c) remain unchanged.
   (d) remain unchanged if taxes are fully deductible from income; otherwise, shift up and to the right.

6. An increase in wealth would cause the *IS* curve to
   (a) shift up and to the right.
   (b) shift down and to the left.
   (c) remain unchanged.
   (d) shift up and to the right only if people face borrowing constraints.

7. The *IS* curve will shift down and to the left when
   (a) desired saving declines.
   (b) government purchases increase.
   (c) consumption increases.
   (d) expected future marginal product of capital declines.

8. A rise in the price of a bond causes the yield of the bond to
   (a) rise.
   (b) fall.
   (c) remain unchanged.
   (d) rise if it's a short-term bond, fall if it's a long-term bond.

9. The *LM* curve illustrates that when income increases, the
   (a) price level must increase to clear the asset market.
   (b) real interest rate on nonmonetary assets must increase to clear the asset market.
   (c) price level must increase to clear the goods market.
   (d) real interest rate on nonmonetary assets must increase to clear the goods market.

10. Looking at the macroeconomic statistics for Friedmanland, you discover that at the beginning of the year, the national money supply was equal to $400 million and by the end of the year it was equal to $420 million. You also found out that the inflation rate in Friedmanland was 7%. In this case, you would expect the *LM* curve to
    (a) shift up and to the left as the real money supply falls.
    (b) shift up and to the left as the real money supply rises.
    (c) shift down and to the right as the real money supply falls.
    (d) shift down and to the right as the real money supply rises.

11. A financial innovation, such as money market mutual funds, which increases the liquidity of alternatives to money, would
    (a) increase money demand, shifting the *LM* curve up and to the left.
    (b) increase money demand, shifting the *LM* curve down and to the right.
    (c) decrease money demand, shifting the *LM* curve up and to the left.
    (d) decrease money demand, shifting the *LM* curve down and to the right.

12. People have reduced their expectations of inflation from 5% to 3%, directly causing
    (a) a relative increase in real money demand, shifting the *LM* curve up and to the left.
    (b) a relative decrease in real money demand, shifting the *LM* curve down and to the right.
    (c) a relative increase in real money demand, shifting the *LM* curve down and to the right.
    (d) a relative decrease in real money demand, shifting the *LM* curve up and to the left.

13. A decrease in the effective tax rate on capital would cause the *IS* curve to _____ and the *LM* curve to _____.
    (a) shift down and to the left; be unchanged
    (b) shift down and to the left; shift up and to the left
    (c) shift up and to the right; be unchanged
    (d) shift up and to the right; shift down and to the right

14. The *IS-LM* model predicts that a temporary adverse supply shock
    (a) reduces output, national saving, and investment, but not the real interest rate.
    (b) reduces output, national saving, and the real interest rate, but not investment.
    (c) reduces the real interest rate, investment, and output, but not national saving.
    (d) reduces output, national saving, investment, and the real interest rate.

15. After a temporary adverse supply shock hits the economy, general equilibrium is restored by
    (a) a shift down and to the left of the *IS* curve.
    (b) a shift to the left of the *FE* line.
    (c) a shift up and to the left of the *LM* curve.
    (d) a shift down and to the right of the *LM* curve.

16 An increase in money supply causes the real interest rate to _____ and output to _____ in the short
    run, before prices adjust to restore equilibrium.
    (a) rise; rise
    (b) rise; fall
    (c) fall; rise
    (d) fall; fall

17. Suppose the intersection of the *IS* and *LM* curves is to the right of the *FE* line. An increase in
    the price level would most likely eliminate a disequilibrium among the asset, labor, and goods
    markets by
    (a) shifting the *LM* curve up and to the left.
    (b) shifting the *IS* curve up and to the right.
    (c) shifting the *IS* curve down and to the left.
    (d) shifting the *FE* curve to the left.

18. A decrease in taxes (when Ricardian equivalence doesn't hold) causes the real interest rate to _____
    and the price level to _____ in general equilibrium.
    (a) rise; rise
    (b) rise; fall
    (c) fall; rise
    (d) fall; fall

19. In classical *IS-LM* analysis, the effects of a decline in desired investment include
    (a) a decline in output.
    (b) an increase in the price level.
    (c) a decline in the real interest rate.
    (d) an increase in unemployment.

20. A decrease in the money supply, in the short run (before the price level has adjusted to restore general
    equilibrium), causes output to _____ and the real interest rate to _____.
    (a) increase; rise
    (b) increase; fall
    (c) decline; fall
    (d) decline; rise

21. An increase in the money supply, in general equilibrium, causes output to _____ and the real interest rate to _____.
    (a) increase; decline
    (b) increase; not change
    (c) not change; not change
    (d) not change; decline

22. Classical economists believe that a market economy will normally
    (a) suffer from extended periods of sustained unemployment.
    (b) achieve full-employment output.
    (c) degenerate into pure monopolies in most industries.
    (d) eliminate the problem of economic scarcity.

23. Keynesians contend that in a recession caused by a decline in aggregate demand, a policy of increasing the nominal money supply would
    (a) raise the level of aggregate demand, which would help return the economy to full-employment output.
    (b) lower the level of aggregate demand, which would help return the economy to full-employment output.
    (c) shift the *LM* curve to left, which would help return the economy to full-employment output.
    (d) not affect the position of the *LM* curve, because the real money supply would not change.

24. The theory of monetary neutrality suggests that
    (a) a change in the nominal money supply has no effect on real variables.
    (b) changes in the real money supply will not affect the real interest rate.
    (c) money is not an asset.
    (d) a decline in nominal money supply growth could create a recession.

25. At a given output level, a temporary reduction in government purchases will
    (a) increase desired saving, causing the *IS* curve to shift down and to the left.
    (b) increase desired saving, causing the *IS* curve to shift up and to the right.
    (c) decrease desired saving, causing the *IS* curve to shift down and to the left.
    (d) decrease desired saving, causing the *IS* curve to shift up and to the right.

26. Which of the following changes shifts the *AD* curve up and to the right?
    (a) A temporary decrease in government purchases
    (b) A decline in the nominal money supply
    (c) An increase in corporate taxes
    (d) An increase in consumer confidence

27. Which of the following changes shifts the *AD* curve down and to the left?
    (a) A decline in the nominal money supply
    (b) A decrease in income taxes
    (c) A decrease in the risk on nonmonetary assets
    (d) An increase in the future marginal productivity of capital

28. Which of the following changes shifts the *SRAS* curve up?

    (a) A decrease in the labor force
    (b) A decrease in the money supply
    (c) An increase in government purchases
    (d) An increase in firms' costs

29. When the money supply declines by 10%, in the short run (before the price level adjusts to restore general equilibrium), output _____ and the price level _____.

    (a) is unchanged; is unchanged
    (b) declines; falls
    (c) is unchanged; falls
    (d) declines; is unchanged

30. An increase in the effective tax rate on capital causes the real interest rate to _____ and the price level to _____ in general equilibrium.

    (a) rise; rise
    (b) rise; fall
    (c) fall; rise
    (d) fall; fall

■ Review Questions

1. Briefly describe the relationship between output and the interest rate on the *FE* line and explain why this relationship exists.

2. Identify changes in three variables that would cause the *FE* line to shift to the right.

3. Identify two variables that change in value as we move down the *IS* curve and state the direction in which they are changing.

4. Can monetary policy be used to offset the real interest rate effects of an adverse supply shock or a decline in desired investment, if prices adjust quickly to restore general equilibrium? Briefly explain.

■ Numerical Problems

1. Calculate the price of a bond that pays no interest but pays its face value of $1,000 at maturity in one year for each of the following nominal interest rates: (a) 3%; (b) 6%; (c) 9%.

2. Calculate the real money supply growth rate when the nominal money supply increases by 10% and the price level increases by each of the following percentages: (a) 2%; (b) 8%; (c) 10%; (d) 15%.

■ Analytical Questions

1. Draw a saving-investment diagram to show how each of the following changes shifts the *IS* curve.
   (a) Future income declines.
   (b) The future marginal productivity of capital declines.
   (c) Government purchases increase temporarily.
   (d) The effective corporate tax rate declines.

2. Describe the effects, in both the short run and the long run, of a decline in the money supply. Explain what happens to real output and the price level.

3. Suppose monetary policymakers decide they will increase output in the economy by increasing the money supply. Beginning from a position of general equilibrium, what effect does this have in the very short run (before general equilibrium is restored)? What must happen to restore general equilibrium? What would happen if the monetary policymaker persistently increased the money supply to try to increase output?

4. For each of the following changes, what happens to the real interest rate and output in the very short run, before the price level has adjusted to restore general equilibrium?
   (a) Wealth declines.
   (b) Money supply declines.
   (c) The future marginal productivity of capital declines.
   (d) Expected inflation rises.
   (e) Future income rises.

■ Answers

Multiple Choice

1. c	7. d	13. c	19. c	25. a
2. b	8. b	14. a	20. d	26. d
3. c	9. b	15. c	21. c	27. a
4. a	10. a	16. c	22. b	28. d
5. b	11. d	17. a	23. a	29. d
6. a	12. a	18. a	24. a	30. d

Review Questions

1. Along the *FE* line, output is independent of the current interest rate, because the *FE* line is vertical.

2. An increase in productivity, an increase in the supply of capital, or an increase in the supply of labor would increase the full-employment level of output, as illustrated by a rightward shift in the *FE* line.

3. As we move down an *IS* curve, output (Y) increases and the real interest rate (r) declines.

4. No. Given flexible prices, monetary policy cannot shift the *LM* curve; therefore, it cannot offset either of these changes. Although the Federal Reserve can change the nominal money supply, any change in *M* creates a proportional change in *P*, so that the real money supply, *M/P*, does not change.

Numerical Problems

1. If B is the price or present value of the bond, i is the nominal interest rate, and F is the face value of the bond, then $B(1 + i) = F$. Dividing through by $1 + i$ gives $B = F/(1 + i)$.

    (a) $i = 3\%$, $B = \$1{,}000/1.03 = \$970.87$.

    (b) $i = 6\%$, $B = \$1{,}000/1.06 = \$943.40$.

    (c) $i = 9\%$, $B = \$1{,}000/1.09 = \$917.43$.

2. Real money supply growth rate = nominal money supply growth rate minus the price level growth rate. (The price level growth rate is the inflation rate.)

    (a) Real money supply growth rate = $10\% - 2\% = 8\%$.

    (b) Real money supply growth rate = $10\% - 8\% = 2\%$.

    (c) Real money supply growth rate = $10\% - 10\% = 0\%$.

    (d) Real money supply growth rate = $10\% - 15\% = -5\%$.

Analytical Questions

1. (a) *IS* shifts down and to the left.

    (b) *IS* shifts down and to the left.

    (c) *IS* shifts up and to the right.

    (d) *IS* shifts up and to the right.

2. In the short run, a decline in the money supply reduces output and has no effect on the price level. In the long run, a decline in the money supply has no effect on output and reduces the price level.

3. In the very short run, output increases and the real interest rate declines, as shown in Figure 9.15. But the price level must rise and the *LM* curve must shift up and to the left to restore general equilibrium. An attempt to persistently increase the money supply causes persistent inflation.

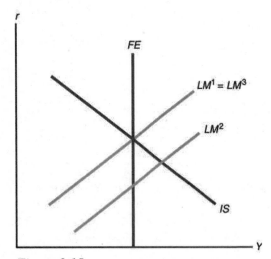

Figure 9.15

4. (a) The *IS* curve shifts down and to the left, so r falls and Y falls.

    (b) The *LM* curve shifts up and to the left, so r rises and Y falls.

    (c) The *IS* curve shifts down and to the left, so r falls and Y falls.

    (d) The *LM* curve shifts down and to the right, so r falls and Y rises.

    (e) The *IS* curve shifts up and to the right, so r rises and Y rises.

Chapter 10
Classical Business Cycle Analysis: Market-Clearing Macroeconomics

■ **Introduction**

This chapter uses a version of the *IS-LM* model with rapidly adjusting wages and prices to represent the classical model. Section 10.1 introduces real business cycle theory, the modern version of the classical model, and discusses some of the current research that uses it. Then, Section 10.2 looks at the role of money in the classical model, and the issues involved in modeling it. Section 10.3 presents the misperceptions theory, a model in which people's expectations about prices matter. Appendix 10.A provides an algebraic model of the misperceptions theory.

Some of the hottest research in macroeconomics today is taking place using classical business cycle analysis. Many researchers are working with real business cycle models to create better empirical models of the U.S. economy. So, if you want to get a good handle on the most recent work in macroeconomics, read Section 10.1 very carefully. Also, the misperceptions model of Section 10.3 represents an older strand of classical analysis, but was very important in leading macro researchers to the real business cycle model in use today. The distinction between anticipated changes in the money supply and unanticipated changes is important.

■ **Outline**

I. **Business Cycles in the Classical Model (Sec. 10.1)**

    A) The real business cycle theory

        1. Two key questions about business cycles

            a. What are the underlying economic causes?

            b. What should government policymakers do about them?

        2. Any business cycle theory has two components

            a. A description of the types of shocks believed to affect the economy the most

            b. A model that describes how key macroeconomic variables respond to economic shocks

        3. Real business cycle (*RBC*) theory (Kydland and Prescott)

            a. Real shocks to the economy are the primary cause of business cycles

                (1) Examples: Shocks to the production function, the size of the labor force, the real quantity of government purchases, the spending and saving decisions of consumers (affecting the *IS* curve or the *FE* line)

                (2) Nominal shocks are shocks to money supply or demand (affecting the *LM* curve)

    b. The largest role is played by shocks to the production function, which the text has called supply shocks, and *RBC* theorists call *productivity shocks*

       (1) Examples: Development of new products or production techniques, introduction of new management techniques, changes in the quality of capital or labor, changes in the availability of raw materials or energy, unusually good or bad weather, changes in government regulations affecting production

       (2) Most economic booms result from beneficial productivity shocks; most recessions are caused by adverse productivity shocks

    c. The recessionary impact of an adverse productivity shock

       (1) Results from Chapter 3: Real wage, employment, output, consumption, and investment decline, while the real interest rate and price level rise

       (2) So an adverse productivity shock causes a recession (output declines), whereas a beneficial productivity shock causes a boom (output increases); but output always equals full-employment output

    d. Real business cycle theory and the business cycle facts

       (1) The *RBC* theory is consistent with many business cycle facts

          (a) If the economy is continuously buffeted by productivity shocks, the theory predicts recurrent fluctuations in aggregate output, which we observe

          (b) The theory correctly predicts procyclical employment and real wages

          (c) The theory correctly predicts procyclical average labor productivity. If booms weren't due to productivity shocks, we would expect average labor productivity to be countercyclical because of diminishing marginal productivity of labor

       (2) The theory predicts countercyclical movements of the price level, which seems to be inconsistent with the data

          (a) But Kydland and Prescott, when using some newer statistical techniques for calculating the trends in inflation and output, find evidence that the price level is countercyclical

          (b) Though the Great Depression appears to have been caused by a sequence of large, adverse aggregate demand shocks, Kydland and Prescott argue that since World War II, large adverse supply shocks have caused the price level to rise while output fell

          (c) The surge in inflation during the recessions associated with the oil price shocks of 1973–1974 and 1979–1980 is consistent with *RBC* theory

  4. Application: Calibrating the business cycle

    a. A major element of *RBC* theory is that it attempts to make quantitative, not just qualitative, predictions about the business cycle

    b. *RBC* theorists use the method of *calibration* to work out a detailed numerical example of the theory

       (1) First they write down specific functions explaining the behavior of people in the economy; for example, they might choose as the production function for the economy, $Y = AK^a N^{1-a}$

       (2) Then they use existing studies of the economy to choose numbers for parameters like a in the production function; for example, $a = 0.3$

       (3) Next they simulate what happens when the economy is hit by various shocks to different sectors of the economy

       (4) Prescott's computer simulations (text Figures 10.1 and 10.2) match post–World War II data fairly well

5. Are productivity shocks the only source of recessions?
   a. Critics of the *RBC* theory suggest that except for the oil price shocks of 1973, 1979, and 1990, there are no productivity shocks that one can easily identify that caused recessions
   b. One *RBC* response is that it doesn't have to be a big shock; instead, the cumulation of many small shocks can cause a business cycle (text Figure 10.3)
6. Does the Solow residual measure technology shocks?
   a. *RBC* theorists measure productivity shocks as the *Solow residual*
      (1) Named after Robert Solow, the originator of modern growth theory
      (2) Given a production function, $Y = AK^aN^{1-a}$, and data on Y, K, and N, the Solow residual is

   $$A = Y/(K^aN^{1-a}) \tag{10.1}$$

      (3) It's called a residual because it can't be measured directly
   b. The Solow residual is strongly procyclical in U.S. data
      (1) This accords with *RBC* theory, which says the cycle is driven by productivity shocks
   c. But should the Solow residual be interpreted as a measure of technology?
      (1) If it's a measure of technology, it should not be related to factors that don't directly affect scientific and technological progress, like government purchases or monetary policy
      (2) But statistical studies show a correlation between these
   d. Measured productivity can vary even if the actual technology doesn't change
      (1) Capital and labor are used more intensively at times
      (2) More intensive use of inputs leads to higher output
      (3) Define the utilization rate of capital u_K and the utilization rate of labor u_N
      (4) Define capital services as $u_K K$ and labor services as $u_N N$
      (5) Rewrite the production function as

   $$Y = AF(u_K K, u_N N) = A(u_K K)^a (u_N N)^{1-a} \tag{10.2}$$

      (6) Use this to substitute for Y in Eq. (10.1) to get

   $$\text{Solow residual} = Au_K^a u_N^{1-a} \tag{10.3}$$

      (7) So the Solow residual isn't just A, but depends on u_K and u_N
      (8) Utilization is procyclical, so the measured Solow residual is more procyclical than is the true productivity term A
         (a) Burnside-Eichenbaum-Rebelo evidence on procyclical utilization of capital
         (b) Fay-Medoff and Braun-Evans evidence on procyclical utilization of labor
            (1) Labor hoarding: firms keep workers in recessions to avoid incurring hiring and firing costs
            (2) Hoarded labor doesn't work as hard, or performs maintenance
            (3) The lower productivity of hoarded labor doesn't reflect technological change, just the rate of utilization
   e. Conclusion: Changes in the measured Solow residual don't necessarily reflect changes in technology
7. Technology shocks may not lead to procyclical productivity
   a. Research by Basu and Fernald shows that technology shocks are not closely related to cyclical movements in output
   b. Shocks to technology are followed by a transition period in which resources are reallocated
   c. Initially, less capital and labor are needed to produce the same amount of output
   d. Later, resources are adjusted and output increases

8. Also, the critics suggest that shocks other than productivity shocks, such as wars and military buildups, have caused business cycles

9. Models allowing for other shocks are DSGE models (dynamic, stochastic, general equilibrium models)

B) Fiscal policy shocks in the classical model

1. The effects of a temporary increase in government expenditures (Figure 10.1; like text Figure 10.4)

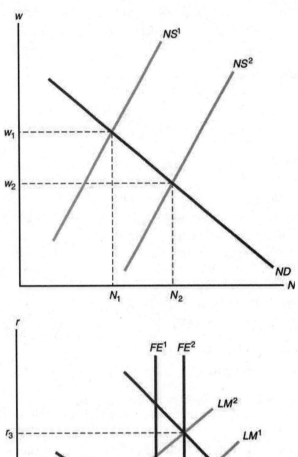

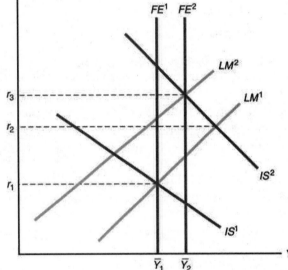

Figure 10.1

a. The current or future taxes needed to pay for the government expenditures effectively reduce people's wealth, causing an income effect on labor supply

b. The increased labor supply leads to a fall in the real wage and a rise in employment

c. The rise in employment increases output, so the *FE* line shifts to the right

    d. The temporary rise in government purchases shifts the *IS* curve up and to the right as national saving declines

    e. It's reasonable to assume that the shift of the *IS* curve is bigger than the shift of the *FE* line, so prices must rise to shift the *LM* curve up and to the left to restore equilibrium

    f. Because employment rises, average labor productivity declines; this helps match the data better, because without fiscal policy the *RBC* model shows a correlation between output and average labor productivity that is too high

    g. So adding fiscal policy shocks to the model increases its ability to match the actual behavior of the economy

  2. Should fiscal policy be used to dampen the cycle?

    a. Classical economists oppose attempts to dampen the cycle, because prices and wages adjust quickly to restore equilibrium

    b. Besides, fiscal policy increases output by making workers worse off, because they face higher taxes

    c. Instead, government spending should be determined by cost-benefit analysis

    d. Also, there may be lags in enacting the correct policy and in implementing it

      (1) So choosing the right policy today depends on where you think the economy will be in the future

      (2) This creates problems, because forecasts of the future state of the economy are imperfect

    e. It's also not clear how much to change fiscal policy to get the desired effect on employment and output

C) Unemployment in the classical model

  1. In the classical model there is no unemployment; people who aren't working are voluntarily not in the labor force

  2. In reality measured unemployment is never zero, and it is the problem of unemployment in recessions that concerns policymakers the most

  3. Classical economists have a more sophisticated version of the model to account for unemployment

    a. Workers and jobs have different requirements, so there is a matching problem

    b. It takes time to match workers to jobs, so there is always some unemployment

    c. Unemployment rises in recessions because productivity shocks cause increased mismatches between workers and jobs

    d. A shock that increases mismatching raises frictional unemployment and may also cause structural unemployment if the types of skills needed by employers change

    e. So the shock causes the natural rate of unemployment to rise; there's still no cyclical unemployment in the classical model

  4. Davis and Haltiwanger show that there is a tremendous amount of churning of jobs both within and across industries

  5. But this worker match theory can't explain all unemployment

    a. Many workers are laid off temporarily; there's no mismatch, just a change in the timing of work

    b. If recessions were times of increased mismatch, there should be a rise in help-wanted ads in recessions, but in fact they fall

      6. So can the government use fiscal policy to reduce unemployment?

        a. Doing so doesn't improve the mismatch problem

        b. A better approach is to eliminate barriers to labor-market adjustment by reducing burdensome regulations on businesses or by getting rid of the minimum wage

  D) Household production

    1. The RBC model matches U.S. data better if the model accounts explicitly for output produced at home

    2. Household production is not counted in GDP but it represents output

    3. Rogerson and Wright used a model with household production to show that such a model yields a higher standard deviation of (market) output than a standard RBC model, thus more closely matching the data

    4. Parente, Rogerson, and Wright showed that after household production is accounted for, income differences across countries are not as large as the GDP data show

II. Money in the Classical Model (Sec. 10.2)

  A) Monetary policy and the economy
    Money is neutral in both the short run and the long run in the classical model, because prices adjust rapidly to restore equilibrium

  B) Monetary nonneutrality and reverse causation

    1. If money is neutral, why do the data show that money is a leading, procyclical variable?

      a. Increases in the money supply are often followed by increases in output

      b. Reductions in the money supply are often followed by recessions

    2. The classical answer: Reverse causation

      a. Just because changes in money growth precede changes in output doesn't mean that the money changes cause the output changes

      b. Example: People put storm windows on their houses before winter but it's the coming winter that causes the storm windows to go on; the storm windows don't cause winter

      c. Reverse causation means money growth is higher because people expect higher output in the future; the higher money growth doesn't cause the higher future output

      d. If so, money can be procyclical and leading even though money is neutral

    3. Why would higher future output cause people to increase money demand?

      a. Firms, anticipating higher sales, would need more money for transactions to pay for materials and workers

      b. The Fed would respond to the higher demand for money by increasing money supply; otherwise, the price level would decline

  C) The nonneutrality of money: Additional evidence

    1. Friedman and Schwartz have extensively documented that often monetary changes have had an independent origin; they weren't just a reflection of changes or future changes in economic activity

      a. These independent changes in money supply were followed by changes in income and prices

      b. The independent origins of money changes include such things as gold discoveries, changes in monetary institutions, and changes in the leadership of the Fed

      2. More recently, Romer and Romer documented additional episodes of monetary nonneutrality since 1960

        a. One example is the Fed's tight money policy begun in 1979 that was followed by a minor recession in 1980 and a deeper one in 1981

        b. That was followed by monetary expansion in 1982 that led to an economic boom

      3. So money does not appear to be neutral

      4. There is a version of the classical model in which money isn't neutral—the misperceptions theory discussed next

III. The Misperceptions Theory and the Nonneutrality of Money (Sec. 10.3)

    A) Introduction to the misperceptions theory

      1. In the classical model, money is neutral because prices adjust quickly

        a. In this case, the only relevant supply curve is the long-run aggregate supply curve

        b. So movements in aggregate demand have no effect on output

      2. But if producers misperceive the aggregate price level, then the relevant aggregate supply curve in the short run isn't vertical

        a. This happens because producers have imperfect information about the general price level

        b. As a result, they misinterpret changes in the general price level as changes in relative prices

        c. This leads to a short-run aggregate supply curve that isn't vertical

        d. But prices still adjust rapidly

    B) The misperceptions theory is that the aggregate quantity of output supplied rises above the full-employment level $\bar{Y}$ when the aggregate price level P is higher than expected

      1. This makes the *AS* curve slope upward

      2. Example: A bakery that makes bread

        a. The price of bread is the baker's nominal wage; the price of bread relative to the general price level is the baker's real wage

        b. If the relative price of bread rises, the baker may work more and produce more bread

        c. If the baker can't observe the general price level as easily as the price of bread, he or she must estimate the relative price of bread

        d. If the price of bread rises 5% and the baker thinks inflation is 5%, there's no change in the relative price of bread, so there's no change in the baker's labor supply

        e. But suppose the baker expects the general price level to rise by 5%, but sees the price of bread rising by 8%; then the baker will work more in response to the wage increase

      3. Generalizing this example, if everyone expects prices to increase 5% but they actually increase 8%, they'll work more

      4. So an increase in the price level that is higher than expected induces people to work more and thus increases the economy's output

      5. Similarly, an increase in the price level that is lower than expected reduces output

      6. The equation $Y = \bar{Y} + b(P - P^e)$ [Eq. (10.4)] summarizes the misperceptions theory

7. In the short run, the aggregate supply (*SRAS*) curve slopes upward and intersects the long-run aggregate supply (*LRAS*) curve at $P = P^e$ (Figure 10.2; like text Figure 10.6)

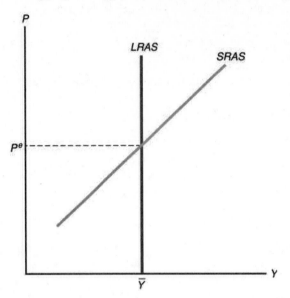

Figure 10.2

C) Monetary policy and the misperceptions theory

1. Because of misperceptions, unanticipated monetary policy has real effects; but anticipated monetary policy has no real effects because there are no misperceptions

2. Unanticipated changes in the money supply (Figure 10.3; like text Figure 10.7)

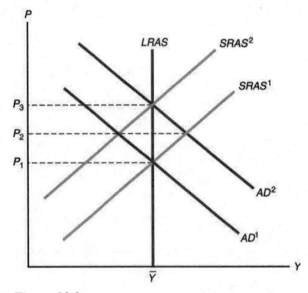

Figure 10.3

a. Initial equilibrium where AD^1 intersects $SRAS^1$ and *LRAS*

b. Unanticipated increase in money supply shifts *AD* curve to AD^2

c. The price level rises to P_2 and output rises above $\overline{Y}$, so money isn't neutral

d. As people get information about the true price level, their expectations change, and the *SRAS* curve shifts left to $SRAS^2$, with output returning to $\overline{Y}$

e. So unanticipated money isn't neutral in the short run, but it is neutral in the long run

3. Anticipated changes in the money supply

   a. If people anticipate the change in the money supply and thus in the price level, they aren't fooled, there are no misperceptions, and the *SRAS* curve shifts immediately to its higher level

   b. So anticipated money is neutral in both the short run and the long run

D) Rational expectations and the role of monetary policy

   1. The only way the Fed can use monetary policy to affect output is to surprise people

   2. But people realize that the Fed would want to increase the money supply in recessions and decrease it in booms so they won't be fooled

   3. The rational expectations hypothesis suggests that the public's forecasts of economic variables are well-reasoned and use all the available data

   4. If the public has rational expectations, the Fed won't be able to surprise people in response to the business cycle; only random monetary policy has any effects

   5. So even if smoothing the business cycle were desirable, the combination of misperceptions theory and rational expectations suggests that the Fed can't systematically use monetary policy to stabilize the economy

   6. Propagating the effects of unanticipated changes in the money supply

      a. It doesn't seem like people could be fooled for long, because money supply figures are reported weekly and inflation is reported monthly

      b. Classical economists argue that *propagation mechanisms* allow short-lived shocks to have long-lived effects

      c. Example of propagation: The behavior of inventories

         (1) Firms hold a normal level of inventories against their normal level of sales

         (2) An unanticipated increase in the money supply increases sales

         (3) Because the firm can't produce many more goods immediately, it draws down its inventories

         (4) Even after the money supply change is known, the firm must produce more to restore its inventory level

         (5) Thus the short-term monetary shock has a long-lived effect on the economy

E) Box 10.1: Are price forecasts rational?

   1. Economists can test whether price forecasts are rational by looking at surveys of people's expectations

   2. The forecast error of a forecast is the difference between the actual value of the variable and the forecast value

   3. If people have rational expectations, forecast errors should be unpredictable random numbers; otherwise, people would be making systematic errors and thus not have rational expectations

   4. Many statistical studies suggest that people don't have rational expectations

   5. But people who answer surveys may not have a lot at stake in making forecasts, so couldn't be expected to produce rational forecasts

   6. Instead, professional forecasters are more likely to produce rational forecasts

   7. Keane and Runkle, using a survey of professional forecasters, find evidence that these forecasters do have rational expectations

   8. Croushore used inflation forecasts made by the general public, as well as economists, and found evidence broadly consistent with rational expectations, though expectations tend to lag in reality when inflation changes sharply

IV. Appendix 10.A: An Algebraic Version of the Classical *AD-AS* Model with Misperceptions

A) The aggregate demand curve

1. From Appendix 9.A, the *AD* curve is

$$Y = [\alpha_{IS} - \alpha_{LM} + (1/\ell_r)(M/P)]/[\beta_{IS} + \beta_{LM}] \qquad (10.A.1)$$

B) The aggregate supply curve (*SRAS*)

1. Based on the misperceptions theory:

$$Y = \bar{Y} + b(P - P^e) \qquad (10.A.2)$$

C) General equilibrium

1. The *AD* curve intersects the *SRAS* curve at the point found by setting the right-hand sides of Eqs. (10.A.1) and (10.A.2) equal and rearranging terms to get

$$a_2 P^2 + a_1 P - a_0 = 0, \qquad (10.A.3)$$

where

$$a_2 = (\beta_{IS} + \beta_{LM})b, \quad a_1 = (\beta_{IS} + \beta_{LM})(\bar{Y} - bP^e) - \alpha_{IS} + \alpha_{LM}, \quad \text{and} \quad a_0 = M/\ell_r$$

2. The solution for *P* is given by the quadratic formula,

$$P = \left[-a_1 + \left(a_1^2 + 4a_2 a_0 \right)^{1/2} \right]/2a_2 \qquad (10.A.4)$$

3. Then output is determined by taking this value of *P* and using it in Eqs. (10.A.1) or (10.A.2)

4. It's easy to see that an increase in the nominal money supply increases a_0 and thus *P*

5. If the increase in money supply in unanticipated, so that P^e doesn't change, then output rises in the short run, according to Eq. (10.A.2)

6. In the long run, of course, $P = P^e$, so from Eq. (10.A.2), $Y = \bar{Y}$

■ Multiple Choice Questions

1. According to real business cycle theory, which of the following events is least likely to cause a recession?
    (a) A decline in the money supply
    (b) A decline in the capital stock
    (c) A decline in productivity
    (d) A decline in labor supply

2. Which of the following would *not* be an example of a productivity shock?
    (a) The introduction of new management techniques
    (b) A change in government regulations affecting production
    (c) A change in the level of government transfer programs
    (d) A spell of unusually good or unusually bad weather

3. A temporary beneficial productivity shock would
    (a) shift the labor supply curve downward.
    (b) increase the level of employment.
    (c) increase future income.
    (d) increase the expected future marginal product of capital.

4. How do *RBC* economists face the business cycle fact that inflation is procyclical?

    (a) They argue that even though inflation doesn't fit their theory, everything else does, and inflation is not important.

    (b) They note that inflation would not be procyclical if monetary policy were conducted properly.

    (c) They argue that inflation is procyclical only because monetary policy shocks are the main cause of business cycles.

    (d) They use alternative statistical methods that suggest that inflation is countercyclical.

5. *RBC* economists argue that inflation appears to be procyclical based on data from _____; but that data from _____ shows that inflation is countercyclical.

    (a) 1918–1941; 1947–on

    (b) 1918–1941; 1983–on

    (c) 1947–on; 1918–1941

    (d) 1983–on; 1918–1941

6. What do *RBC* economists mean by the term calibration?

    (a) Modifying the structure of an economic theory to strengthen its logic

    (b) Changing a theory as the economy changes

    (c) Working out a detailed numerical example of a more general theory

    (d) Writing out the implications of a theory for all the main economic variables

7. Prescott's calibrated RBC model showed that the actual and simulated _____ of five key macroeconomic variables were very close.

    (a) magnitudes

    (b) slopes

    (c) volatilities

    (d) betas

8. Prescott's calibrated RBC model was able to match the data in terms of the _____ between many key macroeconomic variables and GNP; that is, in terms of how closely they moved with GNP over the business cycle.

    (a) correlation

    (b) interdependence

    (c) gamma coefficient

    (d) sigma ratio

9. Research on productivity shocks has shown that

    (a) productivity shocks have only nominal effects.

    (b) there have been no identifiable productivity shocks in the U.S. economy since World War II.

    (c) small productivity shocks can explain large business cycle fluctuations.

    (d) large productivity shocks produce only small deviations in aggregate output.

10. The most common measure of productivity shocks used by real business cycle theorists is

    (a) the Solow residual.

    (b) average labor productivity.

    (c) the change in the capital stock.

    (d) unit labor costs.

11. In U.S. data, the Solow residual is
    (a) strongly countercyclical.
    (b) strongly procyclical.
    (c) weakly procyclical.
    (d) weakly countercyclical.

12. If the utilization rates of capital and labor are procyclical, then
    (a) output will rise in recessions and decline in expansions.
    (b) measured productivity will be constant.
    (c) the Solow residual will be procyclical.
    (d) prices will be countercyclical.

13. When, because of hiring and firing costs, firms retain workers in a recession that they would otherwise lay off, there is said to be
    (a) labor hoarding.
    (b) a decline in capacity utilization.
    (c) voluntary unemployment.
    (d) involuntary unemployment.

14. Classical economists who allow for shocks other than productivity shocks to affect the economy use _____ models rather than RBC models.
    (a) Keynesian
    (b) monetarist
    (c) nonlinear
    (d) DSGE

15. A temporary decrease in government purchases in the classical model would
    (a) shift the production function to the left.
    (b) shift the marginal product of labor curve to the right.
    (c) shift the labor demand curve to the left.
    (d) shift the labor supply curve to the left.

16. Classical economists think that the government _____ use fiscal policy to dampen the business cycle because prices and wages adjust _____.
    (a) should not; rapidly
    (b) should not; slowly
    (c) should; slowly
    (d) should; rapidly

17. Output produced at home instead of in a market is known as
    (a) the underground economy.
    (b) household production.
    (c) nonmarket output.
    (d) overemployment.

18. Assuming that money is neutral, a reduction in the nominal money supply would cause
    (a) an excess demand for goods.
    (b) a decrease in the real money supply.
    (c) a fall in the price level.
    (d) a rise in nominal wages.

19. Assuming money neutrality in the classical model, a 10% decrease in the nominal money supply would cause
    (a) a 10% decrease in the real money supply.
    (b) a 10% increase in the real money supply.
    (c) no change in the real money supply.
    (d) a less-than-10% change in the price level due to a shift in the aggregate supply curve.

20. A decline in the money supply usually precedes a decline in business cycle activity; according to *RBC* theorists, this shows that the Federal Reserve
    (a) intentionally causes most recessions.
    (b) should not be allowed to control the money supply.
    (c) does not know what it is doing.
    (d) reduces the money supply when money demand falls prior to a recession.

21. Research by Friedman and Schwartz on the monetary history of the United States for 1867–1960 and the recent updating of this research by Romer and Romer suggests that
    (a) reverse causality can explain why the nominal money supply is a leading, procyclical variable.
    (b) the Federal Reserve can accurately forecast turning points in the business cycle created by small, random changes in productivity.
    (c) money is often nonneutral in the short run.
    (d) money is often nonneutral in the long run.

22. Misperceptions theory best explains why
    (a) the aggregate demand curve is negatively sloped.
    (b) the aggregate supply curve is vertical.
    (c) the *SRAS* curve is positively sloped.
    (d) the *LM* curve is positively sloped.

23. According to the misperceptions theory, when the aggregate price level is lower than expected,
    (a) the aggregate quantity of output supplied rises above the full-employment level.
    (b) the aggregate quantity of output supplied falls below the full-employment level.
    (c) the aggregate quantity of output demanded falls below the full-employment level.
    (d) the aggregate quantity of output demanded rises above the full-employment level.

24. In the misperceptions model, a 5% decline in the money supply that is unanticipated will
    (a) cause both output and employment to decline in the short run.
    (b) cause output to increase in the long run.
    (c) cause employment to decline in the long run.
    (d) not change employment in the short run or long run.

25. You are likely to think that the relative price of your good has declined and you should decrease your output if
    (a) you expected inflation of 10% and the price of your good rose 7%.
    (b) you expected inflation of 10% and the price of your good rose 10%.
    (c) you expected inflation of 10% and the price of your good rose 13%.
    (d) you expected inflation of 0% and the price of your good rose 10%.

26. The misperceptions theory and the rational expectations hypothesis together suggest that systematic attempts by the Federal Reserve to increase aggregate output will
    (a) cause the price level to exceed the expected price level in the short run.
    (b) not have any real economic effects.
    (c) not increase the price level.
    (d) cause the *AD* curve to shift up and to the right along a fixed *SRAS* curve.

27. In the extended classical model, some kind of propagation mechanism is needed to explain
    (a) the persistence of a recession caused by a nominal shock.
    (b) imperfect information.
    (c) why money is neutral.
    (d) the difference between correlation and causation.

28. According to the misperceptions theory, when $P > P^e$, output is _____ its full-employment level and the short-run aggregate supply curve must shift _____ to restore full employment.
    (a) below; upward
    (b) below; downward
    (c) above; upward
    (d) above; downward

29. According to the misperceptions theory, after an unanticipated decrease in the money supply has occurred, the *SRAS* curve must shift _____ to restore general equilibrium; as it does so, the price level _____.
    (a) downward; rises
    (b) downward; falls
    (c) upward; rises
    (d) upward; falls

30. The Fed had announced to Congress that it would allow M2 to grow by 8% this year, and M2 did grow by 8% this year. You would *not* expect
    (a) money to be neutral in the short run.
    (b) money to be neutral in the long run.
    (c) output to remain unchanged.
    (d) a movement along the short-run aggregate supply curve.

■ Review Questions

1. According to the real business cycle theory, what is the principal cause of business cycle fluctuations?

2. Define real shocks, define nominal shocks, and give an example of each.

3. How do *RBC* theorists answer the objection that there have been few examples of large and easily measurable real shocks to the U.S. economy in recent decades?

4. During a recession, would classical economists propose that changes in government spending or taxes be used to improve economic conditions? Briefly explain.

5. How do *RBC* theorists answer the objection that the money supply is a leading, procyclical variable?

6. During a recession, would classical economists propose that changes in the money supply be used to improve economic conditions? Briefly explain.

7. In the misperceptions model, is money neutral? Can nominal shocks create business cycle fluctuations? Briefly explain.

8. Briefly state the rational expectations hypothesis.

9. Does the extended classical model explain the persistence of business cycle contractions and expansions? Briefly explain.

■ Analytical Questions

1. Use the classical (*RBC*) *IS-LM-FE* model to show the effects on the economy of a temporary *decrease* in government spending. You should show the impact on the real wage, employment, output, the real interest rate, consumption, investment, and the price level.

2. What are the effects of an unanticipated decline in the money supply in the short run and long run in the misperceptions model?

3. What are the effects of an anticipated decline in the money supply in the short run and long run in the misperceptions model?

■ Answers

Multiple Choice

1. a	7. c	13. a	19. c	25. a
2. c	8. a	14. d	20. d	26. b
3. b	9. c	15. d	21. c	27. a
4. d	10. a	16. a	22. c	28. c
5. a	11. b	17. b	23. b	29. b
6. c	12. c	18. c	24. a	30. d

Review Questions

1. According to the real business cycle theory, real shocks, especially productivity shocks, are the principal cause of business cycle fluctuations in aggregate economic activity.

2. Real shocks are changes that disturb labor market equilibrium or goods market equilibrium. Nominal shocks are changes that disturb the asset market. A change in aggregate saving is an example of a real shock. A change in the money supply is an example of a nominal shock.

3. Computer simulations of RBC statistical models have shown that frequent, small, randomly generated productivity shocks can produce large business cycle fluctuations. Therefore large business cycle fluctuations occur even in the absence of large productivity shocks.

4. No. Classical economists do not endorse changes in government spending or taxes designed to offset business cycle fluctuations; the classical model shows that such policy attempts are not likely to improve macroeconomic conditions. From a classical viewpoint, government spending and tax decisions should be long-run decisions based on cost-benefit analysis.

5. The money supply is a leading, procyclical variable, but correlation does not prove causation. One plausible explanation is that the Federal Reserve anticipates changes in the business cycle, then reduces the money supply prior to a recession, and increases it prior to an expansion to achieve its policy goal of maintaining price level stability.

6. No. In the classical model, an increase in the money supply cannot improve economic conditions, because it has no real economic effects. Money is neutral in the classical model.

7. In the misperceptions model, money is neutral in the long run. In the short run, anticipated changes in the money supply are neutral, but unanticipated changes in the money supply are nonneutral.

8. The rational expectations hypothesis states that market actors will use all available information in predicting the values of important economic variables, and they will learn to improve the accuracy of their predictions over time.

9. No. Although the model shows that a monetary surprise can create short-run business cycle fluctuations in aggregate economic activity, the frequent publication of money supply data and price level data suggests that these errors will not persist. The persistence of a business cycle contraction requires some additional propagation mechanism to explain it. One such propagation mechanism is the process of adjusting inventories to their desired level once misperceptions have been corrected.

Analytical Questions

1. The decrease in government spending reduces current or future taxes, so there's a positive wealth effect that increases people's desire for leisure and reduces their labor supply, as shown in Figure 10.4. The decline in labor supply leads to a rise in the real wage and a decline in employment. The fall in employment leads to less output, so the FE line shifts left, as shown in Figure 10.5. However, the decline in government spending increases national saving, so the IS curve shifts down and to the left, most likely shifting left by more than the FE line does. As a result, the price level must decline to restore equilibrium by shifting the LM curve down and to the right. This results in a decline in the real interest rate, so investment increases. The effect on consumption is ambiguous.

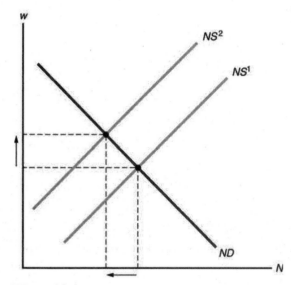

Figure 10.4

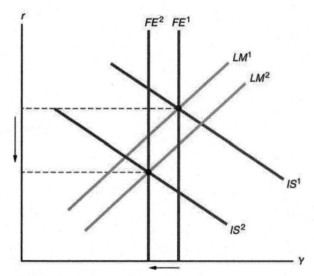

Figure 10.5

2.   In the misperceptions model, an unanticipated decline in the money supply causes the price level to decline and output to decline, as shown in Figure 10.6. In the long run, the price level declines further, as the expected price level declines, but there is no output effect in the long run.

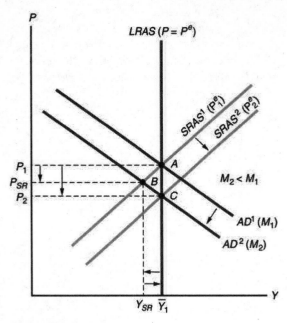

Figure 10.6

3.   In the misperceptions model, an anticipated decline in the money supply causes the price level and the expected price level to immediately decline without producing any change in real output, as shown in Figure 10.7.

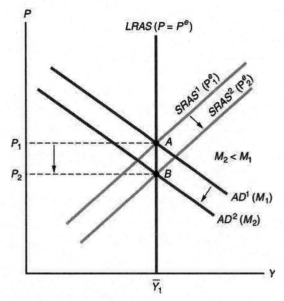

Figure 10.7

Chapter 11
Keynesianism: The Macroeconomics of Wage and Price Rigidity

■ Introduction

This chapter presents the central ideas of Keynesian macroeconomics. Basically, the Keynesian model of the economy is one in which wages and prices don't adjust quickly to restore general equilibrium, the economy may be in disequilibrium for long periods of time, and the government should act to stabilize the economy. The chapter also discusses the potential causes of wage and price rigidity that lead to these results.

The chapter begins with a discussion of real-wage rigidity in Section 11.1, developing a theory that firms pay workers what are known as "efficiency wages." Then, Section 11.2 discusses price stickiness—the reasons why firms are slow to change their prices. Section 11.3 discusses policy—both monetary and fiscal. Section 11.4 shows how well the Keynesian model fits the business cycle facts and looks at the possibility of using policy to stabilize the economy.

The classical model in Chapter 10 is identical to the Keynesian model in the long run. In the short run, the Keynesian model differs in two major aspects: (1) the labor market is characterized by efficiency wages, which are a bit different than the usual supply and demand model of the labor market; and (2) prices are sticky, so the short-run aggregate supply curve is horizontal. Given these differences, however, the type of analysis that is done is the same as you saw in Chapter 10. When there's some shock to the economy, you need to identify which curve or curves are affected and which direction they shift, then see what happens as the economy moves to the new equilibrium.

■ Outline

I.   Real-Wage Rigidity (Sec. 11.1)

    A)   Wage rigidity is important in explaining unemployment

        1. In the classical model, unemployment is due to mismatches between workers and firms

        2. Keynesians are skeptical, believing that recessions lead to substantial cyclical employment

        3. To get a model in which unemployment persists, Keynesian theory posits that the real wage is slow to adjust to equilibrate the labor market

    B)   Some reasons for real-wage rigidity

        1. For unemployment to exist, the real wage must exceed the market-clearing wage

        2. If the real wage is too high, why don't firms reduce the wage?

            a. One possibility is that the minimum wage and labor unions prevent wages from being reduced

                (1) But most U.S. workers aren't minimum wage workers, nor are they in unions

                (2) The minimum wage would explain why the nominal wage is rigid, but not why the real wage is rigid

                (3) This might be a better explanation in Europe, where unions are far more powerful

      b. Another possibility is that a firm may want to pay high wages to get a stable labor force and avoid turnover costs—costs of hiring and training new workers

      c. A third reason is that workers' productivity may depend on the wages they're paid—the efficiency wage model

C) The Efficiency Wage Model

    1. Workers who feel well treated will work harder and more efficiently (the "carrot"); this is Akerlof's *gift exchange motive*

    2. Workers who are well paid won't risk losing their jobs by shirking (the "stick")

    3. Both the gift exchange motive and shirking model imply that a worker's effort depends on the real wage (Figure 11.1)

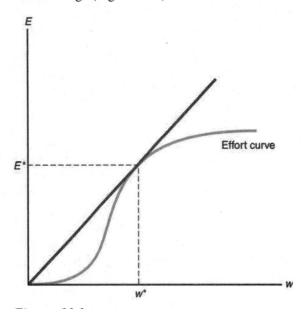

Figure. 11.1

    4. The effort curve, plotting effort against the real wage, is S-shaped

      a. At low levels of the real wage, workers make hardly any effort

      b. Effort rises as the real wage increases

      c. As the real wage becomes very high, effort flattens out as it reaches the maximum possible level

D) Wage determination in the efficiency wage model

    1. Given the effort curve, what determines the real wage firms will pay?

    2. To maximize profit, firms choose the real wage that gets the most effort from workers for each dollar of real wages paid

    3. This occurs at point *B* in Figure 11.1, where a line from the origin is just tangent to the effort curve

    4. The wage rate at point *B* is called the efficiency wage

    5. The real wage is rigid, as long as the effort curve doesn't change

E) Employment and Unemployment in the Efficiency Wage Model
  1. The labor market now determines employment and unemployment, depending on how far above the market-clearing wage is the efficiency wage (Figure 11.2)

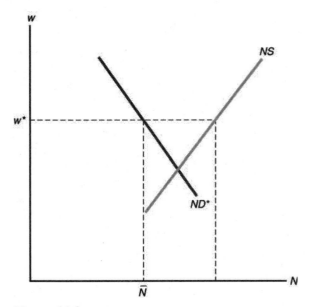

Figure 11.2

  2. The labor supply curve is upward sloping, while the labor demand curve is the marginal product of labor when the effort level is determined by the efficiency wage
  3. The difference between labor supply and labor demand is the amount of unemployment
  4. The fact that there's unemployment puts no downward pressure on the real wage, because firms know that if they reduce the real wage, effort will decline
  5. Does the efficiency wage theory match up with the data?
     a. It seems to have worked for Henry Ford in 1914
     b. Plants that pay higher wages appear to experience less shirking
     c. But the theory implies that the real wage is completely rigid, whereas the data suggests that the real wage moves over time and over the business cycle
     d. It is possible to jazz up the model to allow for the efficiency wage to change over time
        (1) Workers would be less likely to shirk and would work harder during a recession if the probability of losing their jobs increased
        (2) This would cause the effort curve to rise and may cause the efficiency wage to decline somewhat
        (3) This would lead to a lower real wage rate in recessions, which is consistent with the data

F) Efficiency wages and the *FE* line
  1. The *FE* line is vertical, as in the classical model, because full-employment output is determined in the labor market and doesn't depend on the real interest rate
  2. But in the Keynesian model, changes in labor supply don't affect the *FE* line, because they don't affect equilibrium employment
  3. A change in productivity does affect the *FE* line, because it affects labor demand

II.   Price Stickiness (Sec. 11.2)

A)   Price stickiness is the tendency of prices to adjust slowly to changes in the economy

  1.   The data suggest that money is not neutral, so Keynesians reject the classical model (without misperceptions)

  2.   Keynesians developed the idea of price stickiness to explain why money isn't neutral

  3.   An alternative version of the Keynesian model (discussed in Appendix 11.A) assumes that nominal wages are sticky, rather than prices; that model also suggests that money isn't neutral

B)   Sources of price stickiness: Monopolistic competition and menu costs

  1.   Monopolistic competition

   a.   If markets had perfect competition, the market would force prices to adjust rapidly; sellers are price takers, because they must accept the market price

   b.   In many markets, sellers have some degree of monopoly; they are price setters under monopolistic competition

   c.   Keynesians suggest that many markets are characterized by monopolistic competition

   d.   In monopolistically competitive markets, sellers do three things

    (1)   They set prices in nominal terms and maintain those prices for some period

    (2)   They adjust output to meet the demand at their fixed nominal price

    (3)   They readjust prices from time to time when costs or demand change significantly

   e.   Menu costs and price stickiness

    (1)   The term menu costs comes from the costs faced by a restaurant when it changes prices—it must print new menus

    (2)   Even small costs like these may prevent sellers from changing prices often

    (3)   Because competition isn't perfect, having the wrong price temporarily won't affect the seller's profits much

    (4)   The firm will change prices when demand or costs of production change enough to warrant the price change

   f.   Empirical evidence on price stickiness

    (1)   Industrial prices seem to be changed more often in competitive industries, less often in more monopolistic industries (Carlton study)

    (2)   Blinder and his students found a high degree of price stickiness in their survey of firms (Table 11.1)

     (a)   The main reason for price stickiness was managers' fear that if they raised their prices, they'd lose customers to rivals

    (3)   But catalog prices also don't seem to change much from one issue to the next and often change by only small amounts, suggesting that while prices are sticky, menu costs may not be the reason (Kashyap)

    (4)   Price stickiness may not be pervasive, as prices change on average every 4.3 months (Bils-Klenow)

    (5)   Relative prices may respond quickly to supply or demand shocks for a particular good, but the price level may change slowly to changes in monetary policy (Boivin-Giannoni-Mihov), so in our macroeconomic model, the assumption of price stickiness is useful

g. Meeting the demand at the fixed nominal price

   (1) Because firms have some monopoly power, they price goods at a markup over their marginal cost of production:

$$P = (1 + \eta)MC \tag{11.1}$$

   (2) If demand turns out to be larger at that price than the firm planned, the firm will still meet the demand at that price, because it earns additional profits due to the markup

   (3) Because the firm is paying an efficiency wage, it can hire more workers at that wage to produce more goods when necessary

   (4) This means that the economy can produce an amount of output that is not on the *FE* line during the period in which prices haven't adjusted

h. Effective labor demand

   (1) The firm's labor demand is thus determined by the demand for its output

   (2) The effective labor demand curve, $ND^e(Y)$, shows how much labor is needed to produce the output demanded in the economy (Figure 11.3)

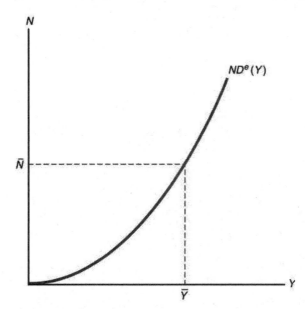

Figure 11.3

   (3) It slopes upward from left to right because a firm needs more labor to produce additional output

III. Monetary and Fiscal Policy in the Keynesian Model (Sec. 11.3)

A) Monetary policy

   1. Monetary policy in the Keynesian *IS-LM* model

     a. The Keynesian *FE* line differs from the classical model in two respects

       (1) The Keynesian level of full employment occurs where the efficiency wage line intersects the labor demand curve, not where labor supply equals labor demand, as in the classical model

       (2) Changes in labor supply don't affect the *FE* line in the Keynesian model; they do in the classical model

b. Because prices are sticky in the short run in the Keynesian model, the price level doesn't adjust to restore general equilibrium
   (1) Keynesians assume that when not in general equilibrium, the economy lies at the intersection of the *IS* and *LM* curves, and may be off the *FE* line
   (2) This represents the assumption that firms meet the demand for their products by adjusting employment
c. Analysis of an increase in the nominal money supply (Figure 11.4)

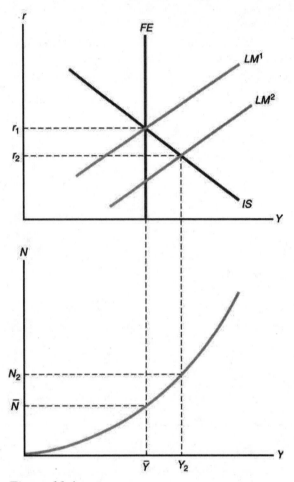

Figure 11.4

   (1) *LM* curve shifts down from LM^1 to LM^2
   (2) Output rises and the real interest rate falls
   (3) Firms raise employment and production due to increased demand
   (4) The increase in money supply is an expansionary monetary policy (easy money); a decrease in money supply is contractionary monetary policy (tight money)
   (5) Easy money increases real money supply, causing the real interest rate to fall to clear the money market
      (a) The lower real interest rate increases consumption and investment
      (b) With higher demand for output, firms increase production and employment
   (6) Eventually firms raise prices, the *LM* curve shifts back to its original level, and general equilibrium is restored
   (7) Thus money is neutral in the long run, but not in the short run

B) Monetary Policy in the Keynesian *AD-AS* framework

   1. We can do the same analysis in the *AD-AS* framework, as was done in text Figure 9.14

   2. The main difference between the Keynesian and classical approaches is the speed of price adjustment

      a. The classical model has fast price adjustment, so the *SRAS* curve is irrelevant

      b. In the Keynesian model, the short-run aggregate supply (*SRAS*) curve is horizontal, because monopolistically competitive firms face menu costs

   3. The effect of a 10% increase in money supply is to shift the *AD* curve up by 10%

      a. Thus output rises in the short run to where the *SRAS* curve intersects the *AD* curve

      b. In the long run the price level rises, causing the *SRAS* curve to shift up such that it intersects the *AD* and *LRAS* curves

   4. So in the Keynesian model, money is not neutral in the short run, but it is neutral in the long run

C) Fiscal policy

   1. The effect of increased government purchases (Figure 11.5)

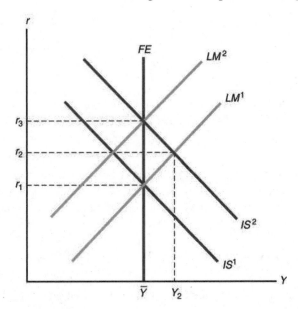

Figure 11.5

      a. A temporary increase in government purchases shifts the *IS* curve up

      b. In the short run, output and the real interest rate increase

      c. The *multiplier*, $\Delta Y/\Delta G$, tells how much increase in output comes from the increase in government spending

         (1) Keynesians think the multiplier is bigger than one, so that not only does total output rise due to the increase in government purchases, but output going to the private sector increases as well

         (2) Classical analysis also gets an increase in output, but only because higher current or future taxes caused an increase in labor supply, a shift of the *FE* line

         (3) In the Keynesian model, the *FE* line doesn't shift, only the *IS* curve does

      d. When prices adjust, the *LM* curve shifts up and equilibrium is restored at the full-employment level of output with a higher real interest rate than before

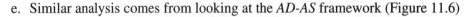

e. Similar analysis comes from looking at the *AD-AS* framework (Figure 11.6)

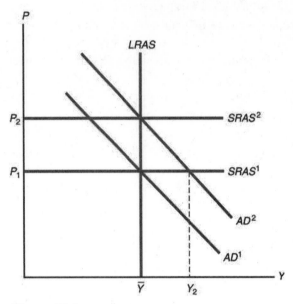

Figure 11.6

2. The effect of lower taxes

   a. Keynesians believe that a reduction of (lump-sum) taxes is expansionary, just like an increase in government purchases

   b. Keynesians reject Ricardian equivalence, believing that the reduction in taxes increases consumption spending, reducing desired national saving and shifting the *IS* curve up

   c. The only difference between lower taxes and increased government purchases is that when taxes are lower, consumption increases as a percentage of full-employment output, whereas when government purchases increase, government purchases become a larger percentage of full-employment output

IV. The Keynesian Theory of Business Cycles and Macroeconomic Stabilization (Sec. 11.4)

A) Keynesian business cycle theory

1. Keynesians think aggregate demand shocks are the primary source of business cycle fluctuations

2. Aggregate demand shocks are shocks to the *IS* or *LM* curves, such as fiscal policy, changes in desired investment arising from changes in the expected future marginal product of capital, changes in consumer confidence that affect desired saving, and changes in money demand or supply

3. A recession is caused by a shift of the aggregate demand curve to the left, either from the *IS* curve shifting down, or the *LM* curve shifting up

4. The Keynesian theory fits certain business cycle facts
   a. There are recurrent fluctuations in output
   b. Employment fluctuates in the same direction as output
   c. Money is procyclical and leading
   d. Investment and durable goods spending is procyclical and volatile
      (1) This is explained by the Keynesian model if shocks to investment and durable goods spending are a main source of business cycles
      (2) Keynes believed in "animal spirits," waves of pessimism and optimism, as a key source of business cycles
   e. Inflation is procyclical and lagging
      (1) The Keynesian model fits the data on inflation, because the price level declines after a recession has begun, as the economy moves toward general equilibrium

5. Procyclical labor productivity and labor hoarding
   a. As discussed in Section 11.1, firms may hoard labor in a recession rather than fire workers, because of the costs of hiring and training new workers
   b. Such hoarded labor is used less intensively, being used on make-work or maintenance tasks that don't contribute to measured output
   c. Thus in a recession, measured productivity is low, even though the production function is stable
   d. So labor hoarding explains why labor productivity is procyclical in the data without assuming that recessions and expansions are caused by productivity shocks

B) Macroeconomic stabilization
   1. Keynesians favor government actions to stabilize the economy
   2. Recessions are undesirable because the unemployed are hurt
   3. Suppose there's a shock that shifts the *IS* curve down, causing a recession (Figure 11.7; like text Figure 11.8)

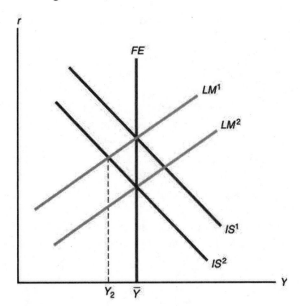

Figure 11.7

a. If the government does nothing, eventually the price level will decline, restoring general equilibrium. But output and employment may remain below their full-employment levels for some time

b. The government could increase the money supply, shifting the *LM* curve down to move the economy to general equilibrium

c. The government could increase government purchases to shift the *IS* curve back up to restore general equilibrium

4. Using monetary or fiscal policy to restore general equilibrium has the advantage of acting quickly, rather than waiting some time for the price level to decline

5. But the price level is higher in the long run when using policy than it would be if the government took no action

6. The choice of monetary or fiscal policy affects the composition of spending

a. An increase in government purchases crowds out consumption and investment spending, because of a higher real interest rate

b. Tax burdens are also higher when government purchases increase, further reducing consumption

7. Difficulties of macroeconomic stabilization

a. *Macroeconomic stabilization* is the use of monetary and fiscal policies to moderate the business cycle; also called *aggregate demand management*

b. In practice, macroeconomic stabilization hasn't been terribly successful

c. One problem is in gauging how far the economy is from full employment, because we can't measure or analyze the state of the economy perfectly

d. Another problem is that we don't know the quantitative impact on output of a change in policy

e. Also, because policies take time to implement and take effect, using them requires good forecasts of where the economy will be six months or a year in the future; but our forecasting ability is quite imprecise

f. These problems suggest that policy shouldn't be used to "fine-tune" the economy, but should be used to combat major recessions

8. Application: The Zero Bound

a. The Japanese economy slumped in the 1990s, with growth near zero

    (1) Japan was in a liquidity trap

    (2) Nominal interest rates became essentially zero (text Fig. 11.9)

    (3) Because nominal interest rates can't go below zero, monetary policy was ineffective

b. Bernanke suggested three strategies for dealing with the zero bound

    (1) Affect interest rate expectations by committing to keep short-term interest rates low for a long period; which was implemented by the Fed in 2003 (text Fig. 11.10)

    (2) Influence the yield curve by buying long-term securities (rather than short-term securities) with open-market operations

    (3) Increase the size of the central bank's balance sheet (quantitative easing)

c. Bernanke argued that the central bank should take these steps early, before the public thinks the central bank cannot help the economy

C) Supply shocks in the Keynesian model

1. Until the mid-1970s, Keynesians focused on demand shocks as the main source of business cycles

2. But the oil price shock that hit the economy beginning in 1973 forced Keynesians to reformulate their theory

3. Now Keynesians concede that supply shocks can cause recessions, but they don't think supply shocks are the main source of recessions

4. An adverse oil price shock shifts the *FE* line left (Figure 11.8; like text Figure 11.11)

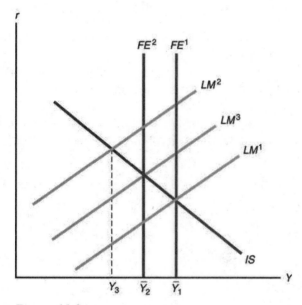

Figure 11.8

a. The average price level rises, shifting the *LM* curve up (from LM^1 to LM^2), because the large increase in the price of oil outweighs the menu costs that would otherwise hold prices fixed

b. The *LM* curve could shift farther than the *FE* line, as in the figure, though that isn't necessary

c. So in the short run, inflation rises and output falls

d. There's not much that stabilization policy can do about the decline in output that occurs, because of the lower level of full-employment output

e. Inflation is already increased due to the shock; expansionary policy to increase output would increase inflation further

D) Box 11.2: DSGE Models and the Classical-Keynesian Debate

1. Until recently, classicals and Keynesians used very different models

2. Recently, each group has incorporated ideas from the other group; Keynesian economists began using DSGE models and classicals began using sticky prices and imperfect competition

3. Economists were able to reconcile aggregative models with models of microeconomic foundations

4. Classicals and Keynesians still disagree about the speed of wage and price adjustment and the role of government policy, but now speak the same language in modeling the economy

V.   Appendix 11.A: Labor Contracts and Nominal-Wage Rigidity

A) Some Keynesians think the nonneutrality of money is because of nominal-wage rigidity, not nominal-price rigidity

1. Nominal wages could be rigid because of long-term contracts between firms and unions
2. With nominal-wage rigidity, the short-run aggregate supply curve slopes upward instead of being horizontal
3. Even so, the main results of the Keynesian model still hold

B) The short-run aggregate supply curve with labor contracts

1. U.S. labor contracts usually specify employment conditions and the nominal wage rate for three years
2. Employers decide on workers' hours and must pay them the contracted nominal wage
3. The result is an upward-sloping short-run aggregate supply curve
    a. As the price level rises, the real wage declines, because the nominal wage is fixed
    b. As the real wage declines, firms hire more workers and thus increase output

C) Nonneutrality of money

1. Money isn't neutral in this model, because as the money supply increases, the *AD* curve shifts along the fixed (upward-sloping) *SRAS* curve (Figure 11.9; like text Figure 11.A.1)

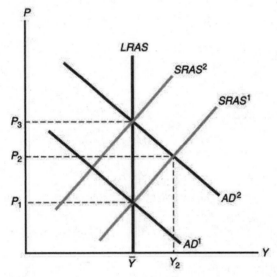

Figure 11.9

2. As a result, output and the price level increase
3. Over time, workers will negotiate higher nominal wages and the *SRAS* curve will shift left to restore general equilibrium
4. Thus money is nonneutral in the short run but neutral in the long run
5. There are several objections to this theory
    a. Less than one-sixth of the U.S. labor force is unionized and covered by long-term wage contracts; however, some nonunion workers get wages similar to those in union contracts, and other workers may have implicit contracts that act like long-term contracts
    b. Some labor contracts are indexed to inflation, so the real wage is fixed, not the nominal wage; however, most contracts aren't completely indexed
    c. The theory predicts that real wages will be countercyclical, but in fact they are procyclical; however, if there are both aggregate supply shocks and aggregate demand shocks, real wages may turn out on average to be procyclical, but could still be countercyclical for demand shocks

VI.   Appendix 11.C: The Multiplier in the Short-Run Keynesian Model

A) The multiplier shows the change in output resulting from a one-unit change in government purchases

1. First, calculate the effect on the intercept of the *IS* curve, α_{IS}, of a change in *G*

a. $\alpha_{IS} = (c_0 + i_0 + G - c_y t_0)/(c_r + i_r)$ (11.B.1)

same as (9.A.15)

b. If *G* increases by ΔG, $\Delta\alpha_{IS} = \Delta G/(c_r + i_r)$ (11.B.2)

2. Second, calculate the effect on *Y* of a change in α_{IS}

a. The *AD* curve intersects the *SRAS* curve at

$$Y = [\alpha_{IS} - \alpha_{LM} + (1/\ell_r)(M/\overline{P})]/[\beta_{IS} + \beta_{LM}] \tag{11.B.3}$$

same as (9.A.27)

b. From (11.B.3),

$$\Delta Y = \Delta\alpha_{IS}/(\beta_{IS} + \beta_{LM}) \tag{11.B.4}$$

3. Finally, combine both effects

a. Substituting (11.B.2) in (11.B.4) we get

$$\Delta Y/\Delta G = 1/[(c_r + i_r)(\beta_{IS} + \beta_{LM})] \tag{11.B.5}$$

b. This is the government purchases multiplier

c. The multiplier is positive, because all the terms in it are positive; it may be greater or less than one

d. The multiplier will be large if the *LM* curve is flat (β_{LM} is zero), because then the shift in the *IS* curve has a large effect on output

(1) In this special case,

$$\Delta Y/\Delta G = 1/[1 - (1 - t)c_y] \tag{11.B.6}$$

(2) For example, if the *MPC* is $c_y = 0.8$ and $t = 0.25$, then the multiplier is 2.5

e. The multiplier will be small if the *LM* curve is steep (β_{LM} is large)

■ Multiple Choice Questions

1. The existence of labor unions could contribute to real-wage rigidity, except that in the United States
(a) labor unions are outlawed.
(b) most workers aren't in unions.
(c) unions are interested in benefits, not wages.
(d) unions try to increase employment rather than negotiating over wages.

2. Real-wage rigidity in the Keynesian efficiency wage diagram of the labor market is depicted by
(a) a vertical labor supply curve at the efficient level of employment.
(b) a vertical labor demand curve at the efficient level of employment.
(c) a horizontal line at the efficiency wage.
(d) a steep, positively sloped labor supply curve depicting various efficiency wages at various employment levels.

3. A firm faces the following relationship between the real wage it pays and the effort exerted by its workers:

Real Wage	Effort (E)
10	14
14	20
18	27
22	32
26	36

The marginal product of labor for this firm is given by $MPN = E(50 - N)/3$. The firm will choose to pay a wage such that the effort level is

(a) 14.

(b) 20.

(c) 27.

(d) 32.

4. A firm faces the following relationship between the real wage it pays and the effort exerted by its workers:

Real Wage	Effort (E)
10	14
14	20
18	27
22	32
26	36

The marginal product of labor for this firm is given by $MPN = E(50 - N)/3$. How many workers will the firm employ?

(a) 48

(b) 46

(c) 44

(d) 40

5. In the Keynesian model, the full-employment level of output is the amount of output produced when

(a) the quantity of labor demanded equals the quantity of labor supplied.

(b) the market wage exceeds the efficiency wage.

(c) labor is paid an efficiency wage, and the real wage equals the marginal product of labor.

(d) the real wage exceeds the nominal wage.

6. In the efficiency wage model, a decrease in productivity would

(a) decrease output but increase the real wage.

(b) increase the real wage but have no effect on output.

(c) decrease output but have no effect on the real wage.

(d) have no effect on either output or the real wage.

7. In an economy where firms in most industries are purely competitive firms, individual firms in each industry would produce _____ products and have a _____ share of industry output.
   (a) differentiated; large
   (b) differentiated; small
   (c) standardized; large
   (d) standardized; small

8. In the Keynesian model, a firm's high menu costs cause
   (a) real-wage rigidity.
   (b) full employment.
   (c) price stickiness.
   (d) efficiency wages.

9. If firms are price setters, a small decline in the demand for their outputs will cause them to
   (a) reduce price and reduce the level of output produced.
   (b) reduce output in the short run, but reduce price in the long run.
   (c) reduce price in the short run, but reduce output only in the long run.
   (d) increase price in the short run to offset the effect on profits of a decline in output.

10. Firms that charge a price for their output in excess of marginal cost in the short run
    (a) are not maximizing profits.
    (b) cannot find buyers for their output.
    (c) are charging a markup.
    (d) will suffer huge losses.

11. As the economy moves down an effective labor demand curve,
    (a) output declines and employment declines.
    (b) output declines and employment rises.
    (c) output rises and employment rises.
    (d) output rises and employment declines.

12. In the Keynesian model, if equilibrium output is less than the full-employment level of output in the short run,
    (a) the price level will rise in the long run.
    (b) the price level will decline in the long run.
    (c) the LM curve will shift up and to the left in the long run.
    (d) the FE line will shift to the left in the long run.

13. In the Keynesian model in the short run, an increase in the money supply will cause
    (a) an increase in output and a decrease in the real interest rate.
    (b) a decrease in the real interest rate but no change in output.
    (c) an increase in the real interest rate and an increase in output.
    (d) no change in either the real interest rate or output.

14. Starting from a point of general (full employment) equilibrium, in the Keynesian model in the long run, an increase in the money supply will cause
    (a) an increase in output and a decrease in the real interest rate.
    (b) a decrease in the real interest rate but no change in output.
    (c) an increase in the real interest rate and an increase in output.
    (d) no change in either the real interest rate or output.

15. In the Keynesian model, which curve is horizontal?
    (a) *LRAS*
    (b) *SRAS*
    (c) *AD*
    (d) *NS*

16. Starting from a point of general (full employment) equilibrium, in the Keynesian model in the long run, an increase in the money supply will cause _____ in the real interest rate and _____ in the price level.
    (a) an increase; an increase
    (b) a decrease; an increase
    (c) no change; an increase
    (d) no change; no change

17. Using the Keynesian model, the effect of a decrease in the effective tax rate on capital would be to cause _____ in the real interest rate and _____ in output in the short run.
    (a) a decrease; a decrease
    (b) a decrease; no change
    (c) an increase; an increase
    (d) no change; a decrease

18. Starting from a point of general (full employment) equilibrium, in the Keynesian model in the long run, a decrease in taxes causes the price level to _____ and the real interest rate to _____.
    (a) fall; rise
    (b) fall; fall
    (c) rise; rise
    (d) rise; fall

19. Tight monetary policy and easy fiscal policy lead to
    (a) high real interest rates.
    (b) low real interest rates.
    (c) roughly unchanged real interest rates.
    (d) roughly unchanged real interest rates only when Ricardian equivalence holds; otherwise, low real interest rates.

20. During a severe and persistent recession, Keynesians would most likely propose
    (a) tax increases.
    (b) a tight money policy.
    (c) annually balanced federal budgets.
    (d) macroeconomic stabilization.

21. Keynesians believe that the most important shocks for affecting the business cycle are
    (a) productivity shocks.
    (b) aggregate supply shocks.
    (c) aggregate demand shocks.
    (d) government spending shocks.

22. Examples of aggregate demand shocks include all of the following *except* changes in:
    (a) fiscal policy.
    (b) the price of oil.
    (c) consumer confidence about the future that affect desired saving.
    (d) the demand for money.

23. Keynesians explain the procyclical behavior of average labor productivity by introducing the concept of
    (a) menu costs.
    (b) sticky prices.
    (c) sticky wages.
    (d) labor hoarding.

24. Keynesians believe that in the event of a recession, the government should consider
    (a) increasing taxes.
    (b) decreasing government spending.
    (c) increasing the money supply.
    (d) increasing the minimum wage.

25. Keynesians believe that the difference between using an increase in the money supply compared with an increase in government spending to increase aggregate demand in the event of a recession is that if government spending is increased, _____ will be _____ than if the money supply is increased.
    (a) the real interest rate; higher
    (b) the real interest rate; lower
    (c) the price level; lower
    (d) the price level; higher

26. In practice, one of the principal problems with aggregate demand management is that
    (a) changes in aggregate demand do not affect output.
    (b) changes in aggregate demand cannot reduce unemployment.
    (c) changes in aggregate demand are highly inflationary.
    (d) stabilization policies could increase aggregate demand too much and at the wrong times.

27. When policymakers are unable to reduce the nominal interest rate to stimulate the economy because the interest rate is at its lower bound of zero, the economy
    (a) is in a liquidity trap.
    (b) is in a recession.
    (c) is in a depression.
    (d) has an inverted yield curve.

28. The Federal Reserve announced that "policy accommodation can be maintained for a considerable period" in 2003 because it was trying to
    (a) introduce inflation targeting.
    (b) deal with the zero bound.
    (c) move to the left on the short-run Phillips curve.
    (d) increase its credibility.

29. From mid-2002 to early 2005, U.S. monetary policy was accommodative, as witnessed by the fact that
    (a) the government reduced taxes.
    (b) the Fed reduced the growth rate of the money supply.
    (c) the inflation rate declined.
    (d) the Federal funds interest rate was less than the inflation rate.

30. In the short run in the Keynesian model, a sharp decline in oil prices would leave the economy with a _____ level of output and a _____ real interest rate.
    (a) higher; lower
    (b) lower; higher
    (c) lower; lower
    (d) higher; higher

■ Review Questions

1. Why might firms pay an efficiency wage rather than a market-clearing wage?

2. How do Keynesians explain real-wage rigidity during a recession?

3. Briefly define price stickiness.

4. Briefly explain how monopolistic competition and high menu costs can explain price stickiness.

5. Do the real effects of aggregate demand shocks differ in the short run and long run in the Keynesian sticky-price model from the effects of these shocks in the classical model of perfectly flexible prices? Briefly explain.

6. Is money neutral in both the classical model and the Keynesian model? Briefly explain.

7. Could monetary stabilization policy be used to reduce or offset the negative short-run output effect of a temporary decline in consumption spending? Briefly explain.

8. What is the principal goal of macroeconomic stabilization, and how can fiscal policy be used to achieve this goal?

9. Do Keynesians and classicals agree on the effectiveness and desirability of macroeconomic stabilization? Briefly explain.

10. What critique does the real business cycle theory make of the Keynesian belief that most recessions are caused by aggregate demand shocks?

11. What are the major difficulties the government faces in attempting to stabilize the economy?

12. Discuss the major problems that arise in practice in attempting to use aggregate demand management to stabilize the economy.

■ Analytical Questions

1. A firm faces the following relationship between the real wage it pays and the effort exerted by its workers:

Real Wage	Effort (E)
5	15
6	19
7	24
8	28
9	31

The marginal product of labor for this firm is given by $MPN = E (20 - N)/2$. What wage will a firm choose to pay its workers? How many workers will the firm hire?

2. In the Keynesian model, what are the short-run effects and long-run effects (on output, employment, the real interest rate, and the price level) of a temporary decline in investment spending?

3. In the Keynesian model, what are the short-run effects and long-run effects (on output, employment, the real interest rate, and the price level) of a temporary increase in consumption spending?

4. In the Keynesian model, what are the effects (on output, the real interest rate, and the price level) of an adverse productivity (i.e., aggregate supply) shock?

5. According to the Keynesian *IS-LM* model, what is the effect of each of the following on output, the real interest rate, employment, and the price level? Distinguish between the short run and the long run.
    (a) Expected inflation declines
    (b) Wealth declines
    (c) Labor supply increases due to a change in demographics
    (d) The future marginal product of capital increases

■ Answers

Multiple Choice

1. b	7. d	13. a	19. a	25. a
2. c	8. c	14. d	20. d	26. d
3. c	9. b	15. b	21. c	27. a
4. a	10. c	16. c	22. b	28. b
5. c	11. a	17. c	23. d	29. d
6. c	12. b	18. c	24. c	30. a

Review Questions

1. An efficiency wage is better than a market-clearing wage because it maximizes effort per dollar of wage income paid to labor. This means that labor productivity per dollar spent on labor is maximized, which means that labor cost per unit of output is minimized. The gift-exchange motive and the shirking model provide two explanations for why an efficiency wage that is above the market-clearing wage may increase productivity per wage dollar. The gift-exchange motive suggests that workers who believe their employer is treating them fairly will want to do a good job. The shirking model views the wage as the reward that workers risk losing if they are so unproductive that they get fired; a higher wage increases productivity by increasing the expected cost of shirking (i.e., having low productivity).

2. In the Keynesian efficiency wage model, firms pay each worker the efficiency wage. A recession reduces labor demand, which causes employment to decline, but firms do not lower the wage. Because the efficiency wage is the wage that maximizes effort per dollar of real wage paid to labor, reducing the real wage would reduce the productivity of labor, which would increase production cost. Another problem with lowering the wage enough to induce the desired number of workers to quit during a recession is that the most productive workers are the most likely workers to quit.

3. Price stickiness means that prices are not perfectly flexible; they do not quickly adjust to long-run market-clearing levels. If prices are slow to adjust to changes in market conditions, they may be viewed, for analytic purposes, as fixed or rigid for some short-run time period.

4. Unlike perfectly competitive firms, monopolistically competitive firms set their prices in nominal terms and leave them set for some time; they meet the demand at their fixed price; and they readjust price from time to time. Because monopolistically competitive firms incur menu costs when they change their prices, they don't change them often. Thus prices are sticky.

5. In the Keynesian model, aggregate demand shocks affect real output, employment, and unemployment in the short run. There is no short-run adjustment period in the classical model, because economic shocks cause prices to adjust immediately to their long-run, general equilibrium values. Keynesian and classical economists agree that aggregate demand shocks have no real output or employment effects in the long run.

6. Money is neutral in the classical model, which is a long-run model with perfectly flexible wages and prices. In the Keynesian model of imperfectly flexible wages and prices, money is nonneutral in the short run, but it is still neutral in the long run. In the Keynesian model, quantities adjust in the short run (e.g., employment and output), rather than wages and prices.

7. Yes, an increase in the money supply would shift the *LM* curve down and to the right and shift the *AD* curve up and to the right to offset the output effect of a decline in consumer spending. The increase in the money supply returns the *AD* curve to its original position, at the full-employment level of output.

8. The principal goal of macroeconomic stabilization is to maintain aggregate demand (*AD*) at the full-employment level of output. Countercyclical changes in government purchases, and possibly taxes, can be used to offset the output effects of private sector *AD* shocks, to maintain *AD* at the full-employment level of output. For example, a shift down and to the left in *IS* and *AD*, caused by a decline in investment spending, can be offset by a temporary increase in government purchases, causing *IS* and *AD* to shift back to their original positions.

9. No, Keynesians and classical economists disagree on the effectiveness and desirability of macroeconomic stabilization. In the classical model, business cycles fluctuations are the optimal response of the economy to various shocks that hit the economy; thus they should not be offset by macroeconomic policy. In the Keynesian model, large and persistent business cycle fluctuations are usually caused by aggregate demand shocks in the presence of price stickiness. Macroeconomic stabilization policies can effectively reduce business cycle fluctuations, so these policies are desirable in that they can help the economy to maintain output at the full-employment level.

10. As classical economists, real business cycle theorists believe that aggregate supply shocks cause most business cycle fluctuations. *RBC* theorists highlight the importance of productivity shocks. *RBC* theorists believe that Keynesians are wrong in their contention that aggregate demand shocks cause most recessions, because aggregate demand shocks would cause productivity to be countercyclical, when in fact it is procyclical.

11. It's difficult to tell how far the economy is from full employment, there's uncertainty about how much the economy responds to monetary and fiscal policy, and there's a need to know where the economy will be in six months to a year.

12. There are problems in gauging how far the economy is from full employment, knowing how much output responds to a change in monetary or fiscal policy, and forecasting the economy reasonably well.

Analytical Questions

1. The maximum of E/w is 3.5, which occurs when $w = 8$. At that wage, because $MPN = (20 - N)/2$, then $8 = (20 - N)/2$; so $16 = 20 - N$; so $N = 4$.

2. See Figure 11.10. Point *A* is the starting point, point *B* shows the short-run equilibrium after the change, and point *C* shows the long-run equilibrium after the change. When there's a decline in investment spending, in the short run, the aggregate demand curve shifts to the left, while the aggregate supply curve doesn't shift, so output declines and the price level doesn't change. Because output declines, employment declines. The decline in investment spending shifts the *IS* curve down and to the left, so that, in addition to the decline in output, the real interest rate falls. In the long run, the price level declines to restore general equilibrium. This shifts the short-run aggregate supply curve down, returning output to its full-employment level. Because there's no change in output in the long run, there's no change in employment either. As the price level falls, the *LM* curve shifts down and to the right, so that it intersects the *IS* curve at the full-employment level of output. As a result, the real interest rate declines further.

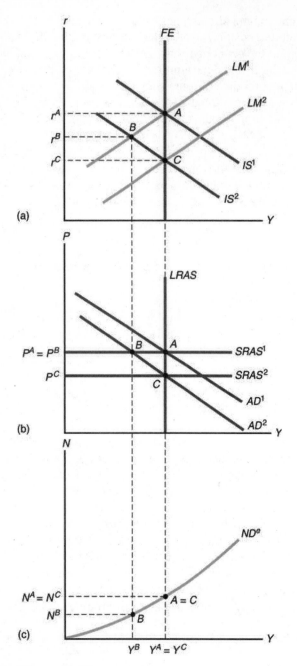

Figure 11.10

3. See Figure 11.11. Point *A* is the starting point, point *B* shows the short-run equilibrium after the change, and point *C* shows the long-run equilibrium after the change. When there's an increase in consumption spending, in the short run, the aggregate demand curve shifts to the right, while the aggregate supply curve doesn't shift, so output increases and the price level doesn't change. Because output rises, employment increases. The increase in consumption spending shifts the *IS* curve up and to the right, so that, in addition to the rise in output, the real interest rate rises. In the long run, the

price level rises to restore general equilibrium. This shifts the short-run aggregate supply curve up, returning output to its full-employment level. Because there's no change in output in the long run, there's no change in employment either. As the price level rises, the *LM* curve shifts up and to the left, so that it intersects the *IS* curve at the full-employment level of output. As a result, the real interest rate rises further.

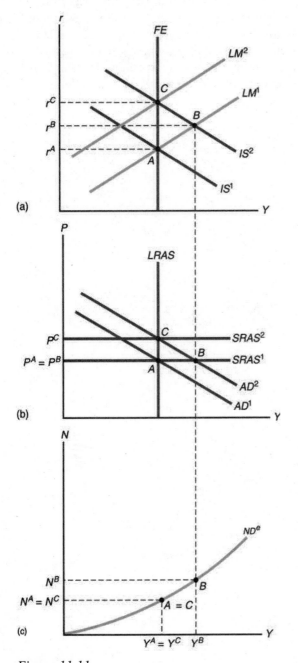

Figure 11.11

4. See Figure 11.12. Point *A* is the starting point, point *B* shows the short-run equilibrium after the change, and point *C* shows the long-run equilibrium after the change. When there's an adverse productivity shock, the long-run aggregate supply curve shifts to the left, while the aggregate demand curve doesn't shift, and the short-run aggregate supply curve shifts up as well. As a result, output decreases and the price level rises (assuming the short-run aggregate supply curve shifts sufficiently far up). The productivity shock shifts the *FE* line to the left, while the rise in the price level shifts the *LM* curve up and to the left. At the new intersection of the *IS* and *LM* curves, the real interest rate is higher. Assuming the *LM* curve shifts sufficiently far, in the long run the price level must fall to restore general equilibrium. This reduces the real interest rate somewhat, but it remains higher than it was initially. The fall in the price level shifts the short-run aggregate supply curve down, so output rises somewhat, but remains less than it was initially. The price level also remains higher than it was initially.

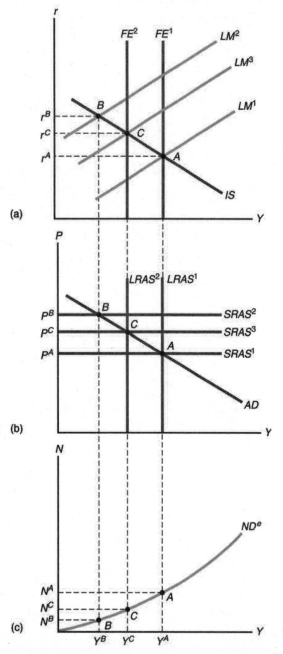

Figure 11.12

5. (a) Short run: Y and N decline, r rises, P is unchanged. Long run: P declines; Y, r, and N are unchanged.

    (b) Short run: Y, r, and N decline; P is unchanged. Long run: r and P decline; Y and N are unchanged.

    (c) Nothing happens to any of the variables.

    (d) Short run: Y, r, and N rise; P is unchanged. Long run: r and P rise; Y and N are unchanged.

Chapter 12
Unemployment and Inflation

■ Introduction

This is the first chapter of Part 4, the section of the textbook that explains how macroeconomic policy works and how it can best be used. This chapter discusses unemployment and inflation, Chapter 13 looks at policy in an open economy—international trade and finance, Chapter 14 covers monetary institutions and policy, and Chapter 15 discusses fiscal institutions and policy.

In this chapter, we study unemployment and inflation together because they are the most important macroeconomic problems and because they are related according to the Phillips curve relationship. In Section 12.1, we study this relationship between inflation and unemployment, looking at whether it has changed over time and if there really is a trade-off. In the following two sections, we study the costs of unemployment (Section 12.2) and inflation (Section 12.3) and consider the implications for macroeconomic policy making.

The only analytical concept that may prove difficult in this chapter is the expectations-augmented Phillips curve in Section 12.1. You should be sure you understand why the Phillips curve shifts with changes in expected inflation. Note that the unemployment rate equals the natural rate of unemployment at the point at which inflation equals expected inflation.

■ Outline

I. **Unemployment and Inflation: Is There a Trade-Off? (Sec. 12.1)**

    A) Many people think there is a trade-off between inflation and unemployment

        1. The idea originated in 1958 when A.W. Phillips showed a negative relationship between unemployment and nominal wage growth in Britain

        2. Since then economists have looked at the relationship between unemployment and inflation

        3. In the 1950s and 1960s many nations seemed to have a negative relationship between the two variables

        4. The United States appears to be on one Phillips curve in the 1960s (text Figure 12.1)

        5. This suggested that policymakers could choose the combination of unemployment and inflation they most desired

        6. But the relationship fell apart in the following three decades (text Figure 12.2)

        7. The 1970s were a particularly bad period, with both high inflation and high unemployment, inconsistent with the Phillips curve

B) The expectations-augmented Phillips curve

   1. Friedman and Phelps: The *cyclical* unemployment rate (the difference between actual and natural unemployment rates) depends only on *unanticipated* inflation (the difference between actual and expected inflation)

      a. This theory was made before the Phillips curve began breaking down in the 1970s

      b. It suggests that the relationship between inflation and the unemployment rate isn't stable

   2. How does this work in the extended classical model?

      a. First case: Anticipated increase in money supply (Figure 12.1; like text Figure 12.3)

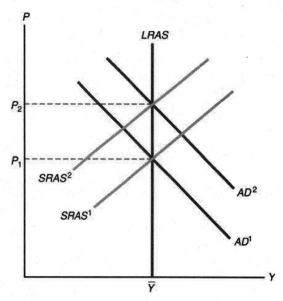

Figure 12.1

      (1) *AD* shifts up and *SRAS* shifts up, with no misperceptions

      (2) Result: *P* rises, *Y* unchanged

      (3) Inflation rises with no change in unemployment

      b. Second case: Unanticipated increase in money supply (Figure 12.2; like text Figure 12.4)

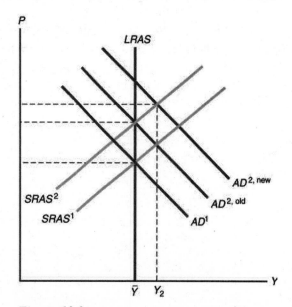

Figure 12.2

(1) *AD* expected to shift up to $AD^{2, \text{old}}$ (money supply expected to rise 10%), but unexpectedly money supply rises 15%, so *AD* shifts further up to $AD^{2,\text{new}}$

(2) *SRAS* shifts up based on expected 10% rise in money supply

(3) Result: *P* rises and *Y* rises as misperceptions occur

(4) So higher inflation occurs with lower unemployment

(5) Long run: *P* rises further, *Y* declines to full-employment level

    c. Expectations-augmented Phillips curve:

$$\pi = \pi^e - h(u - \bar{u}) \tag{12.1}$$

(1) When $\pi = \pi^e$, $u = \bar{u}$

(2) When $\pi < \pi^e$, $u > \bar{u}$

(3) When $\pi > \pi^e$, $u < \bar{u}$

C) The shifting Phillips curve

    1. The Phillips curve shows the relationship between unemployment and inflation for a given expected rate of inflation and natural rate of unemployment

    2. Changes in the expected rate of inflation (Figure 12.3; like text Figure 12.5)

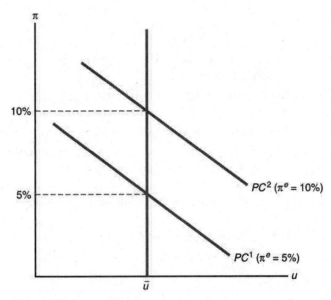

Figure 12.3

    a. For a given expected rate of inflation, the Phillips curve shows the trade-off between cyclical unemployment and actual inflation

    b. The Phillips curve is drawn such that $\pi = \pi^e$ when $u = \bar{u}$

    c. Higher expected inflation implies a higher Phillips curve

3. Changes in the natural rate of unemployment (Figure 12.4; like text Figure 12.6)

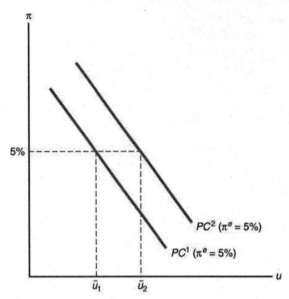

Figure 12.4

   a. For a given natural rate of unemployment, the Phillips curve shows the trade-off between unemployment and unanticipated inflation
   b. A higher natural rate of unemployment shifts the Phillips curve to the right
4. Supply shocks and the Phillips curve
   a. A supply shock increases both expected inflation and the natural rate of unemployment
      (1) A supply shock in the classical model increases the natural rate of unemployment, because it increases the mismatch between firms and workers
      (2) A supply shock in the Keynesian model reduces the marginal product of labor and thus reduces labor demand at the fixed real wage, so the natural unemployment rate rises
   b. So an adverse supply shock shifts the Phillips curve up and to the right
   c. The Phillips curve will be unstable in periods with many supply shocks
5. The shifting Phillips curve in practice
   a. Why did the original Phillips curve relationship apply to many historical cases?
      (1) The original relationship between inflation and unemployment holds up as long as expected inflation and the natural rate of unemployment are approximately constant
      (2) This was true in the United States in the 1960s, so the Phillips curve appeared to be stable
   b. Why did the U.S. Phillips curve disappear after 1970?
      (1) Both the expected inflation rate and the natural rate of unemployment varied considerably more in the 1970s than they did in the 1960s
      (2) Especially important were the oil price shocks of 1973–1974 and 1979–1980
      (3) Also, the composition of the labor force changed in the 1970s and there were other structural changes in the economy as well, raising the natural rate of unemployment
      (4) Monetary policy was expansionary in the 1970s, leading to high and volatile inflation
      (5) Plotting unanticipated inflation against cyclical unemployment shows a fairly stable relationship since 1970 (text Figure 12.7)

D) Macroeconomic policy and the Phillips curve

    1. Can the Phillips curve be exploited by policymakers? Can they choose the optimal combination of unemployment and inflation?

        a. Classical model: NO

           (1) The unemployment rate returns to its natural level quickly, as people's expectations adjust

           (2) So unemployment can change from its natural level only for a very brief time

           (3) Also, people catch on to policy games; they have rational expectations and try to anticipate policy changes, so there is no way to fool people systematically

        b. Keynesian model: YES, temporarily

           (1) The expected rate of inflation in the Phillips curve is the forecast of inflation at the time the oldest sticky prices were set

           (2) It takes time for prices and expected prices to adjust, so unemployment may differ from the natural rate for some time

    2. Box 12.1: The Lucas critique

        a. When the rules of the game change, behavior changes

        b. For example, if batters in baseball were called out after two strikes instead of three, they'd swing more often when they have one strike than they do now

        c. Lucas applied this idea to macroeconomics, arguing that historical relationships between variables won't hold up if there's been a major policy change

        d. The Phillips curve is a good example—it fell apart as soon as policymakers tried to exploit it

        e. Evaluating policy requires an understanding of how behavior will change under the new policy, so both economic theory and empirical analysis are necessary

E) The long-run Phillips curve

    1. Long run: $u = \bar{u}$ for both Keynesians and classicals

    2. The long-run Phillips curve is vertical, because when $\pi = \pi^e$, $u = \bar{u}$ (Figure 12.5; like text Figure 12.8)

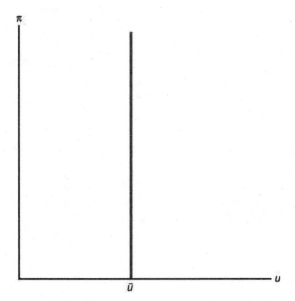

Figure 12.5

3. Changes in the level of money supply have no long-run real effects; changes in the growth rate of money supply have no long-run real effects, either

4. Even though expansionary policy may reduce unemployment only temporarily, policymakers may want to do so if, for example, timing economic booms right before elections helps them (or their political allies) get reelected

II.   The Problem of Unemployment (Sec. 12.2)

A) The costs of unemployment

1. Loss in output from idle resources

a. Workers lose income

b. Society pays for unemployment benefits and makes up lost tax revenue

c. Using Okun's law (each percentage point of cyclical unemployment is associated with a loss equal to 2% of full-employment output), if full-employment output is $7.5 trillion, each percentage point of unemployment sustained for one year costs $150 billion

2. Personal or psychological cost to workers and their families

a. Especially important for those with long spells of unemployment

3. There are some offsetting factors

a. Unemployment leads to increased job search and acquiring new skills, which may lead to increased future output

b. Unemployed workers have increased leisure time, though most wouldn't feel that the increased leisure compensated them for being unemployed

B) The long-term behavior of the unemployment rate

1. The changing natural rate

a. How do we calculate the natural rate of unemployment?

b. CBO's estimates: 5% to 5½% today, similar to 1950s and 1960s; over 6% in 1970s and 1980s

c. Why did the natural rate rise from the 1950s to the late 1970s?

(1) Partly demographics; more teenagers and women with higher unemployment rates

d. Since 1980, demographic forces have reduced the natural rate of unemployment

(1) The proportion of the labor force ages 16–24 years fell from 25% in 1980 to 16% in 1998

(2) Research by Shimer showed this is the main reason for the fall in the natural rate of unemployment

e. Some economists think the natural rate of unemployment is 4.5% or even lower

(1) The labor market has become more efficient at matching workers and jobs, reducing frictional and structural unemployment

(2) Temporary help agencies have become prominent, helping the matching process and reducing the natural rate of unemployment

f. Increased labor productivity may increase the natural rate of unemployment

(1) If increases in real wages lag changes in productivity, firms hire more workers and the natural rate of unemployment will decline temporarily

(2) Ball and Mankiw found evidence supporting this hypothesis in the 1990s

2. Measuring the natural rate of unemployment

   a. Policymakers need a measure of the natural rate of unemployment to use the unemployment rate for setting policy

   b. Economists disagree about how to measure the natural rate of unemployment and the CBO has often revised its measure

   c. Staiger, Stock, and Watson found that the natural rate cannot be measured precisely with econometric methods, as the confidence interval is very large

   d. What should policymakers do in response to uncertainty about the natural rate of unemployment?

      (1) They may wish to be less aggressive with policy than they would be if they knew the natural rate more precisely

      (2) Research (Orphanides-Williams) suggests that the rise of inflation in the 1970s can be blamed on bad estimates of the natural rate

III. The Problem of Inflation (Sec. 12.3)

A) The costs of inflation

  1. Perfectly anticipated inflation

   a. No effects if all prices and wages keep up with inflation

   b. Even returns on assets may rise exactly with inflation

   c. Shoe-leather costs: People spend resources to economize on currency holdings; the estimated cost of 10% inflation is 0.3% of GNP

   d. Menu costs: the costs of changing prices (but technology may mitigate this somewhat)

  2. Unanticipated inflation $(\pi - \pi^e)$

   a. Realized real returns differ from expected real returns

      (1) Expected $r = i - \pi^e$

      (2) Actual $r = i - \pi$

      (3) Actual r differs from expected r by $\pi^e - \pi$

      (4) Numerical example: $i = 6\%$, $\pi^e = 4\%$, so expected $r = 2\%$; if $\pi = 6\%$, actual $r = 0\%$; if $\pi = 2\%$, actual $r = 4\%$

   b. Similar effect on wages and salaries

   c. Result: transfer of wealth

      (1) From lenders to borrowers when $\pi > \pi^e$

      (2) From borrowers to lenders when $\pi < \pi^e$

   d. So people want to avoid risk of unanticipated inflation

      (1) They spend resources to forecast inflation

      (2) Box 12.2: Indexed contracts

         (a) People could use indexed contracts to avoid the risk of transferring wealth because of unanticipated inflation

         (b) Most U.S. financial contracts are not indexed, with the exception of some long-term contracts like adjustable-rate mortgages and inflation-indexed bonds issued by the U.S. Treasury beginning in 1997

         (c) Many U.S. labor contracts are indexed by COLAs (cost-of-living adjustments)

         (d) Indexed contracts are more prevalent in countries with high inflation

   e. Loss of valuable signals provided by prices

      (1) Confusion over changes in aggregate prices versus changes in relative prices

      (2) People expend resources to extract correct signals from prices

   3. The costs of hyperinflation
      a. Hyperinflation is a very high, sustained inflation (for example, 50% or more per month)
         (1) Hungary in August 1945 had inflation of 19,800% per month
         (2) Bolivia had annual rates of inflation of 1281% in 1984, 11,750% in 1985, 276% in 1986
      b. There are large shoe-leather costs, as people minimize cash balances
      c. People spend many resources getting rid of money as fast as possible
      d. Tax collections fall, as people pay taxes with money whose value has declined sharply
      e. Prices become worthless as signals, so markets become inefficient

B) Fighting inflation: The role of inflationary expectations
   1. If rapid money growth causes inflation, why do central banks allow the money supply to grow rapidly?
      a. Developing or war-torn countries may not be able to raise taxes or borrow, so they print money to finance spending
      b. Industrialized countries may try to use expansionary monetary policy to fight recessions, then not tighten monetary policy enough later on
   2. Disinflation is a reduction in the rate of inflation
      a. But disinflations may lead to recessions
      b. An unexpected reduction in inflation leads to a rise in unemployment along the Phillips curve
   3. The costs of disinflation could be reduced if expected inflation fell at the same time actual inflation fell
   4. Rapid versus gradual disinflation
      a. The classical prescription for disinflation is cold turkey—a rapid and decisive reduction in money growth
         (1) Proponents argue that the economy will adjust fairly quickly, with low costs of adjustment, if the policy is announced well in advance
         (2) Keynesians disagree
            (a) Price stickiness due to menu costs and wage stickiness due to labor contracts make adjustment slow
            (b) Cold turkey disinflation would cause a major recession
            (c) The strategy might fail to alter inflation expectations, because if the costs of the policy are high (because the economy goes into recession), the government will reverse the policy
      b. The Keynesian prescription for disinflation is gradualism
         (1) A gradual approach gives prices and wages time to adjust to the disinflation
         (2) Such a strategy will be politically sustainable because the costs are low

5. Box 12.3: The sacrifice ratio
   a. When unanticipated tight monetary and fiscal policies are used to reduce inflation, they reduce output and employment for a time, a cost that must be weighed against the benefits of lower inflation
   b. Economists use the sacrifice ratio as a measure of the costs
      (1) The sacrifice ratio is the number of percentage points of output lost in reducing inflation by one percentage point
      (2) For example, a study of past disinflations by Laurence Ball found that U.S. inflation fell by 8.83 percentage points in the early 1980s, with a loss in output of 16.18% of the nation's potential output
         (a) The sacrifice ratio was 16.18 divided by 8.83, which equals 1.832
   c. Ball studied the sacrifice ratios for many different disinflations around the world in the 1960s, 1970s, and 1980s
      (1) The sacrifice ratios varied substantially across countries, from less than 1 to almost 3
      (2) One factor affecting the sacrifice ratio is the flexibility of the labor market
         (a) Countries with slow wage adjustment (for example, because of heavy government regulation of the labor market) have higher sacrifice ratios
      (3) Ball also found a lower sacrifice ratio from cold turkey disinflation than from gradualism
   d. Ball's results should be interpreted with caution, because it isn't easy to calculate the loss of output and because supply shocks can distort the calculation of the sacrifice ratio
6. Wage and price controls
   a. Pro: Controls would hold down inflation, thus lowering expected inflation and reducing the costs of disinflation
   b. Con: Controls lead to shortages and inefficiency; once controls are lifted, prices will rise again
   c. The outcome of wage and price controls may depend on what happens with fiscal and monetary policy
      (1) If policies remain expansionary, people will expect renewed inflation when the controls are lifted
      (2) If tight policies are pursued, expected inflation may decline
   d. The Nixon wage-price controls from August 1971 to April 1974 led to shortages in many products; the controls reduced inflation when they were in effect, but prices returned to where they would have been soon after the controls were lifted
7. Credibility and reputation
   a. Key determinant of the costs of disinflation: how quickly expected inflation adjusts
   b. This depends on credibility of disinflation policy; if people believe the government and if the government carries through with its policy, expected inflation should drop rapidly
   c. Credibility can be enhanced if the government gets a reputation for carrying out its promises
   d. Also, having a strong and independent central bank that is committed to low inflation provides credibility

C) The U.S. disinflation of the 1980s and 1990s
   1. Fed chairmen Volcker and Greenspan gradually reduced the inflation rate in the 1980s and 1990s
      a. They sought to eliminate inflation as a source of economic instability
      b. They wanted people to be confident that inflation would never be very high again

2. To judge the Fed's success, we look at inflation expectations (text Fig. 12.10)

    a. Inflation expectations were erratic before 1990

    b. Inflation expectations fell gradually from 1990 to 1998 and have been stable since then

3. Inflation expectations were slow to decline initially (in the late 1970s and early 1980s) because Volcker and the Fed lacked credibility

4. But as inflation continued to fall, the Fed's credibility increased, and inflation expectations declined gradually

■ Multiple Choice Questions

1. The Phillips curve is a negative empirical relationship between

   (a) unemployment and inflation.

   (b) unemployment and output.

   (c) inflation and the real interest rate.

   (d) bond prices and interest rates.

2. The Phillips curve suggests that monetary policymakers could use monetary policy to

   (a) reduce the unemployment rate at the expense of higher inflation.

   (b) reduce the unemployment rate while reducing inflation.

   (c) reduce the unemployment rate without affecting the inflation rate.

   (d) reduce inflation without affecting the unemployment rate.

3. Cyclical unemployment is caused by

   (a) people entering the labor force to search for jobs.

   (b) technological progress, which causes some industries to expand employment and others to reduce employment.

   (c) reducing international trade barriers, which causes some industries to expand employment and others to reduce employment.

   (d) recessions.

4. Friedman and Phelps argued that a negative relationship should exist between _____ inflation and _____ unemployment.

   (a) anticipated; structural

   (b) anticipated; cyclical

   (c) unanticipated; cyclical

   (d) unanticipated; structural

5. Based on the theory of the expectations-augmented Phillips curve, if the expected inflation rate is 15%, the short-run Phillips curve will

   (a) be the same as the Phillips curve.

   (b) be the same as the long-run Phillips curve.

   (c) intersect the long-run Phillips curve at the natural unemployment rate, when the inflation rate is 15%.

   (d) be horizontal at an expected inflation rate of 15%.

6. In the extended classical model, an anticipated increase in the money supply would cause output to _____ and the price level to _____ in the short run.

   (a) increase; increase
   (b) increase; not change
   (c) not change; increase
   (d) decrease; increase

7. In the extended classical model, an unanticipated decrease in the money supply would cause output to _____ and the price level to _____ in the short run.

   (a) increase; increase
   (b) decrease; not change
   (c) not change; increase
   (d) decrease; decrease

8. In the expectations-augmented Phillips curve $\pi = \pi^e - 3(u - .06)$, the natural rate of unemployment is

   (a) .02.
   (b) .03.
   (c) .06.
   (d) .18.

9. In the expectations-augmented Phillips curve $\pi = \pi^e - 3(u - .05)$, when $\pi = .09$ and $\pi^e = .03$, the unemployment rate is

   (a) .03.
   (b) .04.
   (c) .05.
   (d) .06.

10. Based on the expectations-augmented Phillips curve, if the natural rate of unemployment is 5%, and if the actual inflation rate exceeds the expected inflation rate, then the unemployment rate is

   (a) 5%.
   (b) less than 5%.
   (c) more than 5%.
   (d) 5%, if cyclical unemployment is greater than zero.

11. Suppose most people had anticipated that inflation would increase by 10% in the coming year because the Fed would increase the money supply by 10%. Instead, the Fed increases the money supply by only 5%. In the short run, this would cause actual output to be _____ full-employment output and prices to increase by _____ 5%.

   (a) above; more than
   (b) above; less than
   (c) below; more than
   (d) below; less than

12. If the expected inflation rate is unchanged, a rise in the natural rate of unemployment would
    (a) shift both the short-run and long-run Phillips curves to the right.
    (b) not shift either the short-run or long-run Phillips curves.
    (c) shift both the short-run and long-run Phillips curves to the left.
    (d) shift the short-run Phillips curve to the left and shift the long-run Phillips curve to the right.

13. An adverse supply shock would cause
    (a) a movement up the short-run Phillips curve.
    (b) a movement down the short-run Phillips curve.
    (c) the short-run Phillips curve to shift upward and to the right.
    (d) the short-run Phillips curve to shift downward and to the left.

14. Classicals argue that a beneficial supply shock would
    (a) lower neither the natural rate of unemployment nor the actual rate of unemployment.
    (b) lower the actual rate of unemployment, but not the natural rate of unemployment.
    (c) lower the natural rate of unemployment, but not the actual rate of unemployment.
    (d) lower both the natural rate of unemployment and the actual rate of unemployment.

15. The idea that new policies change the economic rules and affect economic behavior, so that no one can safely assume that historical relationships between variables will hold when policies change, is known as
    (a) Okun's law.
    (b) Say's law.
    (c) the equation of exchange.
    (d) the Lucas critique.

16. Which of the following forms of unemployment probably imposes the greatest personal costs?
    (a) Frictional unemployment
    (b) Structural unemployment
    (c) Cyclical unemployment
    (d) Voluntary unemployment

17. The natural rate of unemployment generally
    (a) fell from 1960 to 1980.
    (b) was stable from 1960 to 1980.
    (c) fell from 1980 to 2000.
    (d) rose from 1980 to 2000.

18. One reason for the rise in the natural rate of unemployment from 1960 to 1980 is
    (a) changes in the demographic composition of the work force.
    (b) the rise in inflation.
    (c) increased competition from foreign workers.
    (d) the depreciation of the dollar relative to foreign currencies.

19. In years when teenagers become a greater percentage of the labor force
    (a) the natural rate of unemployment falls.
    (b) the natural rate of unemployment rises.
    (c) the inflation rate rises.
    (d) the inflation rate falls.

20. The costs of quickly trading money for nonmonetary assets to reduce one's holdings of money are the
    (a) menu costs of anticipated inflation.
    (b) menu costs of unanticipated inflation.
    (c) shoe-leather costs of anticipated inflation.
    (d) relative price distortion costs of unanticipated inflation.

21. One cost of a perfectly anticipated inflation is that it
    (a) transfers wealth from lenders to borrowers.
    (b) transfers wealth from borrowers to lenders.
    (c) erodes the value of currency.
    (d) damages the role of prices as signals in the economy.

22. When actual inflation is less than expected inflation
    (a) unemployment falls, according to Phillips-curve analysis.
    (b) cyclical unemployment falls, according to Phillips-curve analysis.
    (c) there are transfers from borrowers to lenders.
    (d) there are transfers from lenders to borrowers.

23. An economically efficient way to reduce the costs of unanticipated inflation is to
    (a) impose wage and price controls.
    (b) make raising prices illegal.
    (c) always have tight monetary policy.
    (d) use indexed contracts.

24. When there is a hyperinflation, all of the following occur EXCEPT
    (a) people spend a lot of time and energy getting rid of currency as fast as possible.
    (b) the government finds it difficult to collect taxes.
    (c) markets become inefficient because prices are no longer reliable signals.
    (d) people make fixed-rate loans to protect themselves against inflation.

25. Most economists would agree that the best way to reduce hyperinflation is to
    (a) reduce the nominal money supply growth rate.
    (b) increase transfer payments.
    (c) institute wage-price controls.
    (d) reduce taxes.

26. In analyzing the disinflationary period of the early 1980s in the United States, Keynesians concluded that
   (a) political business cycle theory best explains this monetary policy attempt to reduce unemployment just prior to the 1980 presidential election.
   (b) the rational expectations hypothesis correctly predicts that systematic monetary policies are anticipated and are neutral.
   (c) the basic classical model is correct in showing that changes in the money supply have only price effects.
   (d) the cold turkey approach to reducing inflation can create a costly recession with a sharp increase in cyclical unemployment.

27. Which of the following disinflationary monetary policies would classical economists prefer?
   (a) A cold turkey approach that is announced and credible.
   (b) A cold turkey approach that is announced, but not credible.
   (c) A gradual approach that is announced and credible.
   (d) A gradual approach that is unannounced.

28. The most important factor determining how quickly expected inflation adjusts when the government attempts to reduce inflation is
   (a) the slope of the Phillips curve.
   (b) the credibility of the government's disinflationary policy.
   (c) the degree of gradualism in the government's disinflationary policy.
   (d) the slope of the *IS* curve.

29. Countries in which the government heavily regulates the labor market are likely to have _____ sacrifice ratio.
   (a) an infinite
   (b) a high
   (c) a low
   (d) a negative

30. From 1980 to 2000, the expected inflation rate in the United States declined by about
   (a) 1 percentage point.
   (b) 3 percentage points.
   (c) 5 percentage points.
   (d) 7 percentage points.

■ Review Questions

1. What trade-off is demonstrated by the simple Phillips curve?

2. State and briefly explain whether or not the empirical evidence generally supports the belief that there is a fixed trade-off between unemployment and inflation, such that monetary policymakers can achieve the combination they prefer.

3. Briefly explain why the expectations-augmented Phillips curve is superior to the Phillips curve.

4. State and briefly explain whether or not the empirical evidence generally supports the belief that a change in expected inflation or the natural unemployment rate will shift the expectations-adjusted Phillips curve.

5. Why did the government use expansionary monetary policies in the late 1970s, and what was the principal negative macroeconomic effect of these policies?

6. State and briefly explain whether or not the empirical evidence generally supports the belief that government policy attempts to improve economic conditions by exploiting an existing relationship among economic variables may change the relationship in such a way as to prevent the policies from achieving their objectives.

7. Identify and briefly explain the two principal costs of anticipated inflation.

8. Identify and briefly explain the two principal costs of unanticipated inflation.

9. Compare and contrast the classical cold turkey approach and the Keynesian gradualism approach to reducing inflation.

10. What are the pros and cons of using cold turkey disinflation compared to a policy of gradualism?

■ Numerical Problems

1. Suppose Okun's law holds and a one percentage point increase in the unemployment rate reduces real output by 2% of full-employment output. The expectations-augmented Phillips curve is given by

$$\pi = \pi^e - 2\,(u - .05).$$

Suppose $\pi = .06$ and $\pi^e = .02$.
(a) What is the natural rate of unemployment?
(b) What is the actual rate of unemployment?
(c) How much is actual GDP compared with full-employment GDP?

2. Suppose expected inflation in the economy is 5%. Banks set nominal interest rates so they'll earn a 2% expected real return. Employers set nominal wages based on a 2% expected real wage increase. Suppose the nominal interest rate and nominal wages are determined this way, but actual inflation turns out to differ from the expected inflation rate. Calculate the actual real interest rate and the percent increase in the real wage for each of the following actual inflation rates: a) 2%; b) 5%; c) 10%.

■ Analytical Question

1. Suppose the natural rate of unemployment is 6% and that the expected inflation rate is 5%. Compare and contrast the effects of an unanticipated and anticipated increase in money supply growth rate.

■ Answers

Multiple Choice

1. a	7. d	13. c	19. b	25. a
2. a	8. c	14. d	20. c	26. d
3. d	9. a	15. d	21. c	27. a
4. c	10. b	16. b	22. c	28. b
5. c	11. c	17. c	23. d	29. b
6. c	12. a	18. a	24. d	30. d

Review Questions

1. The Phillips curve depicts various possible combinations of unemployment and inflation that could exist in the economy. The negative slope of the Phillips curve shows that these variables are negatively related. Therefore a trade-off exists between them; any decline in the unemployment rate increases the inflation rate. Any decline in the inflation rate increases the unemployment rate. The simple Phillips curve suggests that policymakers could choose the particular combination of unemployment and inflation that they prefer, and that they could use monetary policy to move the economy to that preferred point on the Phillips curve.

2. The Phillips curve suggests that there is a stable set of unemployment rate and inflation rate combinations, and that monetary policymakers could achieve the combination they prefer. The macroeconomic data for the 1950s and 1960s for many countries seemed consistent with this view, but further research using data for the 1970s and 1980s failed to show that a stable trade-off exists. The empirical evidence suggests that a stable trade-off exists only during the time period in which expected inflation and the natural unemployment rate remain unchanged. The extended classical model suggests that a nonsystematic expansionary monetary policy attempt to move up a fixed expectations-augmented Phillips curve to a lower unemployment rate and higher inflation rate will achieve its objective only for the short-run period in which the increase in inflation is not anticipated. Systematic monetary policies will be anticipated, so they cannot achieve their objective of temporarily reducing unemployment below the natural unemployment rate.

3. The expectations-augmented Phillips curve critique is that the Phillips curve fails to include the expected inflation rate as a determinant of the actual inflation rate. The Phillips curve suggests that there is a stable relationship between unemployment and inflation that policymakers can exploit, but the expectations-augmented Phillips curve shows that this relationship is not stable and therefore not exploitable. Any attempt to reduce the unemployment rate below the natural unemployment rate will be effective only if unanticipated and, even then, only during the short-run period of misperceptions or wage-price rigidities. Once expectations, wages, and prices have adjusted, the Phillips curve will shift up to the right and unemployment will return to the natural unemployment rate at a higher inflation rate.

4. The Friedman-Phelps theory suggests that a change in expected inflation or the natural unemployment rate will shift the expectations-augmented Phillips curve. The empirical evidence generally supports this theory. For example, structural and demographic changes in the United States after 1970 caused the natural unemployment rate to increase; the curve also shifted to the right when expected inflation increased, then shifted to the left when expected inflation declined.

5. In the late 1970s the U.S. government used expansionary monetary policies in an attempt to reduce the unemployment rate and to increase the growth rate of output. Relying on the Keynesian model to explain the slowdown in economic growth, policymakers concluded that aggregate demand had declined and that expansionary monetary stabilization policies could pull aggregate demand back to the full-employment level of output. However, aggregate demand had not declined. The recession was created by a decline in aggregate supply caused by an increase in the price of oil. Expansionary monetary policies caused aggregate demand to increase along the new aggregate supply curve, which caused inflation to increase further.

6. The Lucas critique is that government policy attempts to improve economic conditions by exploiting an existing relationship among economic variables may change the relationship in such a way as to prevent the policies from achieving their objectives. The empirical evidence generally supports this critique. A good example of this policy problem is the U.S. government's attempts to reduce the unemployment rate by exploiting the Phillips curve trade-off between inflation and unemployment. While successful in the 1960s, it was not effective in the 1970s because the policy attempts increased expected inflation, causing the Phillips curve to shift to the right.

7. (1) Menu costs: The costs of changing prices are called menu costs. Classical economists believe these costs are small, assuming perfectly competitive market conditions. Keynesians believe these costs are large enough to create price stickiness, assuming monopolistically competitive market conditions.

    (2) Shoe leather costs: The transactions costs incurred by households and firms in reducing the share of their assets they hold as money are called shoe-leather costs. These costs are likely to be larger than menu costs.

8. (1) Risk of redistribution of wealth cost: Unanticipated inflation creates a redistribution of wealth; what some people and firms lose, others gain. For example, creditors lose and debtors gain, because unanticipated inflation lowers the real interest rate on existing loans. Although there is no aggregate income loss from redistribution, the costs incurred by market participants trying to reduce their risk of losses may be large. For example, creditors may charge an inflation risk premium on all loans to cover their risk, even during periods when inflation is constant, thereby increasing the real interest rate in the long run.

    (2) Relative price distortions cost: Unanticipated inflation causes firms to misperceive a change in the price level as changes in the relative prices of their products. This misperception causes firms to charge inefficient prices for their products, produce inefficient levels of output, and employ efficient amounts of labor at inefficient wages. These relative price distortions cause inefficiencies that are costly.

9. (1) Cold turkey approach: Classical economists propose a rapid reduction in money supply growth to achieve disinflation, assuming that prices, wages, and expectations adjust quickly. Unemployment costs and inflation costs are most likely to be small if the classical assumptions about rapid market adjustments are correct, the policy is announced in advance, and the announcement is credible. Both classical economists and Keynesians agree that the inflation costs would be smaller for a cold turkey approach than for gradualism, because inflation is being reduced more quickly. However, Keynesians believe that the unemployment costs could be very high.

(2) Gradualism approach: Keynesians propose a gradualism approach of slowly reducing money supply growth over several years to achieve disinflation, assuming wages, prices, and expectations adjust slowly to changes in the inflation rate. Both classical economists and Keynesians believe that this approach would have small unemployment costs, but the inflation costs would be greater, because the inflation rate would be higher for a long period of time. Classicals contend inflation costs could be much higher than for a cold turkey approach, because an announced gradualism approach is unlikely to be credible.

10. Cold turkey disinflation reduces inflation quickly and could be successful if expected inflation fell at the same time; that requires that policy be credible, however. But Keynesians suggest that menu costs and nominal wage contracts will prevent prices and wages from adjusting quickly, so a cold turkey strategy will cause a recession. Further, if a cold turkey strategy is begun, but people think the costs will be so large that the strategy will be abandoned, then expected inflation will not decline. For this reason, Keynesians prefer a gradualist approach to allow wages and prices more time to adjust to policy changes. Such a policy is more likely to be sustainable politically.

Numerical Problems

1. (a) .05

    (b) $\pi = \pi^e - 2 (u - .05)$, so $.06 = .02 - 2 (u - .05)$, so $.04 = -2 (u - .05)$, so $-.02 = u - .05$, so $u = .03$.

    (c) 4% higher because the unemployment rate is below the natural rate by two percentage points, so actual GDP exceeds full-employment GDP by the Okun's law coefficient (two) times two percentage points = 4%.

2. The real interest rate (r) = the nominal interest rate – the inflation rate. In percentage terms, the increase in the real wage (w) = the increase in the nominal wage–the inflation rate. It is given that the expected inflation rate = 5%, so the nominal interest rate on bank savings deposits = 7%, and the increase in the nominal wage = 7%. When inflation is

    (a) 2%, then $r = 7\% - 2\% = 5\%$, and the increase in $w = 7\% - 2\% = 5\%$.

    (b) 5%, then $r = 7\% - 5\% = 2\%$, and the increase in $w = 7\% - 5\% = 2\%$.

    (c) 10%, then $r = 7\% - 10\% = -3\%$, and the increase in $w = 7\% - 10\% = -3\%$.

Analytical Question

1. Figure 12.6 shows a Phillips curve diagram in which the natural unemployment rate = 6%. The economic effects of a 3% increase in money supply growth depend on whether the increase is anticipated or unanticipated.

    (1) Anticipated: If the increase in money supply growth is anticipated, then money is neutral. In the diagram, the economy moves quickly from point E to H. There is no unemployment effect or output effect. Wages, prices, and expectations quickly adjust to general equilibrium.

    (2) Unanticipated: In the short run, the 3% increase in money supply growth causes the growth rate of output to increase, the unemployment rate to decline, and the inflation rate to increase as we move from point E to F in the diagram along a fixed, short-run Phillips curve with the expected

inflation rate equal to 5%. In the long run, the expected inflation rate rises to 8%, causing the Phillips curve to shift up. In the diagram, we move from point E to H in the long run. At point H, the inflation rate has increased to 8%, the expected inflation rate has increased to 8%, and unemployment is at the natural rate of 6%.

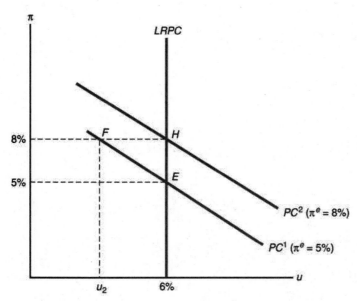

Figure 12.6

Chapter 13
Exchange Rates, Business Cycles, and Macroeconomic Policy in the Open Economy

■ Introduction

This chapter examines the two primary aspects of interdependence between economies of different nations. First, there is international trade in goods and services. Second, financial markets are integrated worldwide. Interdependence means that nations are dependent on each other, so policy changes in one country may affect other countries.

The chapter begins by covering the basics of exchange rates in Section 13.1, including a look at the difference between nominal and real exchange rates. Section 13.2 uses supply-and-demand analysis to examine how exchange rates are determined. These results are then used to develop an *IS-LM* model for the open economy in Section 13.3. Next, the chapter examines the effects of macroeconomic policy in the open economy in Section 13.4. Finally, there's a discussion of how a system of fixed exchange rates works in Section 13.5. Appendix 13.A presents an algebraic version of the model.

This is a very difficult chapter because there are many new concepts. Exchange rates themselves are confusing because they can be written in two different ways: for example, yen per dollar or dollars per yen. Then there are distinctions between real and nominal exchange rates, between depreciation and devaluation, and between fixed- and flexible-exchange rates. Here are a couple of hints to help you. If an exchange rate (such as yen per dollar) rises, it means the second currency (the dollar in this case) has appreciated (become more valuable) relative to the first currency (the yen). Whenever the demand for a currency rises relative to other currencies, because foreigners increase their demand for either its goods (perhaps because the goods have increased in quality or fallen in price) or its assets (such as stocks and bonds, perhaps because their returns have increased), foreigners will need to acquire more of the currency, and it will rise in value (appreciate).

■ Outline

I. **Exchange Rates (Sec. 13.1)**

    A) Nominal exchange rates

        1. The nominal exchange rate tells you how much foreign currency you can obtain with one unit of the domestic currency

           a. For example, if the nominal exchange rate is 110 yen per dollar, 1 dollar can be exchanged for 110 yen

           b. Transactions between currencies take place in the foreign exchange market

           c. Denote the nominal exchange rate (or simply, exchange rate) as e_{nom} in units of the foreign currency per unit of domestic currency

2. Under a flexible-exchange-rate system or floating-exchange-rate system, exchange rates are determined by supply and demand and may change every day; this is the current system for major currencies

3. In the past, many currencies operated under a fixed-exchange-rate system, in which exchange rates were determined by governments

    a. The exchange rates were fixed because the central banks in those countries offered to buy or sell the currencies at the fixed exchange rate

    b. Examples include the gold standard, which operated in the late 1800s and early 1900s, and the Bretton Woods system, which was in place from 1944 until the early 1970s

    c. Even today, though major currencies are in a flexible-exchange-rate system, some smaller countries fix their exchange rates

B) Real exchange rates

1. The real exchange rate tells you how much of a foreign good you can get in exchange for one unit of a domestic good

2. If the nominal exchange rate is 110 yen per dollar, and it costs 1100 yen to buy a hamburger in Tokyo compared to 2 dollars in New York, the price of a U.S. hamburger relative to a Japanese hamburger is 0.2 Japanese hamburgers per U.S. hamburger

3. The real exchange rate is the price of domestic goods relative to foreign goods, or

$$e = e_{\text{nom}} P/P_{\text{For}} \tag{13.1}$$

4. To simplify matters, we'll assume that each country produces a unique good

5. In reality, countries produce many goods, so we must use price indexes to get P and P_{For}

6. If a country's real exchange rate is rising, its goods are becoming more expensive relative to the goods of the other country

C) Appreciation and depreciation

1. In a flexible-exchange-rate system, when e_{nom} falls, the domestic currency has undergone a nominal depreciation (or it has become weaker); when e_{nom} rises, the domestic currency has become stronger and has undergone a nominal appreciation

2. In a fixed-exchange-rate system, a weakening of the currency is called a devaluation, and a strengthening is called a revaluation

3. We also use the terms real appreciation and real depreciation to refer to changes in the real exchange rate

D) Purchasing power parity

1. To examine the relationship between the nominal exchange rate and the real exchange rate, think first about a simple case in which all countries produce the same goods, which are freely traded

    a. If there were no transportation costs, the real exchange rate would have to be $e = 1$, or else everyone would buy goods where they were cheaper

    b. Setting $e = 1$ in Eq. (13.1) gives

$$P = P_{\text{For}}/e_{\text{nom}} \tag{13.2}$$

    c. This means that similar goods have the same price in terms of the same currency, a concept known as *purchasing power parity*, or *PPP*

    d. Empirical evidence shows that purchasing power parity holds in the long run but not in the short run because in reality, countries produce different goods, because some goods aren't traded, and because there are transportation costs and legal barriers to trade

2. When *PPP* doesn't hold, using Eq. (13.1), we can decompose changes in the real exchange rate into parts

$$\Delta e/e = \Delta e_{nom}/e_{nom} + \Delta P/P - \Delta P_{For}/P_{For}$$

3. This can be rearranged as

$$\Delta e_{nom}/e_{nom} = \Delta e/e + \pi_{For} - \pi \qquad (13.3)$$

4. Thus a nominal appreciation is due to a real appreciation or a lower rate of inflation than in the foreign country

5. In the special case in which the real exchange rate doesn't change, so that $\Delta e/e = 0$, the resulting equation in Eq. (13.3) is called *relative purchasing power parity*, because nominal exchange-rate movements reflect only changes in inflation

   a. Relative purchasing power parity works well as a description of exchange-rate movements in high-inflation countries, because in those countries, movements in relative inflation rates are much larger than movements in real exchange rates

6. Box 13.1: McParity

   a. As a test of the *PPP* hypothesis, *The Economist* magazine periodically reports on the prices of Big Mac hamburgers in different countries

   b. The prices, when translated into dollar terms using the nominal exchange rate, range from just over $1 in China to over $4 in Switzerland (using 2003 data), so *PPP* definitely doesn't hold

   c. The hamburger price data forecasts movements in exchange rates

      (1) Hamburger prices might be expected to converge, so countries in which Big Macs are expensive may have a depreciation, while countries in which Big Macs are cheap may have an appreciation

E) The real exchange rate and net exports

   1. The real exchange rate (also called the terms of trade) is important because it represents the rate at which domestic goods and services can be traded for those produced abroad

      a. An increase in the real exchange rate means people in a country can get more foreign goods for a given amount of domestic goods

   2. The real exchange rate also affects a country's net exports (exports minus imports)

      a. Changes in net exports have a direct impact on export and import industries in the country

      b. Changes in net exports affect overall economic activity and are a primary channel through which business cycles and macroeconomic policy changes are transmitted internationally

   3. The real exchange rate affects net exports through its effect on the demand for goods

      a. A high real exchange rate makes foreign goods cheap relative to domestic goods, so there's a high demand for foreign goods (in both countries)

      b. With demand for foreign goods high, net exports decline

      c. Thus the higher the real exchange rate, the lower a country's net exports

   4. The J curve

      a. The effect of a change in the real exchange rate may be weak in the short run and can even go the "wrong" way

      b. Although a rise in the real exchange rate will reduce net exports in the long run, in the short run it may be difficult to quickly change imports and exports

      c. As a result, a country will import and export the same amount of goods for a time, with lower relative prices on the foreign goods, thus increasing net exports

      d. Similarly, a real depreciation will lead to a decline in net exports in the short run and a rise in the long run

      e. This pattern of net exports is known as the J curve (Figure 13.1)

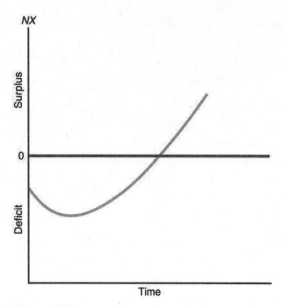

Figure 13.1

5. The analysis in this chapter assumes a time period long enough that the movements along the J curve are complete, so that a real depreciation raises net exports and a real appreciation reduces net exports

F) Application: The value of the dollar and U.S. net exports

1. Our theory suggests that the value of the dollar and U.S. net exports should be inversely related

2. Looking at data since the early 1970s, when the world switched to floating exchange rates, confirms the theory, at least in the 1980s (text Figure 13.2)

a. From 1980 to 1985 the dollar appreciated and net exports declined sharply

b. The dollar began depreciating in 1985, but it wasn't until late 1987 that net exports began to rise

(1) Initially, economists relied on the J curve to explain the continued decline in net exports with the decline of the dollar

(2) But two and one-half years is a long time for the J curve to be in effect

(3) A possible explanation for this long lag in the J curve is a change in competitiveness

(a) The strength of the dollar for such a long period in the first half of the 1980s meant U.S. firms lost many foreign customers

(b) Foreign firms made many inroads into the United States

(c) This is known as the "beachhead effect," because it allowed foreign producers to establish beachheads in the U.S. economy

(4) The U.S. real exchange rate and net exports moved in opposite directions from 1997 to 2001

(a) The strong dollar reduced net exports

(b) But a bigger factor was weak growth in foreign economies

II. How Exchange Rates Are Determined: A Supply-and-Demand Analysis (Sec. 13.2)

A) What causes changes in the exchange rate?

    1. To analyze this, we'll use supply-and-demand analysis, assuming a fixed price level

    2. Holding prices fixed means that changes in the real exchange rate are matched by changes in the nominal exchange rate

    3. The nominal exchange rate is determined in the foreign exchange market by supply and demand for the currency

    4. Demand and supply are plotted against the nominal exchange rate, just like demand and supply for any good (Figure 13.2; like text Figure 13.3)

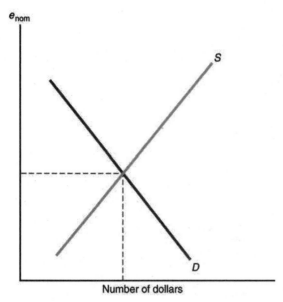

Figure 13.2

        a. Supplying dollars means offering dollars in exchange for the foreign currency

        b. The supply curve slopes upward, because if people can get more units of foreign currency for a dollar, they'll supply more dollars

        c. Demanding dollars means wanting to buy dollars in exchange for the foreign currency

        d. The demand curve slopes downward, because if people need to give up a greater amount of foreign currency to obtain one dollar, they'll demand fewer dollars

    5. Why do people demand or supply dollars?

        a. People need dollars for two reasons:

            (1) To be able to buy U.S. goods and services (U.S. exports)

            (2) To be able to buy U.S. real and financial assets (U.S. financial inflows)

        b. These transactions are the two main categories in the balance of payments accounts: the current account and the capital and financial account

        c. People want to sell dollars for two reasons:

            (1) To be able to buy foreign goods and services (U.S. imports)

            (2) To be able to buy foreign real and financial assets (U.S. financial outflows)

6. Factors that increase demand for U.S. exports and assets will increase demand for dollars, shifting the demand curve to the right and increasing the nominal exchange rate

  a. For example, an increase in the quality of U.S. goods relative to foreign goods will lead to an appreciation of the dollar (Figure 13.3; like text Figure 13.4)

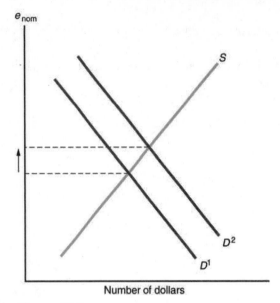

Figure 13.3

B) In touch with the macroeconomy: Exchange rates

  1. Trading in currencies occurs around-the-clock, because some market is open in some country any time of day

  2. The spot rate is the rate at which one currency can be traded for another immediately

  3. The forward rate is the rate at which one currency can be traded for another at a fixed date in the future (for example, 30, 90, or 180 days from now)

  4. A pattern of rising forward rates suggests that people expect the spot rate to be rising in the future

C) Macroeconomic determinants of the exchange rate and net export demand

  1. Look at how changes in real output or the real interest rate are linked to the exchange rate and net exports, to develop an open-economy *IS-LM* model

  2. Effects of changes in output (income)

    a. A rise in domestic output (income) raises demand for goods and services, including imports, so net exports decline

    b. To increase purchases of imports, people must sell the domestic currency to buy foreign currency, increasing the supply of foreign currency, which reduces the exchange rate

    c. The opposite occurs if foreign output (income) rises

      (1) Domestic net exports rise

      (2) The exchange rate appreciates

3. Effects of changes in real interest rates

    a. A rise in the domestic real interest rate (with the foreign real interest rate held constant) causes foreigners to want to buy domestic assets, increasing the demand for domestic currency and raising the exchange rate

    b. The rise in the exchange rate leads to a decline in net exports

    c. The opposite occurs if the foreign real interest rate rises

       (1) Domestic net exports rise

       (2) The exchange rate depreciates

D) Summary Table 16: Determinants of the exchange rate (real or nominal)

    1. A rise in domestic output (income) or the foreign real interest rate causes the exchange rate to fall

    2. A rise in foreign output (income), the domestic real interest rate, or the world demand for domestic goods causes the exchange rate to rise

E) Summary Table 17: Determinants of net exports

    1. A rise in domestic output (income) or the domestic real interest rate causes net exports to fall

    2. A rise in foreign output (income), the foreign real interest rate, or the world demand for domestic goods causes net exports to rise

III. The *IS-LM* Model for an Open Economy (Sec. 13.3)

A) Only the *IS* curve is affected by having an open economy instead of a closed economy; the *LM* curve and *FE* line are the same

    1. Note that we don't use the *AD-AS* model because we need to know what happens to the real interest rate, which has an important impact on the exchange rate

    2. The *IS* curve is affected because net exports are part of the demand for goods

    3. The *IS* curve remains downward sloping

    4. Any factor that shifts the closed-economy *IS* curve shifts the open-economy *IS* curve in the same way

    5. Factors that change net exports (given domestic output and the domestic real interest rate) shift the *IS* curve

       a. Factors that increase net exports shift the *IS* curve up and to the right

       b. Factors that decrease net exports shift the *IS* curve down and to the left

B) The open-economy *IS* curve

    1. The goods-market equilibrium condition is

$$S^d - I^d = NX \tag{13.4}$$

       a. This means that desired foreign lending must equal foreign borrowing

       b. Equivalently,

$$Y = C^d + I^d + G + NX \tag{13.5}$$

       c. This means the supply of goods equals the demand for goods and is derived using the definition of national saving,

$$S^d = Y - C^d - G$$

2. Plotting $S^d - I^d$ and *NX* illustrates goods-market equilibrium (Figure 13.4; like text Figure 13.5)

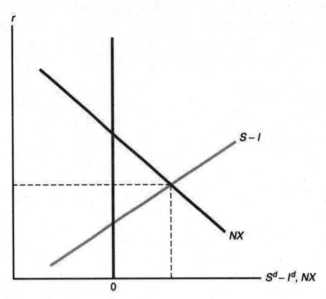

Figure 13.4

a. Net exports can be positive or negative
b. The net export curve slopes downward, because a rise in the real interest rate increases the real exchange rate and thus reduces net exports
c. The $S - I$ curve slopes upward, because a rise in the real interest rate increases desired national saving and reduces desired investment
d. Equilibrium occurs where the curves intersect

3. To get the open-economy *IS* curve, we need to see what happens when domestic output changes (Figure 13.5; like text Figure 13.6)

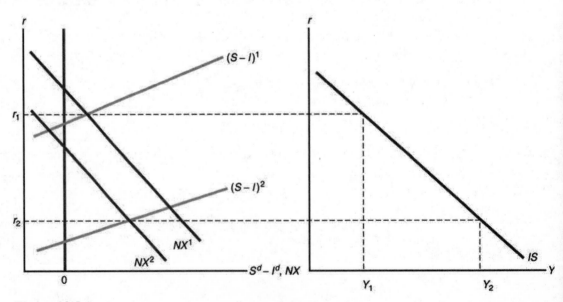

Figure 13.5

   a. Higher output increases saving, so the $S - I$ curve shifts to the right
   b. Higher output reduces net exports, so the NX curve shifts to the left
   c. The new equilibrium occurs at a lower real interest rate, so the IS curve is downward sloping

C) Factors that shift the open-economy IS curve
   1. Any factor that raises the real interest rate that clears the goods market at a constant level of output shifts the IS curve up and to the right
      a. An example is a temporary increase in government purchases (Figure 13.6; like text Figure 13.7)

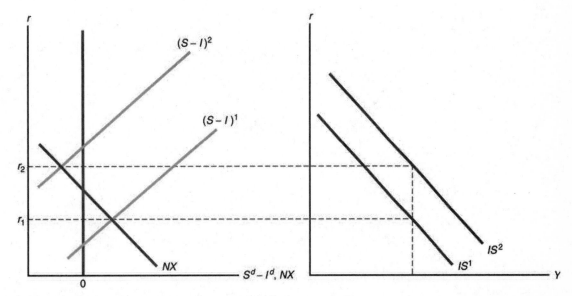

Figure 13.6

   b. The rise in government purchases reduces desired national saving, shifting the $S - I$ curve to the left, shifting the IS curve up and to the right
   c. Anything that reduces desired national saving relative to investment shifts the IS curve up and to the right

2. Anything that raises a country's net exports, given domestic output and the domestic real interest rate, will shift the open-economy *IS* curve up and to the right (Figure 13.7; like text Figure 13.8)

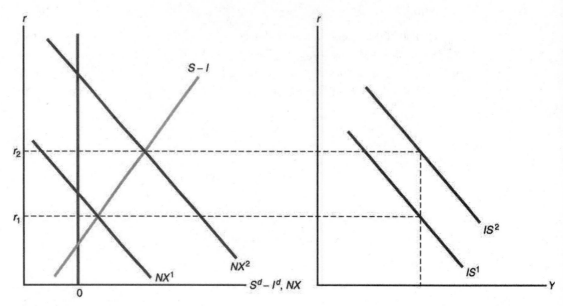

Figure 13.7

a. The increase in net exports is shown as a shift to the right in the *NX* curve
b. This raises the real interest rate for a fixed level of output, shifting the *IS* curve up and to the right
c. Three things could increase net exports for a given level of output and real interest rate
   (1) An increase in foreign output, which increases foreigners' demand for domestic exports
   (2) An increase in the foreign real interest rate, which makes people want to buy foreign assets, causing the exchange rate to depreciate, which in turn causes net exports to rise
   (3) A shift in worldwide demand toward the domestic country's goods, for example, as occurs if the quality of domestic goods improves
3. Summary Table 18: International factors that shift the *IS* curve
   a. An increase in foreign output, the foreign real interest rate, or the demand for domestic goods relative to foreign goods all shift the *IS* curve up and to the right

D) The international transmission of business cycles
   1. The impact of foreign economic conditions on the real exchange rate and net exports is one of the principal ways by which cycles are transmitted internationally
   2. What would be the effect on Japan of a recession in the United States?
      a. The decline in U.S. output would reduce demand for Japanese exports, shifting the Japanese *IS* curve down and to the left
      b. In a Keynesian model, or in the classical misperceptions model, this leads to recession in Japan
      c. In a classical (*RBC*) model, the decline in net exports wouldn't affect Japanese output
   3. A similar effect could occur because of a shift in preferences (or trade restrictions) for Japanese goods

IV. Macroeconomic Policy in an Open Economy with Flexible Exchange Rates (Sec. 13.4)

    A) Two key questions

        1. How do fiscal and monetary policy affect a country's real exchange rate and net exports?

        2. How do the macroeconomic policies of one country affect the economies of other countries?

    B) Three steps in analyzing these questions

        1. Use the domestic economy's *IS-LM* diagram to see the effects on domestic output and the domestic real interest rate

        2. See how changes in the domestic real interest rate and output affect the exchange rate and net exports

        3. Use the foreign economy's *IS-LM* diagram to see the effects of domestic policy on foreign output and the foreign real interest rate

    C) A fiscal expansion

        1. Look at a temporary increase in domestic government purchases using the classical (*RBC*) model

            a. The rise in government purchases shifts the *IS* curve up and to the right and the *FE* line to the right (Figure 13.8; like text Figure 13.9)

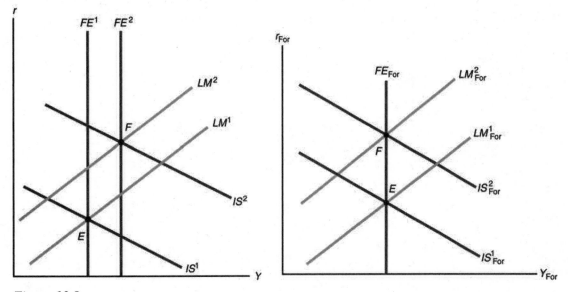

Figure 13.8

            b. The *LM* curve shifts up and to the left to restore equilibrium as the price level rises

            c. Both the real interest rate and output rise in the domestic country

            d. Higher output reduces the exchange rate, while a higher real interest rate increases the exchange rate, so the effect on the exchange rate is ambiguous

            e. Higher output and a higher real interest rate both reduce net exports, supporting the twin deficits idea

2. How do these changes affect a foreign country's economy?
    a. The decline in net exports for the domestic economy means a rise in net exports for the foreign country, so the foreign country's *IS* curve shifts up and to the right
    b. In the classical model, the *LM* curve shifts up and to the left as the price level rises to restore equilibrium, thus raising the foreign real interest rate, but foreign output is unchanged
    c. In a Keynesian model, the shift of the *IS* curve would give the foreign country higher output temporarily
3. In either the classical or Keynesian model, a temporary increase in domestic government purchases raises domestic income (temporarily) and the domestic real interest rate, as in a closed economy
    a. It also reduces domestic net exports, so government spending crowds out both investment and net exports
    b. The effect on the exchange rate is ambiguous
    c. The foreign real interest rate and price level rise
    d. In the Keynesian model, foreign output rises temporarily

D) A monetary contraction
    1. Look at a reduction in the domestic money supply in a Keynesian model
    2. Short-run effects on the domestic and foreign economies (Figure 13.9; like text Figure 13.10)

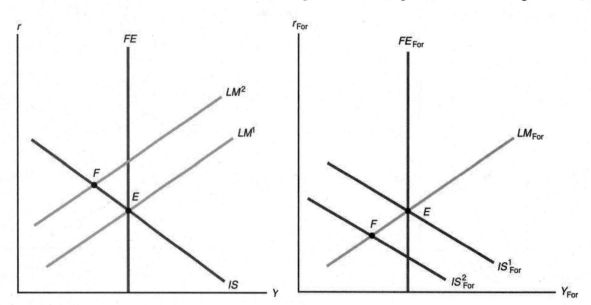

Figure 13.9

    a. The domestic *LM* curve shifts up and to the left
    b. In the short run, domestic output is lower and the real interest rate is higher
    c. The exchange rate appreciates, because lower output reduces demand for imports, thus reducing the supply of the domestic currency to the foreign exchange market, and because a higher real interest rate increases demand for the domestic currency

      (2) A country can't maintain an overvalued currency forever, as it will run out of official reserve assets
        (a) In the gold standard period, countries sometimes ran out of gold and had to devalue their currencies
        (b) A speculative run (or speculative attack) may end the attempt to support an overvalued currency (text Figure 13.12)
          (1) If investors think a currency may soon be devalued, they may sell assets denominated in the overvalued currency, increasing the supply of that currency on the foreign exchange market
          (2) This causes even bigger losses of official reserves from the central bank and speeds up the likelihood of devaluation, as occurred in Mexico in 1994 and Asia in 1997–1998
      (3) Thus an overvalued currency can't be maintained for very long

3. Similarly, in the case of an undervalued currency, the official rate is below the fundamental value (text Figure 13.13)
    a. In this case, a central bank trying to maintain the official rate will acquire official reserve assets
    b. If the domestic central bank is gaining official reserve assets, foreign central banks must be losing them, so again the undervalued currency can't be maintained for long

C) Monetary policy and the fixed exchange rate
1. The best way for a country to make the fundamental value of a currency equal the official rate is through the use of monetary policy
2. Rewrite Eq. (13.1) as

$$e_{nom} = eP_{For}/P \qquad\qquad (13.6)$$

3. For an overvalued currency, a monetary contraction is desirable
    a. In a Keynesian model, a monetary contraction causes a real (and nominal) exchange rate appreciation in the short run and a nominal exchange rate appreciation in the long run (with no long-run effect on the real exchange rate)
    b. Conversely, a monetary expansion causes a nominal exchange rate depreciation in both the short run and the long run

c. Plotting the relationship between the money supply and the nominal exchange rate shows the level of the money supply for which the fundamental value of the exchange rate equals the official rate (Figure 13.11; like text Figure 13.14)

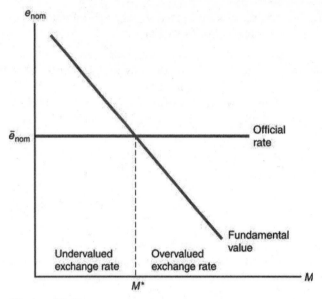

Figure 13.11

(1) A higher money supply yields an overvalued currency
(2) A lower money supply yields an undervalued currency

4. This implies that countries can't both maintain the exchange rate and use monetary policy to affect output
    a. Using expansionary monetary policy to fight a recession would lead to an overvalued currency
    b. So under fixed exchange rates, monetary policy can't be used for macroeconomic stabilization

5. However, a group of countries may be able to coordinate their use of monetary policy
    a. If two countries increase their money supplies together to fight joint recessions, there needn't be an overvaluation
    b. One country increasing its money supply by itself would lead to a depreciation
    c. But when the other country increases its money supply, it provides an offsetting effect
    d. If the money supplies expand in each country, they offset each other, so the exchange rate needn't change (text Figure 13.15)

6. Overall, fixed exchange rates can work well if countries in the system have similar macroeconomic goals and can coordinate changes in monetary policy
    a. But the failure to cooperate can lead to severe problems

D) Fixed versus flexible exchange rates
    1. Flexible-exchange-rate systems also have problems, because the volatility of exchange rates introduces uncertainty into international transactions
    2. There are two major benefits of fixed exchange rates
        a. Stable exchange rates make international trades easier and less costly
        b. Fixed exchange rates help discipline monetary policy, making it impossible for a country to engage in expansionary policy; the result may be lower inflation in the long run

3. But there are some disadvantages to fixed exchange rates
    a. They take away a country's ability to use expansionary monetary policy to combat recessions
    b. Disagreement among countries about the conduct of monetary policy may lead to the breakdown of the system
4. Which system is better may thus depend on the circumstances
    a. If large benefits can be gained from increased trade and integration, and when countries can coordinate their monetary policies closely, then fixed exchange rates may be desirable
    b. Countries that value having independent monetary policies, either because they face different macroeconomic shocks or hold different views about the costs of unemployment and inflation than other countries, should have a floating exchange rate

E) Currency unions
    1. Under a *currency union*, countries agree to share a common currency
        a. They often cooperate economically and politically as well, as was the case with the thirteen original U.S. colonies
    2. To work effectively, a currency union must have just one central bank
        a. Because countries don't usually want to give up control over monetary policy by not having their own central banks, currency unions are very rare
        b. But a currency union has advantages over fixed exchange rates because having a single currency reduces the costs of trading goods and assets across countries and because speculative attacks on a national currency can no longer occur
    3. But the major disadvantage of a currency union is that all countries share a common monetary policy, a problem that also arises with fixed exchange rates
        a. Thus if one country is in recession while another is concerned about inflation, monetary policy can't help both, whereas with flexible exchange rates, the countries could have monetary policies that help their particular situation
    4. Application: European monetary unification
        a. In 1991, countries in the European Community adopted the Maastricht treaty, which provides for a common currency
            (1) The currency, called the euro, came into being on January 1, 1999
            (2) Eleven countries took part in the union
        b. Monetary policy is determined by the Governing Council of the European Central Bank
        c. European monetary union is an important development, whose long-term implications are unknown
            (1) There are many advantages
                (a) Easier movement of goods, capital, and labor among European countries
                (b) Lower costs of financial transactions
                (c) Greater political and economic cooperation
                (d) An integrated market similar in size and wealth to the U.S. market
                (e) The possibility that the euro could become the preferred currency for international transactions, displacing the dollar
            (2) But there are some disadvantages
                (a) Countries may strongly disagree about what monetary policy should do
                (b) For example, in 1999, the countries faced varying degrees of recession, and the European Central Bank faced a tough decision about what to do

    d. The euro was introduced in 1999, but coins and currency were not issued until 2002

       (1) From 1999 to 2001, existing national notes and coins were used at fixed exchange rates

       (2) The euro declined in value in that period relative to the dollar

          (a) The attractiveness of U.S. assets might explain the decline of the euro, but the euro's weakness continued even after U.S. asset markets turned down in 2000

          (b) Sinn and Westermann suggested that demand for the dollar relative to the euro as a store of value in eastern European countries might explain the euro's decline, as foreign holders of German marks could not obtain euro currency yet, so they traded in their marks for dollars

          (c) Their hypothesis seemed to be confirmed when the euro rose relative to the dollar as soon as euro currency came into existence in 2002

F) Application: Crisis in Argentina

  1. Argentina's economy began recovering in 2002 after several years of crisis

  2. Argentina's inflation rate in the 1970s and 1980s was very large, with prices rising by a factor of ten billion from 1975 to 1990

  3. Inflation was reduced to near zero in the 1990s as the budget deficit was reduced and a currency board was implemented

    a. A currency board is a monetary arrangement under which the supply of domestic currency in circulation is strictly limited by the amount of foreign reserves held by the central bank

    b. A currency board works by limiting the money supply, ensuring low inflation

    c. Argentina's peso was backed one-for-one with U.S. dollars, and the exchange rate was fixed at one peso per dollar

  4. The 1990s were a time of economic prosperity for Argentina, with fast economic growth and low inflation

  5. But the end of the decade saw Argentina slip into deep recession and the government's budget deficit increased sharply

    a. Argentina's real exchange rate was overvalued in comparison with trading partners such as Brazil

    b. Argentina ran large current account deficits in the 1990s, and its foreign debt grew to about one-half of one year's GDP

  6. Eventually, Argentina defaulted on foreign debts and in January 2002 it abandoned the currency board, allowing the peso to float relative to the dollar

    a. By July 2003, the peso was worth just $0.36

    b. But the reduced real exchange rate allowed the economy to recover

    c. Unfortunately, the inflation rate returned to double digits, so ultimately the currency board failed to deliver long-term price stability

■ Multiple Choice Questions

1. From November 1984 to April 1987, the yen/dollar exchange rate fell from 240 yen/dollar to 145 yen/dollar, while the dollar/pound exchange rate rose from 1.25 dollars/pound to 1.59 dollars/pound. As a result,

   (a) the dollar appreciated relative to the yen, but depreciated relative to the pound.
   (b) the dollar depreciated relative to the yen, but appreciated relative to the pound.
   (c) the dollar appreciated relative to both the yen and the pound.
   (d) the dollar depreciated relative to both the yen and the pound.

2. The international monetary system in which the exchange rate is determined by the market forces of supply and demand is called

   (a) a managed float.
   (b) a flexible-exchange-rate system.
   (c) an adjustable-peg system.
   (d) a fixed-exchange-rate system.

3. In the post-World War II period, prior to the collapse of the Bretton Woods system in the early 1970s, the exchange rate of the dollar was

   (a) determined in a flexible-exchange-rate system.
   (b) determined by the market forces of supply and demand.
   (c) fixed at $35 per ounce of gold.
   (d) determined by a managed float.

4. The real exchange rate is

   (a) the number of foreign goods that can be obtained in exchange for one unit of the domestic good.
   (b) the nominal exchange rate minus the rate of inflation.
   (c) the amount of foreign currency that can be obtained in exchange for one unit of the domestic currency.
   (d) the amount of domestic currency that can be obtained in exchange for one unit of the foreign currency.

5. For a given nominal exchange rate, an increase in the price of foreign goods relative to the price of domestic goods causes

   (a) domestic residents to buy more foreign goods.
   (b) domestic residents to buy fewer domestic goods.
   (c) the real exchange rate to decline.
   (d) an increase in the number of units of the foreign goods needed to buy a unit of the domestic goods.

6. A fall in the real exchange rate in a flexible-exchange-rate system is called

   (a) a real depreciation.
   (b) a real appreciation.
   (c) a real revaluation.
   (d) a real devaluation.

7: If the nominal exchange rate rises 7%, domestic inflation is 3%, and foreign inflation is 4%, what is the percent change in the real exchange rate?

    (a) 8%

    (b) 6%

    (c) 4%

    (d) 2%

8. The J curve illustrates that a decline in the real exchange rate of the dollar will cause net exports to

    (a) increase immediately, because prices are perfectly flexible.

    (b) increase after some adjustment period, because it takes some time for people to adjust their buying decisions to a change in the terms of trade.

    (c) decrease immediately, because prices are perfectly flexible.

    (d) decrease after some adjustment period, because it takes some time for people to adjust their buying decisions to a change in the real exchange rate.

9. Suppose the pound/yen exchange rate rises while the dollar/yen exchange rate falls. What happens to the price of goods imported into Japan?

    (a) British goods become more expensive while U.S. goods become cheaper.

    (b) British goods become cheaper while U.S. goods become more expensive.

    (c) Both British and U.S. goods become more expensive.

    (d) Both British and U.S. goods become cheaper.

10. An appreciation of the dollar causes

    (a) an increase in U.S. exports.

    (b) a reduction in U.S. imports.

    (c) an increase in the prices of U.S. imports.

    (d) an increase in the prices of U.S. exports.

11. A decline in domestic output would cause a _____ in net exports and a _____ in the exchange rate.

    (a) rise; rise

    (b) rise; fall

    (c) fall; rise

    (d) fall; fall

12. An improvement in the quality of U.S. goods would lead to a _____ in the demand for dollars and a _____ in the exchange rate.

    (a) rise; rise

    (b) rise; fall

    (c) fall; rise

    (d) fall; fall

13. A decline in the exchange rate could have been caused by which of these factors?

    (a) A decline in domestic output (income)

    (b) An increase in the domestic real interest rate

    (c) A decline in the world demand for domestic goods

    (d) An increase in foreign output (income)

14. In an open economy, an increase in net exports because of increased demand for domestic products by foreigners should cause the domestic real interest rate to _____ and should cause desired saving minus desired investment to _____.
   (a) rise; rise
   (b) rise; fall
   (c) fall; rise
   (d) fall; fall

15. In an open economy, an increase in savings because of concerns about the future should cause the domestic real interest rate to _____ and should cause net exports to _____.
   (a) rise; rise
   (b) rise; fall
   (c) fall; rise
   (d) fall; fall

16. In an open economy, a shift down and to the left of the *IS* curve could have been caused by
   (a) a decline in the foreign real interest rate.
   (b) an increase in the demand for domestic goods relative to foreign goods.
   (c) an increase in foreign output.
   (d) a decline in domestic output.

17. In an open economy, an increase in foreign output would cause the *IS* curve to shift _____ and a decrease in the foreign real interest rate would cause the *IS* curve to shift _____.
   (a) down; up
   (b) down; down
   (c) up; down
   (d) up; up

18. You have just noticed that the dollar depreciated and you suspect that the American government was behind this change. Which would you choose as the most likely cause of this depreciation in the real exchange rate?
   (a) An increase in the money supply
   (b) A decrease in the money supply
   (c) A temporary increase in government purchases
   (d) A temporary decrease in taxes

19. A classical *IS-LM* model of the world economy can be used to show that in a flexible-exchange-rate system, a temporary increase in government purchases will cause
   (a) output and the real interest rate to rise, which reduces net exports but has an ambiguous effect on the real exchange rate.
   (b) output and the real interest rate to rise, which increases net exports but has an ambiguous effect on the real exchange rate.
   (c) output to rise and the real interest rate to fall, which reduces net exports and causes the exchange rate to depreciate.
   (d) the real interest rate to fall, which causes the exchange rate to rise, which reduces net exports.

20. Assume the United States is currently running a current account deficit. The most effective way of eliminating this current account deficit would be to temporarily _____ government purchases and _____ the domestic money supply.

    (a) increase; increase
    (b) increase; decrease
    (c) decrease; increase
    (d) decrease; decrease

21. If the fundamental value of the exchange rate is less than the official (fixed) exchange rate, the country has an _____ problem, and it will _____ reserves.

    (a) overvaluation; lose
    (b) overvaluation; gain
    (c) undervaluation; gain
    (d) undervaluation; lose

22. If the fundamental value of the exchange rate is _____ than the official (fixed) exchange rate, the country has an _____ problem, and it will gain reserves.

    (a) less; overvaluation
    (b) greater; overvaluation
    (c) greater; undervaluation
    (d) less; undervaluation

23. If a country has an undervaluation problem, the best solution is to

    (a) lower the official rate.
    (b) buy more of its currency in the foreign exchange market.
    (c) sell less of its currency in the foreign exchange market.
    (d) increase the money supply.

24. In a fixed-exchange-rate system, if the government takes no action, an increase in the world demand for domestic goods will

    (a) increase net exports and create an undervalued domestic currency.
    (b) reduce net exports and create an overvalued domestic currency.
    (c) reduce net exports and create an undervalued domestic currency.
    (d) increase net exports and create an overvalued domestic currency.

25. If a country that fixes its exchange rate increases its money supply, then its currency will become _____ and it will _____ reserves.

    (a) overvalued; gain
    (b) overvalued; lose
    (c) undervalued; lose
    (d) undervalued; gain

26. If a country that fixes its exchange rate has an undervalued exchange rate, then it will _____ reserves, unless it _____ its money supply to the appropriate level.

    (a) gain; increases
    (b) lose; increases
    (c) lose; decreases
    (d) gain; decreases

27. An important advantage of a fixed-exchange-rate system is that it
    (a) prevents an exchange rate from becoming an overvalued exchange rate.
    (b) prevents an exchange rate from becoming an undervalued exchange rate.
    (c) protects the domestic economy from being hit by foreign shocks.
    (d) promotes the growth of international trade and international financial transactions by reducing the risk to market participants that exchange rates will change unexpectedly and substantially.

28. Compared with system of flexible exchange rates, currency unions have the disadvantage of
    (a) requiring all its members to share a common monetary policy.
    (b) allowing exchange rates to float.
    (c) requiring every country to share a common fiscal policy.
    (d) decreasing the sacrifice ratio.

29. From 1999 to 2001, because of black market activity, the value of the euro _____ against the dollar. After the introduction of the euro notes and coins in 2002, the euro _____ against the dollar.
    (a) fell; rose
    (b) fell; fell
    (c) rose; fell
    (d) rose; rose

30. Argentina reformed its currency in 1991 by using
    (a) a currency union.
    (b) a fixed exchange rate against gold.
    (c) a fixed exchange rate against the Brazilian real.
    (d) a currency board.

■ Review Questions

1. How is the real exchange rate related to the nominal exchange rate?

2. Briefly explain the difference between a revaluation and a real depreciation of the exchange rate.

3. Under what conditions would the real exchange rate change by the same percentage as the nominal exchange rate?

4. Identify changes in two variables that would shift the supply curve of dollars to the right. Identify changes in two variables that would shift the demand curve for dollars to the right.

5. Briefly explain how a change in the domestic economy is transmitted to the foreign country in a two-country model of the world.

■ Numerical Problem

1. Given goods market equilibrium in an open economy with $Y = \$7,000$ billion, calculate:
    (a) S^d and NX, when $C^d = 60\%$ of output, $I^d = 15\%$ of output, and $G = 20\%$ of output;
    (b) NX, when $S^d = 25\%$ of output and $I^d = 10\%$ of output.

■ Analytical Questions

1. When the real exchange rate rises, what happens to net exports in the short run? In the long run? What explains the difference between the short-run effect and the long-run effect?

2. What happens to the exchange rate and net exports in each of the following cases?
    (a) The foreign real interest rate rises.
    (b) Foreign output falls.
    (c) Foreign demand for domestic goods falls.
    (d) Domestic output falls.
    (e) The domestic real interest rate rises.

3. In a Keynesian model, what are the short-run effects on output, the real interest rate, and the real exchange rate, for both the domestic economy and a foreign economy, of a decline in investment?

4. In a Keynesian model, what are the short-run effects on output, the real interest rate, and the real exchange rate, for both the domestic economy and a foreign economy, of a decline in foreign demand for domestic goods?

■ Answers

Multiple Choice

1. d	7. b	13. c	19. a	25. b
2. b	8. b	14. a	20. d	26. a
3. c	9. b	15. c	21. a	27. d
4. a	10. d	16. a	22. c	28. a
5. c	11. a	17. c	23. d	29. a
6. a	12. a	18. a	24. a	30. d

Review Questions

1. The real exchange rate is $e = e_{nom} P/P_{For}$.

2. A revaluation is an increase in the exchange rate in a fixed-exchange-rate system. A real depreciation is a decline in the real exchange rate in a flexible-exchange-rate system.

3. The percent change in the nominal exchange rate = the percent change in the real exchange rate + the foreign inflation rate – the domestic inflation rate. When the difference between the foreign inflation rate and the domestic inflation rate remains constant, the percent increase in the nominal exchange rate equals the percent increase in the real exchange rate.

4. An increase in U.S. output or an increase in the foreign real interest rate will cause the supply curve for dollars to shift to the right. A rightward shift in the supply curve causes the exchange rate to depreciate in a flexible-exchange-rate system.

   An increase in foreign output or an increase in the U.S. real interest rate will cause the demand curve for dollars to shift to the right. A rightward shift in the demand curve causes the exchange rate to appreciate in a flexible-exchange-rate system.

5. Domestic economy changes are transmitted to the foreign economy through changes in the exchange rate and through changes in net exports. An economic change in the domestic economy that changes net exports shifts the IS curve in the foreign country. In a two-country model, the exports of one country are the imports of the other; an increase in domestic net exports is also a decline in foreign net exports.

Numerical Problem

1. The goods market equilibrium condition for an open economy is $NX = S^d - I^d$. Because $S^d = Y - C^d - G$, an alternative equation for goods market equilibrium is $NX = Y - C^d - I^d - G$.

   (a) C^d = .60 × \$7,000 billion = \$4,200 billion.

   I^d = .15 × \$7,000 billion = \$1,050 billion.

   G = .20 × \$7,000 billion = \$1,400 billion.

   S^d = \$7,000 billion − \$4,200 billion − \$1,400 billion = \$1,400 billion.

   NX = \$1,400 billion − \$1,050 billion = \$350 billion.

   (b) S^d = .25 × \$7,000 billion = \$1,750 billion.

   I^d = .10 × \$7,000 billion = \$700 billion.

   NX = \$1,750 billion − \$700 billion = \$1,050 billion.

Analytical Questions

1. In the short run, net exports rise, while in the long run net exports fall. The difference is the J curve effect, because quantities are slower to adjust than prices.

2. (a) Exchange rate falls, net exports rise.

   (b) Exchange rate falls, net exports fall.

   (c) Exchange rate falls, net exports fall.

   (d) Exchange rate rises, net exports rise.

   (e) Exchange rate rises, net exports fall.

3.   The *IS* curve shifts down and to the left, causing *Y* to decline and *r* to decline, as the left panel of Figure 13.12 shows. The decline in *Y* causes imports to decline and *NX* to increase. The effect on the exchange rate is ambiguous, because the increase in *NX* causes the exchange rate to rise, while the decline in *r* causes it to fall. The increase in *NX* causes NX_{For} to decline, which causes the foreign *IS* curve to shift down and to the left, causing Y_{For} and r_{For} to decline, as shown in the right panel.

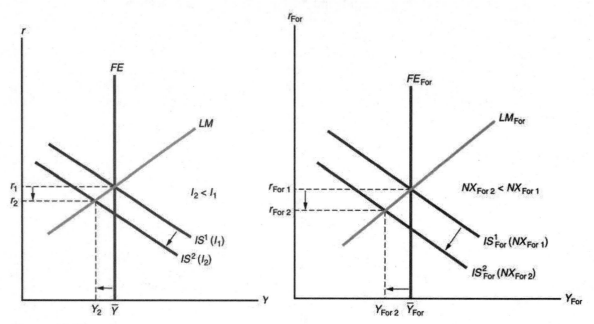

Figure 13.12

4.   The decline in foreign imports causes NX_{For} to increase, causing the foreign *IS* curve to shift up and to the right, causing Y_{For} and r_{For} to increase, as shown in the right panel of Figure 13.13. An increase in NX_{For} is a decline in *NX*. The decline in *NX* and the increase in r_{For} cause the exchange rate to depreciate. The decline in *NX* causes the domestic *IS* curve to shift down and to the left, causing *Y* and *r* to decline, as shown in the left panel.

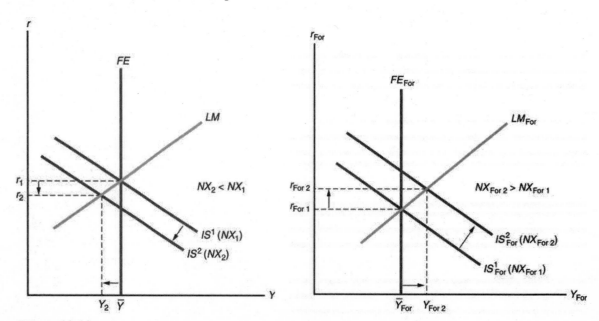

Figure 13.13

Chapter 14
Monetary Policy and the Federal Reserve System

■ Introduction

Chapter 14 looks at how the nation's money supply is determined. It explores the question: How should the central bank conduct monetary policy? This leads to a discussion of the following issues: (1) Should the central bank offset cyclical fluctuations? (2) Should the central bank follow simple rules? (3) How should policy-making institutions be designed?

The chapter begins with a discussion in Section 14.1 of the factors that determine the money supply, including a demonstration of how the Federal Reserve, banks, and the public all make decisions that affect the money supply. Section 14.2 covers the Federal Reserve in more detail, describing its institutional structure, how it affects the money supply, and how it develops its strategy for monetary policy. The issue of whether the Fed should use rules or discretion is taken up in Section 14.3, which includes a discussion of new research into credibility, modeling a game between the Fed and the public.

There are a couple of fairly technical parts of this chapter. First, the money supply is described by a set of equations that relate what the Fed controls (the monetary base and the required reserve ratio) to what banks and the public control (the currency–deposit ratio). These are used to develop the money multiplier, which you need to understand to be able to do many of the problems in this chapter. So spend some time working through the algebra that develops the formula and working on problems that use it. The second technical aspect is the game between the central bank and firms that is developed in Section 14.3. This is a standard example in the economic field called game theory, so you might have seen something similar in other economics courses. If you haven't seen it before, the logic can seem mysterious. However, once you work carefully through the logic of the exercise, it will make sense to you. In fact, economists are doing more and more with game theory, so it's a good idea to invest some time with it to be sure you get the main concepts.

■ Outline

I. **Principles of Money Supply Determination (Sec. 14.1)**

    A) Three groups affect the money supply

        1. The central bank is responsible for monetary policy

        2. Depository institutions (banks) accept deposits and make loans

        3. The public (people and firms) holds money as currency and coin or as bank deposits

    B) The money supply in an all-currency economy

        1. A trading system based on barter is inconvenient

        2. The creation of a central bank to print money can improve matters

            a. The central bank uses money it prints to buy real assets from the public; this gets money in circulation

            b. People accept the paper money if they believe other people will accept it in exchange

            c. The government often decrees that the paper money is *legal tender*, so that it can be used to pay off debts and the government will accept it for tax payments

      d. The central bank's assets are the real assets it buys from the public; its liabilities are the paper money it issued

      e. That money is called the monetary base, or high-powered money

   3. In an all-currency economy, the money supply equals the monetary base

C) The money supply under fractional reserve banking

   1. As an economy becomes more sophisticated financially, banks develop

   2. If currency is easily lost or stolen, people may want to hold all their money in bank deposits and none in currency

      a. In this case, the consolidated balance sheet of banks has assets of all the currency in the economy and liabilities consisting of all the bank deposits

      b. The balance sheet of the central bank is unchanged from the case in the all-currency economy

   3. The currency that banks hold is called *bank reserves*

      a. When bank reserves are equal to deposits, the system is called *100% reserve banking*

      b. To make money, banks would have to charge fees for deposits, because they earn no interest on reserves

   4. Rather than holding reserves that earn no interest, suppose a bank lent some of the reserves

      a. It could do this, because the flow of money in and out of the bank is fairly predictable and only a fraction of reserves are needed to meet the need for outflows

      b. If the bank needs to keep only 25% of the amount of its deposits on reserve to meet the demand for funds, it can lend the other 75%

      c. The *reserve–deposit ratio* would be 25%

      d. When the reserve–deposit ratio is less than 100%, the system is called *fractional reserve banking*

   5. When all the banks catch on to this idea, they will all make loans as the economy undergoes a *multiple expansion of loans and deposits*

   6. The process stops only when the banks' currency holdings (reserves) are exactly 25% of their total deposits, with loans equal to 75% of total deposits

      a. For example, if the monetary base is $1 million, banks would make $3 million in loans, so their total assets would be $4 million

      b. In loaning the $3 million, banks create $3 million in new deposits

      c. Adding the $3 million in new deposits to the $1 million in existing deposits gives total liabilities in the banking system of $4 million

   7. The money supply in this economy is equal to the total amount of bank deposits ($4 million in the example)

   8. The relationship between the monetary base and the money supply can be shown algebraically

      a. Let M = money supply, $BASE$ = monetary base, DEP = bank deposits, RES = bank reserves, res = banks' desired reserve–deposit ratio (RES/DEP)

      b. Because no currency is held by the public,

$$M = DEP \qquad\qquad (14.1)$$

c. Banks want to hold $res \times DEP$ in reserves, which must equal the amount of currency distributed by the central bank, so

$$res \times DEP = BASE \qquad (14.2)$$

d. Using Eqs. (14.1) and (14.2) gives

$$M = DEP = BASE/res \qquad (14.3)$$

e. So an economy with fractional reserve banking and no currency held by the public has money supply equal to the monetary base divided by the reserve–deposit ratio

9. Each unit of monetary base allows $1/res$ of money to be created

10. The monetary base is called high-powered money because each unit of the base that is issued leads to the creation of more money

D) Bank runs
   1. In the example, banks plan on never having to pay out more than 25% of their deposits
   2. If more people wanted to get their money from the bank, the bank would be unable to give them their funds
   3. If people think a bank won't be able to give them their money, they may panic and rush to withdraw their money, causing a bank run

E) The money supply with both public holdings of currency and fractional reserve banking
   1. If there is both public holding of currency and fractional reserve banking, the picture gets more complicated
   2. The money supply consists of currency held by the public and deposits, so

$$M = CU + DEP \qquad (14.4)$$

   3. The monetary base is held as currency by the public and as reserves by banks, so

$$BASE = CU + RES \qquad (14.5)$$

   4. Taking the ratio of these two equations gives

$$M/BASE = (CU + DEP)/(CU + RES) \qquad (14.6)$$

   5. This can be written as

$$M/BASE = [(CU/DEP) + 1]/[(CU/DEP) + (RES/DEP)] \qquad (14.7)$$

   6. The currency–deposit ratio (CU/DEP, or cu) is determined by the public
   7. The reserve–deposit ratio (RES/DEP, or res) is determined by banks
   8. Rewrite Eq. (14.7) as

$$M = [(cu + 1)/(cu + res)]BASE \qquad (14.8)$$

   9. The term $(cu + 1)/(cu + res)$ is the money multiplier
       a. The money multiplier is greater than one for res less than one (that is, with fractional reserve banking)
       b. If $cu = 0$, the multiplier is $1/res$, as when all money is held as deposits
       c. The multiplier decreases when either cu or res rises
       d. Look at U.S. data to illustrate the multiplier (text Table 14.1)

F) Open-market operations

1. The most direct and frequently used way of changing the money supply is by raising or lowering the monetary base through open-market operations

2. To increase the monetary base, the central bank prints money and uses it to buy assets in the market; this is an open-market purchase

    a. If the central bank wishes to increase the money supply by 15%, it purchases 15% more assets and its liabilities increase by 15%, which is the currency it issues

    b. To decrease the monetary base, the central bank sells assets in the market and retires the money it receives; this is an open-market sale

    c. For a constant money multiplier, the decline or fall in the monetary base of 15% is matched by a decline or fall in the money supply of 15%

G) Application: The money multiplier during the Great Depression

1. The money multiplier is usually fairly stable, but it fell sharply in the Great Depression

2. The decline in the multiplier was due to bank panics, which affected the multiplier in two ways

    a. People became mistrustful of banks and increased the currency–deposit ratio (text Figure 14.1)

    b. Banks held more reserves, in anticipation of bank runs, which raised the reserve–deposit ratio

3. Even though the monetary base grew 20% from March 1930 to March 1933, the money supply fell 35% (text Figure 14.2)

4. As a result, the price level fell sharply (nearly one-third) and there was a decline in output (though attributing the drop in output to the decline in the money supply is controversial)

II.   Monetary Control in the United States (Sec. 14.2)

A) The Federal Reserve System

1. The Fed began operation in 1914 for the purpose of eliminating severe financial crises

2. There are twelve regional Federal Reserve Banks (Boston, New York, Philadelphia, Cleveland, Richmond, Atlanta, Chicago, St. Louis, Minneapolis, Kansas City, Dallas, and San Francisco), which are owned by private banks within each district (text Figure 14.3)

3. The leadership of the Fed is provided by the Board of Governors in Washington, D.C.

    a. There are seven governors, who are appointed by the president of the United States, and have fourteen-year terms

    b. The chairman of the Board of Governors has considerable power, and has a term of four years

4. Monetary policy decisions are made by the Federal Open Market Committee (FOMC), which consists of the seven governors plus five presidents of the Federal Reserve Banks on a rotating basis (with the New York president always on the committee)

    a. The FOMC meets eight times a year

    b. It may meet more frequently if economic developments warrant

B) The Federal Reserve's balance sheet and open-market operations

1. Balance sheet of Fed (text Table 14.2)

    a. Largest asset is holdings of Treasury securities

    b. Also owns gold, makes loans to banks, and holds other assets including foreign exchange and federal agency securities

      c. Largest liability is currency outstanding
         (1) Some is held in bank vaults and is called vault cash
         (2) The rest is held by the public
      d. Another liability is deposits by banks and other depository institutions
      e. Vault cash plus banks' deposits at the Fed are banks' total reserves (*RES*)
  2. The monetary base equals banks' reserves plus currency held by the nonbank public (text Figure 14.4)
  3. The primary method for changing the monetary base is open-market operations

C) Other means of controlling the money supply
  1. Reserve requirements
      a. The Fed sets the minimum fraction of each type of deposit that a bank must hold as reserves
      b. An increase in reserve requirements forces banks to hold more reserves, thus reducing the money multiplier
  2. Discount window lending
      a. Discount window lending is lending reserves to banks so they can meet depositors' demands or reserve requirements
      b. The interest rate on such borrowing is called the discount rate
      c. The Fed was set up to halt financial panics by acting as a lender of last resort through the discount window
      d. A discount loan increases the monetary base
      e. Increases in the discount rate discourage borrowing and reduce the monetary base
      f. The Fed modified the discount window in 2003
         (1) Previously, the Fed discouraged banks from borrowing from the Fed and encouraged them to borrow from each other in the Federal funds market
         (2) The interest rate in the Federal funds market is the Fed funds rate
         (3) The Fed funds rate is a market rate of interest, determined by supply and demand
         (4) By contrast, the discount rate is set by the Fed
         (5) Under the new procedure, the Fed sets the discount rate above the Fed funds rate (text Figure 14.5)
         (6) Banks in good condition may take out a primary credit discount loan with no questions asked, at the primary credit discount rate
         (7) Banks that are not in good condition may take out a secondary credit discount loan at a higher interest rate under careful supervision by the Fed
         (8) The new policy is intended to improve the operation of the discount loan procedure and to reduce the volatility of the Federal funds rate
  3. Summary 19: Factors affecting the monetary base, the money multiplier, and the money supply
      a. An increase in *res, cu*, or reserve requirements has no effect on the monetary base, decreases the money multiplier, and decreases the money supply
      b. An open-market purchase, an increase in discount window borrowing, or a decrease in the discount rate increase the monetary base, have no effect on the money multiplier, and increase the money supply

D) Intermediate targets

1. The Fed uses intermediate targets to guide policy as a step between its tools or instruments (such as open-market purchases) and its goals or ultimate targets of price stability and stable economic growth

2. Intermediate targets are variables the Fed can't directly control but can influence predictably, and they are related to the Fed's goals

3. Most frequently used are monetary aggregates such as M1 and M2, and short-term interest rates, such as the Fed funds rate

4. The Fed cannot target both the money supply and the Fed funds rate simultaneously

    a. Suppose both the money supply and the Fed funds rate were above target, so the Fed needs to lower them

    b. Because a decrease in the money supply shifts the *LM* curve up, it will increase the Fed funds rate

5. In recent years the Fed has been targeting the Fed funds rate (Figure 14.1; like text Figure 14.6)

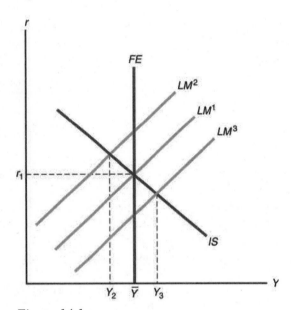

Figure 14.1

a. This strategy works well if the main shocks to the economy are to the *LM* curve (shocks to money supply or money demand)

b. The strategy stabilizes output, the real interest rate, and the price level, as it offsets the shocks to the *LM* curve completely

c. But if other shocks to the economy (such as *IS* shocks) are more important than nominal shocks, the policy may be destabilizing, unless the Fed changes the target for the Fed funds rate

d. Suppose a shock shifts the *IS* curve to the right (text Figure 14.7)

    (1) If the Fed were to maintain the real interest rate, it would increase the money supply, thus making output rise even more, which would be destabilizing

    (2) Instead, the Fed needs to raise the real interest rate to stabilize output

    (3) Research suggests that the optimal Fed funds rate varies substantially over time

E) Making monetary policy in practice

1. The *IS-LM* model makes monetary policy look easy—just change the money supply to move the economy to the best point possible

a. In fact, it isn't so easy because of lags in the effect of policy and uncertainty about the ways monetary policy works

2. Lags in the effects of monetary policy

a. It takes a fairly long time for changes in monetary policy to have an impact on the economy

b. Interest rates change quickly, but output and inflation barely respond in the first four months after the change in money growth (text Figure 14.8)

c. Tighter monetary policy causes real GDP to decline sharply after about 4 months, with the full effect being felt about 16 to 20 months after the change in policy

d. Inflation responds even more slowly, remaining essentially unchanged for the first year, then declining somewhat

e. These long lags make it very difficult to use monetary policy to control the economy very precisely

f. Because of the lags, policy must be made based on forecasts of the future, but forecasts are often inaccurate

g. The Fed under Greenspan has made preemptive strikes against inflation based on forecasts of higher future inflation

3. The channels of monetary policy transmission

a. Exactly how does monetary policy affect economic activity and prices? There are two effects discussed in the textbook so far

(1) The interest rate channel: as seen in the *IS-LM* model, a decline in money supply raises real interest rates, reducing aggregate demand, leading to a decline in output and prices

(2) The exchange rate channel: in an open economy, tighter monetary policy raises the real exchange rate, reducing net exports, and thus aggregate demand

(3) The credit channel: tighter monetary policy reduces both the supply and demand for credit (see the Box 14.1 below)

b. How important are these different channels?

(1) Suppose real interest rates are high, but the dollar has been falling; is monetary policy tight or easy? It depends on the relative importance of the different channels

(2) Or suppose real interest rates are low, but borrowing and lending are weak

4. These practical difficulties make monetary policy "an art as well as a science"

5. Box 14.1: The credit channel of monetary transmission

a. The credit channel refers to the effects monetary policy has on the supply and demand for credit

b. On the supply side, tight monetary policy leads to reduced lending by banks

(1) Tighter monetary policy reduces bank reserves, so banks can't accept as many deposits

(2) With fewer deposits, banks can't lend as much

(3) With fewer loans available, firms can't obtain all the credit they want

(4) So firms spend less on investment, reducing aggregate demand

    c. On the demand side, tight monetary policy makes borrowers less credit-worthy

      (1) A firm with outstanding debt (with a floating interest rate, interest rate tied to the prime rate, or short-term loan) has to pay more interest when tight policy makes interest rates rise, so its costs go up and profits decline

      (2) With lower profits, the firm is more likely to go bankrupt, so banks will be less willing to make loans to it

      (3) Consumers who use stock as collateral for loans find that tighter monetary policy reduces stock values as investors switch from stocks to bonds, so their collateral is worth less and they can't borrow as much

      (4) The overall effect is reduced spending on investment and consumption, leading the *IS* curve to shift down and to the left

    d. Empirical evidence for the credit channel

      (1) On the supply side, the credit channel was powerful in the 1960s and 1970s, but has declined in importance recently because of deregulation in the banking sector and the elimination of most reserve requirements

      (2) On the demand side, the credit channel can be observed by noting that the spending of consumers and small firms is more sensitive to monetary policy than the spending of large firms

        (a) Consumers and small firms are financially riskier than large firms, so when monetary policy tightens they're more likely to be disqualified from loans

        (b) The data show that after a tightening of monetary policy, small firms and consumers are more likely to go bankrupt and receive less credit than large firms

      (3) The quantitative importance of the credit channel, relative to the interest rate channel and exchange rate channel, remains controversial, but it appeared to play a major role in the recession of 1990–1991

III. The Conduct of Monetary Policy: Rules Versus Discretion (Sec. 14.3)

  A) Monetarists and classical macroeconomists advocate the use of rules

    1. Rules make monetary policy automatic, as they require the central bank to set policy based on a set of simple, prespecified, and publicly announced rules

    2. Examples of rules

      a. Increase the monetary base by 1% each quarter

      b. Maintain the price of gold at a fixed level

    3. The rule should be simple; there shouldn't be much leeway for exceptions

    4. The rule should specify something under the Fed's control, like growth of the monetary base, not something like fixing the unemployment rate at 4%, over which the Fed has little control

    5. The rule may also permit the Fed to respond to the state of the economy

  B) Most Keynesian economists support discretion

    1. Discretion means the central bank looks at all the information about the economy and uses its judgment as to the best course of policy

    2. Discretion gives the central bank the freedom to stimulate or contract the economy when needed; it is thus called *activist*

    3. Because discretion gives the central bank leeway to act, while rules constrain its behavior, why would anyone suggest that the central bank follow rules?

  C) Box 14.2: The Taylor rule

    1. John Taylor of Stanford University introduced a rule that allows the Fed to take economic conditions into account

2. The rule is $i = \pi + 0.02 + 0.5y + 0.5\,(\pi - 0.02)$, where i is the nominal Fed funds rate, π is the inflation rate over the last four quarters, $y = (Y - \overline{Y})/\overline{Y}$ = the percentage deviation of output from full-employment output

3. The rule works by having the real Fed funds rate $(i - \pi)$ respond to:
   a. y, the difference between output and full-employment output
   b. $\pi - 0.02$, the difference between inflation and its target of 2%

4. If either y or π increase, the real Fed funds rate is increased, causing monetary policy to tighten (and vice versa)

5. Taylor showed that the rule is similar to what the Fed does in practice

6. Taylor advocates the use of the rule as a guideline for policy, not something to be followed mechanically

D) The monetarist case for rules

1. *Monetarism* is an economic theory emphasizing the importance of monetary factors in the economy

2. The leading monetarist is Milton Friedman, who has argued for many years (since 1959) that the central bank should follow rules for setting policy

3. Friedman's argument for rules comes from four main propositions

   a. Proposition 1: Monetary policy has powerful short-run effects on the real economy. In the longer run, however, changes in the money supply have their primary effect on the price level

   (1) This proposition comes from Friedman's research with Anna Schwartz on monetary history

   (2) Friedman and other monetarists think monetary policy is a main source of business cycles

   b. Proposition 2: Despite the powerful short-run effect of money on the economy, there is little scope for using monetary policy actively to try to smooth business cycles

   (1) First, the information lag makes it difficult to know the current state of the economy

   (2) Second, monetary policy works with a long and variable lag, so it isn't clear how to set policy quantitatively

   (3) Third, wage and price adjustment is fast enough that by the time a change in policy begins to affect the economy, it may be moving the economy in the wrong direction, thus destabilizing the economy

   c. Proposition 3: Even if there is some scope for using monetary policy to smooth business cycles, the Fed cannot be relied on to do so effectively

   (1) Friedman believes the Fed responds to political pressure and tends to stimulate the economy in election years

   (2) Historically, monetary policy has tended to destabilize, rather than stabilize, the economy; so eliminating monetary policy as a source of instability would improve macroeconomic performance

   d. Proposition 4: The Fed should choose a specific monetary aggregate (such as M1 or M2) and commit itself to making that aggregate grow at a fixed percentage rate every year

   (1) The Fed needs to give up activist, or discretionary, policy completely and follow a simple rule

   (2) Friedman prefers a constant money growth rule, because the money supply is controllable by the Fed and the Fed would not follow destabilizing monetary policies

   (3) To reduce inflation to zero, the money growth target should be gradually lowered over time

E) Rules and central bank credibility

   1. New arguments for rules suggest that rules are valuable even if the central bank has a lot of information and forms policy wisely

     a. The new arguments suggest that rules improve the credibility of the central bank

     b. The credibility of the central bank influences how well monetary policy works

   2. Dad, the kids, and the game: Credible threats and commitment

     a. Dad wants to take the kids to a ballgame and the kids want to go too

     b. But the kids like to fight and Dad doesn't like them fighting

     c. To induce them not to fight, Dad says, "If you fight, we won't go to the game"

     d. A *game theory* model can tell us whether the kids will fight or not and whether Dad will take them to the game or not; game theory explores situations (games) in which strategy is used by individuals (players) to achieve their goals, possibly at the expense of other players

     e. First, the value of different actions is specified

       (1) For the kids, fighting is worth one, not fighting zero, going to the game two, not going to the game zero

       (2) For Dad, fighting is worth zero, not fighting one, going to the game two, not going to the game zero

     f. This means the payoffs to the combinations of whether the kids fight or not and whether they all go to the game or not can be laid out as in text Figure 14.9

	Kid's Strategy	
Dad's Strategy	**Fight**	**Don't Fight**
Go to game	Dad: 2	Dad: 3
	Kids: 3	Kids: 2
Don't go to game	Dad: 0	Dad: 1
	Kids: 1	Kids: 0

     g. Dad's statement isn't credible, because he would be worse off if he followed it

       (1) If the kids fight and Dad follows through on not going to the game, he gets a payoff of 0

       (2) But if they fight and Dad backs down from his statement and takes them to the game anyway, Dad's payoff is 2

       (3) Because the kids know that Dad will take them to the game whether they fight or not, and because they prefer to fight, they will fight

     h. Could Dad make his statement credible?

       (1) He could if he could commit himself somehow to following through

       (2) One possibility is to give the tickets to Mom, who doesn't care if they go to the game, who could enforce Dad's decision

       (3) Then both fighting and going to the game would not be possible, so the kids wouldn't fight, because they prefer not fighting and going to the game over fighting and not going to the game

3. A game between the central bank and firms (text Figure 14.10)
    a. Consider a similar game between the central bank and firms
    b. The inflation rate is 10% and the unemployment rate is 6%
    c. The Fed tells firms that it will hold the money supply constant this year
    d. Should the firms believe the Fed and hold prices constant, or should they doubt that the Fed will really hold the money supply constant, in which case they should raise prices?
    e. The payoffs
        (1) For firms, 0% inflation is worth one, 10% inflation is worth zero; unemployment at the natural rate is worth two, unemployment above or below the natural rate is worth zero
        (2) For the Fed, 0% inflation is worth one, 10% inflation is worth zero; unemployment at the natural rate is worth zero, unemployment above the natural rate is worth –one, and unemployment below the natural rate is worth one
    f. If the Fed holds the money supply constant
        (1) If firms don't raise prices, then inflation is zero and the *LM* curve stays put, so unemployment remains at the natural rate
        (2) If firms raise prices, inflation is 10%, the *LM* curve shifts up, and unemployment rises to 9%
    g. If the Fed raises the money supply
        (1) If firms don't raise prices, then inflation is zero and the *LM* curve shifts down, so unemployment falls to 3%
        (2) If firms raise prices, inflation is 10%, the *LM* curve stays put, and unemployment remains at the natural rate
    h. The payoffs can thus be laid out as

	Firm's Strategy	
Fed's Strategy	**Raise *P***	**Don't Raise *P***
Increase *M*	Fed: 0	Fed: 2
	Firms: 2	Firms: 1
Don't Increase *M*	Fed: –1	Fed: 1
	Firms: 0	Firms: 3

    i. The payoffs are such that if firms raise prices, the Fed is better off increasing *M*, so firms reason that the Fed's threat isn't credible
    j. Further, if the firms didn't raise prices, the Fed would increase the money supply, because its payoff is larger
    k. So firms will increase prices and the Fed will increase the money supply, leading to inflation of 10% and unemployment of 6%
    l. If the Fed's statement not to raise the money supply was credible, however, then firms would choose not to raise prices and inflation would fall to zero, with unemployment remaining at the natural rate
4. Rules, commitment, and credibility
    a. How does a central bank (or a dad) gain credibility?
    b. One way to get credibility is by building a reputation for following through on its promises, even if it's costly in the short run
    c. Another, less costly, way is to follow a rule that is enforced by some outside agency (Mom, for example)

      d. Keynesians argue that there may be a trade-off between credibility and flexibility

         (1) To be credible, a rule must be nearly impossible to change

         (2) But if a rule can't be changed, what happens in a crisis situation?

         (3) For example, if a rule is based on economic relationships that change suddenly, then the lack of flexibility may be very costly

         (4) So a rule may create unacceptable risks

F) Application: Monetary-growth targeting and inflation targeting

    1. High unemployment and high inflation in the 1970s led central banks worldwide to experiment with alternative strategies for monetary policy, including targeting money growth and targeting inflation

    2. Money-growth targeting

      a. Germany's Bundesbank introduced money-growth targets in 1975 and used the strategy until the European Monetary Union began in 1999

         (1) The U.S., Canada, the U.K., Switzerland, and others also adopted money targets in the 1970s

      b. Money-growth targeting means the central bank announces a money-growth rate that it will aim for over the next year or so

         (1) The idea is that by having money grow at the optimal rate, inflation and output will be at desired levels

         (2) Germany had been quite successful in targeting money growth

      c. The United States began targeting money in 1975

         (1) But the Fed tried to target three monetary aggregates (M1, M2, and M3) all at the same time, and often missed its targets badly

      d. Most countries that used money-growth targeting (including the United States) were able to reduce inflation in the early 1980s, but output and employment growth were often unstable

         (1) The Fed began to deemphasize money-growth targeting in 1982 because of instability in money demand and moved gradually toward interest-rate targeting

         (2) Many other countries also weakened their reliance on money-growth targets in the 1980s, except for Germany and Switzerland

    3. Inflation targeting

      a. Since 1990, some countries have switched from targeting money growth to targeting inflation

         (1) New Zealand was the pioneer, announcing explicit inflation targets that had to be met or else the central bank's governor could be fired

         (2) Canada, the U.K., Sweden, Australia, Spain, and others followed with some version of inflation targeting

         (3) The new European Central Bank uses a method of inflation targeting that retains a role for money-growth targets

      b. Under inflation targeting, the central bank announces targets for inflation over the next one to four years

      c. Advantages of inflation targeting over money-growth targeting

         (1) It avoids the problem of instability in money demand

         (2) It's easy to explain inflation targets to the public (because they understand what inflation is) than money-growth targeting (which most people don't understand)

         (3) Better communication of the central bank's goals will reduce uncertainty about what the central bank will do and may increase the bank's accountability

      d. Disadvantages of inflation targeting relative to money-growth targeting

        (1) Inflation responds to policy actions with a long lag, so it's hard to judge what policy actions are needed to hit the inflation target and hard for the public to tell if the central bank is doing the right thing

        (2) Thus central banks may miss their targets badly, losing credibility

G) Other ways to achieve central bank credibility besides targeting money growth or inflation

  1. Appointing a "tough" central banker

    a. Appointing someone who has a well-known reputation for being tough in fighting inflation may help establish credibility for the central bank

    b. For example, in 1979 the appointment of Paul Volcker to be chairman of the Fed was designed to convince people that President Carter was serious about stopping inflation

    c. Even in Volcker's case, however, disinflation proved to be costly

  2. Changing central bankers' incentives

    a. People are more likely to believe a central bank is serious about disinflation if it has the incentive to care a lot about inflation

    b. In New Zealand, for example, the head of the central bank must be replaced if inflation targets aren't met; as a result, inflation was reduced significantly, but at a cost of higher unemployment

  3. Increasing central bank independence

    a. If the executive and legislative branches of government can't interfere with the central bank, people are more likely to believe that the central bank is committed to keeping inflation low and won't cause a political business cycle

    b. Looking at evidence across countries (text Figure 14.11), Alesina and Summers showed that the more independent the central bank, the lower the inflation rate from 1955 to 1988; also, the long-run level of unemployment is no higher in those countries

■ Multiple Choice Questions

1. Monetary policy in the United States is controlled by
   (a) the president of the United States.
   (b) the U.S. Senate.
   (c) the Federal Reserve.
   (d) fiscal policymakers.

2. If a currency is legal tender in a country, then
   (a) the government will readily exchange it for gold.
   (b) the government will not accept it in payment of taxes.
   (c) it is the only legal form of wealth.
   (d) creditors are required to accept it in settlement of debts.

3. The monetary base is equal to
   (a) banks' reserves plus their holdings of Treasury securities.
   (b) banks' reserves plus Fed funds.
   (c) banks' reserves plus currency held by the nonbank public.
   (d) M2 minus M1.

4. In a fractional reserve banking system
   (a) most deposits are used to make bank loans.
   (b) 100% of deposits are held as reserves.
   (c) the money supply = high-powered money.
   (d) the money multiplier is less than one.

5. The monetary base (*BASE*) equals
   (a) $CU + RES$.
   (b) RES.
   (c) $CU + DEP$.
   (d) $M - CU$.

6. If the public's demand for currency increased relative to its demand for deposits,
   (a) the monetary base would decrease.
   (b) reserve requirements would decrease.
   (c) the currency–deposit ratio would decrease.
   (d) the money multiplier would decrease.

7. Currently, the currency–deposit ratio is 0.3 and the reserve–deposit ratio is 0.2. The Federal Reserve raises the reserve–deposit ratio to 0.25, as a response to a change in the public's currency–deposit ratio, to maintain the old money multiplier. What is the public's approximate new currency–deposit ratio?
   (a) 0.22
   (b) 0.25
   (c) 0.33
   (d) 0.35

8. Assume that the currency–deposit ratio is 0.5 and the reserve–deposit ratio is 0.2. The Federal Reserve carries out open-market operations, purchasing $1,000,000 worth of bonds from banks. This action will increase the money supply by
   (a) $1,428,571.
   (b) $1,714,285.
   (c) $2,142,857.
   (d) $2,400,000.

9. Suppose the Federal Reserve wanted to increase the money supply without using open-market operations. It could try to get the public to _____ their currency–deposit ratio and _____ banks' reserve requirements, which would in turn change the banks' reserve–deposit ratio.
   (a) decrease; lower
   (b) decrease; raise
   (c) increase; lower
   (d) increase; raise

10. If the Fed increases the monetary base by $100 million and the money multiplier is 3, M1 will
    (a) rise by $300 million.
    (b) fall by $300 million.
    (c) rise by $33 1/3 million.
    (d) fall by $33 1/3 million.

11. Which of the following is *not* a policy instrument of the Fed?
    (a) Open-market operations
    (b) Changes in the discount rate
    (c) Changes in reserve requirements
    (d) Changes in the government deficit

12. The largest liability of the Fed is
    (a) U.S. Treasury securities.
    (b) deposits of depository institutions.
    (c) loans to depository institutions.
    (d) currency outstanding.

13. The policy instrument most frequently used to change the money supply is
    (a) open-market operations.
    (b) changes in reserve requirements.
    (c) changes in margin requirements on stock prices.
    (d) changes in the discount rate.

14. By lending at the discount window, the Fed
    (a) insures bank deposits.
    (b) ensures that banks will make healthy profits.
    (c) eliminates the need for banks to pay market interest rates to attract deposits.
    (d) acts as a lender of last resort to enable banks to meet unexpectedly high withdrawal demands.

15. Banks in good condition may take out a _____ from the Fed.
    (a) secondary credit discount loan
    (b) Fed funds loan
    (c) primary credit discount loan
    (d) class A loan

16. The Fed funds rate is
    (a) the interest rate on federal government bonds.
    (b) the interest rate banks charge other banks for short-term loans.
    (c) the interest rate the Fed charges banks who borrow from it.
    (d) the interest rate penalty on late federal tax payments.

17. If the *IS* curve shifts to the left, and the Fed wants to keep the real interest rate unchanged, it should take action to
     (a) shift the *LM* curve to the left.
     (b) shift the *IS* curve further to the left.
     (c) shift the *IS* curve to the right.
     (d) shift the *LM* curve to the right.

18. In response to an unanticipated tightening of monetary policy, the Fed funds rate _____ at first, then _____ after six to twelve months.
     (a) rises; returns most of the way to its original value
     (b) falls; returns most of the way to its original value
     (c) remains roughly unchanged; rises significantly
     (d) remains roughly unchanged; falls significantly

19. In response to an unanticipated tightening of monetary policy, output _____ at first, then _____ after about four months.
     (a) rises; returns most of the way to its original value
     (b) falls; returns most of the way to its original value
     (c) remains roughly unchanged; rises significantly
     (d) remains roughly unchanged; falls significantly

20. When the Fed reduces the money supply, raising the real interest rate, which reduces aggregate demand, which leads to falling output and prices, the effects of monetary policy on the economy are said to work through the _____ of monetary policy.
     (a) aggregate-demand channel
     (b) aggregate-supply channel
     (c) output channel
     (d) interest rate channel

21. The basic Keynesian argument for discretionary monetary policy is that
     (a) monetary policy is the principal cause of business cycles.
     (b) monetary policy is much more effective than fiscal policy.
     (c) aggregate demand is unstable and monetary policy can help to stabilize it.
     (d) reducing unemployment is much more important than reducing inflation.

22. A monetary policy rule proposed by monetarists is to
     (a) increase the money supply at a low, constant rate of growth every year.
     (b) target a constant Fed funds rate over long periods.
     (c) adjust money supply growth often, to stabilize the economy.
     (d) adjust the Fed Funds rate often, to stabilize the economy.

23. According to Taylor's rule, if output is below its full-employment level and inflation is less than 2%,
     (a) the Fed should raise the Fed funds rate above 4%.
     (b) the Fed should reduce the Fed funds rate below 4%.
     (c) the Fed should make the Fed funds rate exactly 4%.
     (d) what the Fed should do is ambiguous.

24. According to Taylor's rule, if inflation in the last year was 4% and output was at its full-employment level, the nominal Fed funds rate should be
    (a) 4%.
    (b) 5%.
    (c) 6%.
    (d) 7%.

25. The viewpoint that monetary factors are important in the macroeconomy is known as
    (a) monetarism.
    (b) Keynesianism.
    (c) classical theory.
    (d) institutionalism.

26. A monetarist is most likely to believe that monetary policy should
    (a) be based entirely on the discretion of the central bank.
    (b) be guided by the Taylor rule.
    (c) depend on the stance of fiscal policy.
    (d) set a constant growth rate of the money supply.

27. If the Fed announces that it will reduce the growth rate of the money supply to 3% next year but people do not believe it, the Fed is said to
    (a) engage in commitment.
    (b) be an inflation nutter.
    (c) engage in destabilizing policy.
    (d) lack credibility.

28. In New Zealand, if the Reserve Bank fails to meet its inflation targets, then _____ may be fired.
    (a) the country's president
    (b) the country's finance minister
    (c) the Reserve Bank's governor
    (d) the Reserve Bank's chief economist

29. The chief disadvantage of inflation targeting is that
    (a) it's hard to measure inflation.
    (b) it isn't easy for the public to observe inflation.
    (c) people don't understand what inflation is.
    (d) it's hard for the central bank to judge what policy actions are needed.

30. Other than following a rule, a country could do each of the following things to help its central bank achieve credibility EXCEPT
    (a) appoint a tough central banker.
    (b) change the incentives of the central bankers.
    (c) increase central bank independence.
    (d) put the central bank under the government's control.

■ Review Questions

1. Identify the market actors who control each of the following variables, and state whether the money supply is positively related or negatively related to each variable: the monetary base, the reserve–deposit ratio, and the currency–deposit ratio.

2. Identify the most commonly used policy instrument for changing the money supply, and explain how the Fed can use this policy instrument to increase and decrease the money supply.

3. Was the money multiplier stable during the Great Depression? Why would an unstable money multiplier pose a problem for monetary policy?

4. What policy-making body within the Fed controls monetary policy? How are its members chosen?

5. From a Keynesian viewpoint, what is wrong with the monetarist argument against an activist monetary policy?

6. If you could determine the goals of the Fed, what goals would you choose? Should the Fed's policy be activist? Discuss the pros and cons.

7. What is the intermediate target recommended by monetarists? Why do they propose this target?

8. Why don't Keynesians believe the credibility argument in favor of rules for monetary policy?

9. Should the Fed be independent? Or should the Fed be required to confer with Congress to coordinate fiscal and monetary policies? Explain the pros and cons.

10. Why is it important to policymakers that people believe them when they say they are going to reduce inflation? How can they increase their credibility?

■ Numerical Problems

1. Calculate the money multiplier for each of the following cases.
   (a) $cu = .40$ and $res = .07$
   (b) $cu = .40$ and $res = .08$
   (c) $cu = .45$ and $res = .07$

2. The money supply is $12 million, currency held by the public is $2 million, and the reserve–deposit ratio is 0.2.
   (a) What is the quantity of bank deposits?
   (b) What is the quantity of bank reserves?
   (c) What is the quantity of the monetary base?
   (d) What is the money multiplier (give a number)?

■ Analytical Questions

1. Given an economy with no currency and a reserve–deposit ratio of 10%, explain how much money the banking system creates when the Fed buys a $1,000 bond from a bank.

2. The inflation rate is 4% and the unemployment rate is 5%. The central bank tells firms that it will reduce the growth of the money supply over the next year so that prices will rise only 3% instead of 4%. Should the firms believe the central bank and raise their prices only 3%, or should they be doubtful that the central bank will really do what it says, which means firms should raise their prices 4%? The following diagram shows the payoffs.

	Firms' Strategy	
	Raise Prices 4%	**Raise Prices 3%**
Central Bank's Strategy	**Outcome A**	**Outcome B**
Keep money growth same	Fed: 0 Firms: 10 $\pi = 4\%$ $u = 5\%$	Fed: 10 Firms: 0 $\pi = 3\%$ $u = 4\%$
	Outcome C	**Outcome D**
Lower money growth	Fed: –5 Firms: –10 $\pi = 4\%$ $u = 6\%$	Fed: 5 Firms: 20 $\pi = 3\%$ $u = 5\%$

(a) If the central bank can move first, what will be the outcome of this game?

(b) Now suppose the firms move first. What will be the outcome?

■ Answers

Multiple Choice

1. c	7. a	13. a	19. d	25. a
2. d	8. c	14. d	20. d	26. d
3. c	9. a	15. c	21. c	27. d
4. a	10. a	16. b	22. a	28. c
5. a	11. d	17. a	23. b	29. d
6. d	12. d	18. a	24. d	30. d

Review Questions

1. (1) The monetary base (*BASE*) is positively related to the money supply; an increase in the base increases the money supply. The Fed controls the monetary base.

    (2) The reserve–deposit ratio (*res*) is negatively related to the money supply; an increase in the reserve–deposit ratio reduces the money multiplier and thus reduces the money supply. The Fed sets the minimum reserve requirement ratio on bank deposits, but the private banks can change the reserve–deposit ratio by changing their holdings of excess reserves (i.e., reserves in excess of required reserves).

(3) The currency–deposit ratio (*cu*) is negatively related to the money supply; an increase in the currency–deposit ratio reduces the money multiplier and thus reduces the money supply. The public (i.e., everyone except banks, thrifts, and the Fed) controls the currency–deposit ratio by deciding how much of their money they want to retain as currency, rather than as deposits in banks and thrift institutions.

2. Open-market operations are the most commonly used policy instrument for changing the money supply. The Fed can increase the money supply by making an open-market purchase of government securities (bonds) from the public or banks. An open-market purchase increases currency held by the nonbank public and bank reserves, which is an increase in the monetary base. An increase in the monetary base increases the money supply by the amount of the money multiplier times the increase in the money base. Alternatively, the Fed can reduce the monetary base and the money supply by making an open-market sale of government securities.

3. The money multiplier was not stable during the Great Depression. In the 1931 to early 1933 period, the money multiplier declined sharply, because the currency–deposit ratio and the reserve–deposit ratio both rose dramatically. Market actors increased their demand for currency, and banks increased their demand for excess reserves. Instability in the money multiplier creates instability in the money supply for a given monetary base. The Fed could offset any undesirable effect of a change in the money multiplier on the money supply by changing the monetary base. However, the Fed did not sufficiently compensate for the change in the money multiplier, so the money supply declined by 35% in this period. More than one-third of the banks in the country failed or were acquired by other banks in the 1930–1933 period. This financial crisis was stopped in 1933, when President Roosevelt temporarily shut down the banking system by declaring a "bank holiday."

4. The Federal Open Market Committee (FOMC) controls monetary policy. There are twelve members of the FOMC, including the seven members of the Board of Governors, the president of the Federal Reserve Bank of New York, and the presidents of four other Federal Reserve regional banks (on a rotating basis). The members of the Board of Governors are nominated by the U.S. president and confirmed by the U.S. Senate. The presidents of the Federal Reserve district banks are appointed by the directors of each regional bank.

5. Keynesians do not believe that the economy is stable and self-regulating. Consequently, the economy does not quickly recover from recessions. Unlike monetarists, Keynesians believe that the Fed is reasonably efficient and can use monetary stabilization policy efficiently. Keynesians contend that using monetary policy would greatly reduce the magnitude of the business cycle.

6. Goals: Maintain low inflation and unemployment in a stable economic environment with steady interest rates and exchange rates. If you are a Keynesian, you believe that activist policy is desirable, as the Fed can offset shocks to the economy. Monetarists see activist policy as destabilizing, partly because of the long and variable lags associated with monetary policy. Classical (*RBC*) economists see no need for activist policy, because the economy is self-correcting.

7. The monetarists recommend that the Fed choose a monetary aggregate as an intermediate target, such as M2. They propose a monetary aggregate target for several reasons. First, they do not believe that nominal shocks are an important source of instability in the economy. In the monetarist view, money demand is reasonably stable. Second, they believe that the macroeconomy is reasonably stable and self-regulating, and normally operates at full-employment output, consistent with the natural unemployment rate. Third, they believe that the money supply largely determines the level of aggregate demand, and that aggregate demand determines the price level; therefore the money supply determines the price level. Fourth, in a stable economy operating at full employment, the ultimate target of monetary policy should be to maintain price level stability (i.e., zero inflation). Fifth, to hit the price level target, the Fed needs to achieve a constant rate of money supply growth.

8. Rules provide credibility, but there may be a need for flexibility to respond to conditions that the rules didn't anticipate.

9. The value of Fed independence is that it prevents political pressure from influencing the money supply process. On the other hand, if fiscal and monetary policy aren't coordinated, there may be large swings in the real interest rate and/or output if the policies move in opposite directions.

10. If policymakers are credible, inflation expectations will fall quickly, reducing the costs of disinflation. Credibility can be enhanced by building a reputation, following a rule, appointing a tough central banker, changing the incentives of the central banker, or increasing central bank independence.

Numerical Problems

1. The money multiplier $= (cu + 1)/(cu + res)$.
    (a) For $cu = .40$ and $res = .07$, the money multiplier $= 1.40/0.47 = 2.98$.
    (b) For $cu = .40$ and $res = .08$, the money multiplier $= 1.40/0.48 = 2.92$.
    (c) For $cu = .45$ and $res = .07$, the money multiplier $= 1.45/0.52 = 2.79$.

2. (a) $10 million
    (b) $2 million
    (c) $4 million
    (d) 3

Analytical Questions

1. For an economy with no currency and a reserve–deposit ratio of 10%, a $1,000 open-market purchase from a bank increases the bank's excess reserves by $1,000. The bank can make loans up to the limit of its excess reserves, so it makes a $1,000 loan to some borrower. The borrower deposits the amount of the loan in his bank account. The bank retains 10% of the $1,000 deposit as reserves and now makes a $900 loan, using its excess reserves. The amount of the $900 loan is deposited in a second bank, which retains 10% as reserves and makes a loan for the $810 balance. The borrower deposits the amount of the $810 loan in a third bank, which retains 10% as reserves and lends out the balance. When all possible loans have been made by the banking system, this multiple expansion of loans and deposits will increase the money supply by $(1/.10) \times \$1,000 = \$10,000$.

2.   (a) If the central bank can move first, it will reason as follows. If it keeps money growth the same, firms can raise prices 4% and earn a payoff of ten, or they can raise prices 3% and earn a payoff of zero; clearly they'll raise prices 4%. If the central bank lowers money growth, firms can raise prices 4% and earn a payoff of minus ten, or they can raise prices 3% and earn a payoff of twenty; clearly they'll raise prices 3%. So if the central bank keeps money growth the same, firms raise prices 4%, outcome A is reached and the central bank's payoff is zero. If the central bank lowers money growth, firms raise prices 3%, outcome D is reached, and the central bank's payoff is five. Because the central bank is better off with a payoff of five, it will choose to lower money growth.

     (b) If firms can move first, they will reason as follows. If they raise prices 4%, the central bank can keep money growth the same and earn a payoff of zero, or lower money growth and earn a payoff of minus five; clearly they'll keep money growth the same. If firms raise prices 3%, the central bank can keep money growth the same and earn a payoff of ten, or they can lower money growth and earn a payoff of five; clearly they'll keep money growth the same. So if firms raise prices 4%, the central bank will keep money growth the same, outcome A is reached and the firms' payoff is ten. If firms raise prices 3%, the central bank will keep money growth the same, outcome B is reached, and the firms' payoff is zero. Because firms are better off with a payoff of ten, they will choose to raise prices 4%.

Chapter 15
Government Spending and Its Financing

■ Introduction

This chapter examines fiscal policy and its macroeconomic effects. Section 15.1 looks at definitions and facts about the government's budget. Section 15.2 examines the effects of government spending and taxes on economic activity. The burden of government debt on future generations is discussed in Section 15.3. Section 15.4 covers the link between budget deficits and inflation.

This is a very policy-oriented chapter. Pay close attention to the main facts about government debt and deficits in Section 15.1, as some are surprising, and they'll help you understand why the government debt is of such great concern to economists. Also, you'll understand a lot about how economists think about taxes if you understand the different effects of changes in marginal tax rates compared to average tax rates, which are discussed in Section 15.2. They'll help you figure out the incentive effects and distortions caused by taxes.

■ Outline

I. **The Government Budget: Some Facts and Figures (Sec. 15.1)**

A) Government outlays

1. Three categories of government expenditures

a. Government purchases (G)

(1) Government investment, which is about 1/6 of total government purchases, consists of purchases of capital goods

(2) Government consumption expenditures are about 5/6 of total government purchases

b. Transfer payments (TR)

(1) Transfers are expenditures for which the government receives no current goods or services in return

(2) Examples: Social Security benefits, pensions for government retirees, welfare payments

c. Net interest payments (INT)

(1) Interest paid to holders of government bonds less interest received by the government

(2) Government makes loans to students, farmers, small businesses

d. Subsidies less surpluses of government enterprises; relatively small, so we ignore it

2. Total (Federal, state, and local) government outlays are about one-third of GDP (text Figure 15.1)

a. Government purchases increased enormously in World War II

(1) Government purchases rose in other wars as well

(2) Since the late 1960s, government purchases have drifted downward from about 23% of GDP to about 19% of GDP

      b. Transfer payments have been rising steadily
         (1) They're now about 12% of GDP
         (2) Many social programs, including Social Security, Medicare, and Medicaid, have expanded over time
      c. Net interest payments have also changed over time
         (1) They doubled between 1941 and 1946 because of the higher debt to finance World War II
         (2) They nearly doubled in the 1980s, as both the government debt and interest rates increased sharply
         (3) They declined in the 1990s because of lower interest rates and government budget surpluses
   3. Comparing U.S. government spending to that of other countries shows that the United States spends less as a percentage of GDP than almost any other OECD country (text Table 15.1)

B) Taxes
   1. Total tax collections have increased over time, from about 16.5% of GDP in 1940 to about 30% in 2000, though declining to about 27% in 2005 (text Figure 15.2)
   2. Four principal categories
      a. Personal taxes
         (1) Personal income taxes
         (2) Property taxes
         (3) Personal taxes have risen steadily over time, except for the Kennedy–Johnson tax cut of 1964 and the Reagan tax cut of 1981, and the Bush tax cuts in the early 2000s
      b. Contributions for social insurance have increased steadily as a percentage of GDP since World War II
      c. Taxes on production and imports are mostly sales taxes and have been steady relative to GDP since World War II
      d. Corporate taxes declined gradually over time relative to GDP from the mid-1950s to the mid-1980s, and now average about 2% to 3% of GDP
   3. The composition of outlays and taxes: The Federal government versus state and local governments
      a. To see the overall picture of government spending, we usually combine Federal, state, and local government spending
      b. But the composition of the Federal government budget is quite different from state and local government budgets (text Table 15.2)
         (1) Consumption expenditures
             (a) About 75% of state and local current expenditures are purchases of goods and services
             (b) By contrast, about 30% of Federal current expenditures are for purchases, and of those, about 2/3 is for national defense
             (c) Of all government purchases of nondefense goods and services, over 80% is done by state and local governments
         (2) Transfer payments
             (a) The Federal government budget is more heavily weighted to transfers than state and local budgets
         (3) Grants-in-aid are payments from the Federal government to state and local governments

(4) Net interest paid

(a) Net interest is significant and positive for the Federal government

(b) It is small and sometimes negative for state and local governments

(5) Composition of taxes

(a) Personal taxes and contributions for social insurance account for about 80% of Federal receipts, but only about 20% of state and local government receipts

(b) Taxes on production and imports provide about half of state and local government receipts, but only about 5% of Federal receipts

C) Deficits and surpluses

1. When outlays exceed revenues, there is a deficit; when revenues exceed outlays, there is a surplus

2. Formally, deficit = outlays – tax revenues

= government purchases + transfers + net interest – tax revenues

$$= G + TR + INT - T \tag{15.1}$$

3. Another useful deficit definition is the primary government budget deficit, which excludes net interest payments: primary deficit = outlays – net interest – tax revenues

= government purchases + transfers – tax revenues

$$= G + TR - T \tag{15.2}$$

a. The total deficit tells the amount the government must borrow to cover all its expenditures

b. The primary deficit tells if the government's receipts are enough to cover its current purchases and transfers

c. The primary deficit ignores interest payments, because those are payments for past government spending (text Figure 15.3)

4. The separation of government purchases into government investment and government consumption expenditures introduces another set of deficit concepts

a. The current deficit equals the deficit minus government investment

b. The primary current deficit equals the primary deficit minus government investment, which equals the current deficit minus interest payments

5. The current deficit and primary current deficit usually move together over time (text Figure 15.4)

a. Large current deficits occurred in World War II, the mid-1970s, and the early 1980s

b. The primary current deficit became a primary surplus in some years in the 1980s and 1990s, but large interest payments kept the overall deficit large until the late 1990s

II. Government Spending, Taxes, and the Macroeconomy (Sec. 15.2)

A) Fiscal policy and aggregate demand

1. An increase in government purchases increases aggregate demand by shifting the *IS* curve up

2. The effect of tax changes depends on the economic model

a. Classical economists accept the Ricardian equivalence proposition that lump-sum tax changes have no effect on national saving or on aggregate demand

b. Keynesians think a tax cut is likely to increase consumption and decrease saving, thus increasing aggregate demand

3. Classicals and Keynesians disagree about using fiscal policy to stabilize the economy
    a. Classicals oppose activist policy while Keynesians favor it
    b. But even Keynesians admit that fiscal policy is difficult to use
        (1) There is a lack of flexibility, because much of government spending is committed years in advance
        (2) There are long time lags, because the political process takes time to make changes
4. Automatic stabilizers and the full-employment deficit
    a. Automatic stabilizers cause fiscal policy to be countercyclical by changing government spending or taxes automatically
    b. One example is unemployment insurance, which causes transfers to rise in recessions
    c. The most important automatic stabilizer is the income tax system, because people pay less tax when their incomes are low in recessions, and they pay more tax when their incomes are high in booms
    d. Because of automatic stabilizers, the government budget deficit rises in recessions and falls in booms
        (1) The full-employment deficit is a measure of what the government budget deficit would be if the economy were at full employment
        (2) So the full-employment deficit doesn't change with the business cycle, only with changes in government policy regarding spending and taxation
        (3) The actual budget deficit is much larger than the full-employment budget deficit in recessions (text Figure 15.5)

B) Government capital formation
    1. Fiscal policy affects the economy through the formation of government capital—long-lived physical assets owned by the government, like roads, schools, and sewer systems
    2. Also, fiscal policy affects human capital formation through expenditures on health, nutrition, and education
    3. Data on government investment include only physical capital, not human capital
        a. In 2005, 2/3 of federal government investment was on national defense and 1/3 on nondefense capital
        b. Most federal government investment is in equipment, but most state and local government investment is for structures

C) Incentive effects of fiscal policy
    1. Average versus marginal tax rates
        a. Average tax rate = total taxes/pretax income
        b. Marginal tax rate = taxes due from an additional dollar of income
        c. Example: Suppose taxes are imposed at a rate of 25% on income over $10,000 (text Table 15.3)
            (1) For someone earning less than $10,000, the marginal tax rate and average tax rate are both zero
            (2) Anyone earning over $10,000 would have a marginal tax rate of 25%
            (3) Someone earning $18,000 would pay ($18,000 – $10,000) × .25 = $2,000 in taxes, so he or she would have an average tax rate of 11.1%
            (4) Someone earning $50,000 would pay ($50,000 – $10,000) × .25 = $10,000 in taxes, so he or she would have an average tax rate of 20%
            (5) Someone earning $100,000 would pay ($100,000 – $10,000) × .25 = $22,500 in taxes, so he or she would have an average tax rate of 22.5%

    d. The distinction between average and marginal tax rates affects people's decisions about how much labor to supply

        (1) If the average tax rate increases, with the marginal tax rate held constant, a person will increase labor supply

           (a) The higher average tax rate causes an income effect

           (b) With lower income, a person consumes less and wants less leisure, so he or she works more

           (c) The labor supply curve shifts right

        (2) If the marginal tax rate increases, with the average tax rate held constant, a person will decrease labor supply

           (a) The higher marginal tax rate causes a substitution effect

           (b) With a lower after-tax reward for working, a person wants to work less

           (c) The labor supply curve shifts left

2. Tax reform proposals in 2005

    a. The tax code distorts economic behavior

    b. President Bush appointed a panel in 2005 to find ways to make the tax code simpler and fairer

    c. The panel found that

        (1) the tax system should be streamlined and made easier

        (2) marginal tax rates should be reduced for everyone

        (3) tax benefits for homeownership and charitable donations should go to everyone, not just those who itemize deductions

        (4) health insurance should not be taxed

        (5) the tax system should encourage saving and investment

        (6) the Alternative Minimum Tax should be repealed

    d. Passage of the plan faces large political hurdles

3. Application: Labor supply and tax reform in the 1980s

    a. Congress reduced tax rates twice in the 1980s

        (1) At the beginning of the decade the highest marginal tax rate on labor income was 50%

        (2) The 1981 tax act (ERTA) reduced tax rates in three stages, phased in until 1984

        (3) The tax reform of 1986 further reduced personal tax rates, dropping the top marginal tax rate to 28%

    b. Supply-side economists promoted the tax rate reductions, arguing that labor supply, saving, and investment would all increase substantially

    c. Both marginal and average tax rates declined from the 1981 tax cut

        (1) The decline in the marginal tax rate should lead to increased labor supply

        (2) The decline in the average tax rate should lead to decreased labor supply

        (3) The overall effect is ambiguous and may be small

        (4) The data suggest little effect, as the labor force participation rate didn't change much after 1981

    d. The 1986 tax reform lowered marginal tax rates on labor income and raised average tax rates

        (1) Both should lead to increased labor supply

        (2) The data confirm this result, as men's labor force participation, which had been falling over time, leveled off in 1988 and rose in 1989

    e. The changes in labor supply are consistent with theory, but not nearly as dramatic as projected by the supply-siders

4. Tax-induced distortions and tax rate smoothing
   a. In the absence of taxes, the free market works efficiently
      (1) Taxes change economic behavior, reducing welfare
      (2) Thus tax-induced deviations from free-market outcomes are called distortions
   b. The difference between the number of hours a worker would work without taxes and the number of hours he or she actually works when there is a tax reflects the tax distortion
   c. The higher the tax rate, the greater the distortion
   d. Fiscal policymakers would like to raise the needed amount of government revenue while minimizing distortions
   e. It's better to keep the tax rate constant over time than to raise it and lower it, because the higher tax rate has a higher distortion
      (1) For example, keeping the tax rate at a steady 15% is better than having it at 10% one year and 20% the next, because the distortions in the second year are much higher
      (2) Keeping a constant tax rate over time is called tax rate smoothing
      (3) Empirical studies suggest that the Federal government hasn't always smoothed tax rates as much as it could to minimize distortions
      (4) But borrowing to finance wars, thus avoiding the need to raise taxes a lot in war years, is consistent with the idea of tax rate smoothing

III. Government Deficits and Debt (Sec. 15.3)

A) The growth of the government debt
   1. The deficit is the difference between expenditures and revenues in any fiscal year
   2. The debt is the total value of outstanding government bonds on a given date
   3. The deficit is the change in the debt in a year
      a. ΔB = nominal government budget deficit   (15.3)
      b. B = nominal value of government bonds outstanding
   4. A useful measure of government's indebtedness that accounts for the ability to pay off the debt is the debt–GDP ratio
      a. The U.S. debt–GDP ratio (text Figure 15.6) fell from over one after World War II to a low point in the mid-1970s
      b. From 1979 to 1995, the debt–GDP ratio rose significantly, but it fell from 1995 to 2001, then began to rise in 2002

   5. Change in debt–GDP ratio = deficit/nominal GDP – [(total debt/nominal GDP) × growth rate of nominal GDP]   (15.4)
      a. So two things cause the debt–GDP ratio to rise
         (1) A high deficit relative to GDP
         (2) A slow rate of GDP growth
      b. During World War II, large deficits raised the debt–GDP ratio
      c. For the next thirty-five years, deficits were small or negative, and GDP growth was rapid, so the debt–GDP ratio fell
      d. During the 1980s and early 1990s, the debt–GDP ratio rose because of high deficits
      e. Large surpluses reduced the debt–GDP ratio in the late 1990s, but large deficits raised it beginning in 2002

B) Application: Social Security: How can it be fixed?

   1. The Social Security system may not be able to pay future promised benefits

   2. The system is mostly pay as you go, so that most taxes collected today go to paying benefits to current retirees—there is only a small trust fund

   3. The pay-as-you-go system worked as long as the number of workers greatly exceeded the number of retirees, but demographic changes will soon decrease the ratio of workers to retirees

   4. The result will be payouts in excess of tax revenue (text Figure 15.7)

   5. Fixing the Social Security system

      a. Increase tax revenue by raising taxes, but this distorts labor supply decisions

      b. Increase the rate of return by investing in the stock market, but this is risky

      c. Reduce benefits by increasing retirement age

      d. Allow people to invest their own funds in individual accounts

         (1) But then there would not be enough funds to pay current retirees

C) The burden of the government debt on future generations

   1. People worry that their children will have to pay back the debt that past generations have accumulated

   2. But U.S. citizens own most government bonds, so future generations will just be paying themselves

   3. However, there could be a burden, because if tax rates have to be raised in the future to pay off the debt, the higher tax rates could be distortionary

   4. Also, because bondholders are richer on average than nonbondholders, when the debt was repaid there would be a large transfer from the poor to the rich

   5. Finally, government deficits reduce national saving according to many economists

      a. If so, with lower saving there will be lower investment

      b. Lower investment means a smaller capital stock

      c. A smaller capital stock means less output in the future

      d. So the future standard of living will be lower

      e. However, this assumes that government deficits reduce national saving; that is a key and unsettled question

D) Budget deficits and national saving: Ricardian equivalence revisited

   1. When will a government deficit reduce national saving?

      a. It almost certainly does when government spending rises

      b. But it may not for a cut in taxes or increase in transfers

   2. Ricardian equivalence: An example

      a. Suppose the government cuts taxes by $100 per person

      b. Because $S = Y - C - G$,   (15.5)

        national saving declines only if consumption rises (assuming Y is fixed at its full-employment level)

      c. Consumption might not rise if people realize that a tax cut today must be financed by higher taxes in the future

         (1) A tax cut of $100 per person could be financed by a tax increase of $(1 + r)\$100$ next year

         (2) Then taxpayers' ability to consume is the same with or without the tax cut

         (3) People will simply save the tax cut so they can pay off the future taxes

      d. As a result, national saving should be unaffected

3. Ricardian equivalence across generations

    a. What if the higher future taxes are to be paid by future generations?

    b. Then people might consume more today, because they wouldn't have to pay the higher future taxes

    c. But as Barro pointed out, if people care about their children, they'll increase their bequests to their children so their children can pay the higher future taxes

        (1) After all, if people wanted to consume at their children's expense, they could have lowered their planned bequests

        (2) So why should the fact that the government gives people a tax cut cause them to consume at their children's expense?

E) Departures from Ricardian equivalence

    1. The data show that Ricardian equivalence holds sometimes, but not always

      a. It certainly didn't hold in the United States in the 1980s, when high government deficits were accompanied by low savings

      b. It did seem to hold in Canada and Israel sometimes

      c. But overall, there seems to be little relationship between government budget deficits and national saving

    2. What are the main reasons Ricardian equivalence may fail?

      a. Borrowing constraints

        (1) If people can't borrow as much as they would like, a tax cut financed by higher future taxes essentially lets them borrow from the government

      b. Shortsightedness

        (1) If people don't foresee the higher future taxes, or spend based on rules of thumb about their current after-tax income, they may increase consumption in response to a tax cut

      c. Failure to leave bequests

        (1) People may not leave bequests because they don't care about their children, or because they think their children will be richer than they are, so they will increase consumption spending in response to a tax cut

      d. Non–lump-sum taxes

        (1) When taxes aren't lump sum, changes in tax rates affect economic decisions

        (2) However, a tax cut won't necessarily lead to an increase in consumption in this case

IV. Deficits and Inflation (Sec. 15.4)

A) The deficit and the money supply

    1. Inflation results when aggregate demand rises more quickly than aggregate supply

    2. Budget deficits could be related to inflation, but we usually think of expansionary fiscal policy as leading to a one-time jump in the price level, not a sustained inflation

    3. The only way for a sustained inflation to occur is for there to be sustained growth in the money supply

    4. Can government deficits lead to ongoing increases in the money supply?

      a. Yes, if spending is financed by printing money

      b. The revenue that a government raises by printing money is called *seignorage*

      c. Usually, governments don't just buy things directly with newly printed money, they do so indirectly

        (1) The Treasury borrows by issuing government bonds

        (2) The central bank buys the bonds with newly printed money

(3) The relationship between the deficit and the increase in the monetary base is

$$\text{deficit} = \Delta B = \Delta B^p + \Delta B^{cb} = \Delta B^p + \Delta BASE \tag{15.6}$$

(4) ΔB is the increase in government debt, which is divided into government debt held by the public B^p and government debt held by the central bank B^{cb}

(5) Changes in B^{cb} equal changes in the monetary base $BASE$

(6) In an all-currency economy, the change in the monetary base is equal to the change in the money supply:

$$\text{deficit} = \Delta B = \Delta B^p + \Delta B^{cb} = \Delta B^p + \Delta M \tag{15.7}$$

5. Why would governments use money creation to finance deficits, knowing that it causes inflation?

 a. Developed countries rarely use seignorage, because it doesn't raise much revenue

 b. But war-torn or developed countries are unable to raise sufficient tax revenue to cover government spending and may not be able to borrow from the public

B) Real seignorage collection and inflation

 1. The real revenue the government gets from seignorage is closely related to the inflation rate

 2. Consider an all-currency economy with a fixed level of real output and a fixed real interest rate, plus constant rates of money growth and inflation

 a. The real quantity of money demanded is constant, so real money supply must be constant

 b. Thus

$$\pi = \Delta M/M \tag{15.8}$$

 c. Real seignorage revenue R is $\Delta M/P$, but because $\pi = \Delta M/M$, then

$$\Delta M = \pi M, \tag{15.9}$$

so

$$R = \Delta M/P = \pi M/P \tag{15.10}$$

 3. Seignorage is called the inflation tax, because the government's seignorage revenue equals the inflation rate times real money balances

 a. So seignorage is like a tax (at the rate of inflation) on real money balances

 b. The government collects its revenue from the inflation tax when it buys goods with newly printed money

 c. The inflation tax is paid by everyone who holds money

4. Will a rise in money growth increase seignorage revenue?
    a. As the money growth rate rises, inflation rises, but people may hold less real balances
    b. Whether seignorage rises or falls depends on whether inflation rises more or less than the decline in real money holdings (Figure 15.1; like text Figure 15.8)

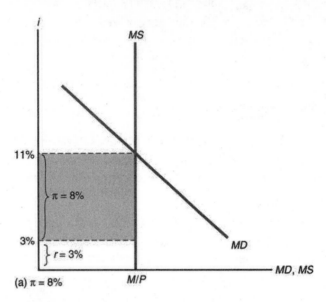

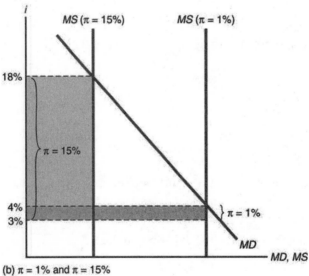

Figure 15.1

    c. Real seignorage revenue is shown by the shaded rectangles in the figures, which represent $\pi M/P$
    d. At low inflation rates, seignorage is low
    e. As the inflation rate rises, seignorage rises
    f. But at some inflation rate, seignorage begins to decline because of the decline in real money demand

g. Plotting inflation against real seignorage revenue illustrates this result (Figure 15.2; like text Figure 15.9)

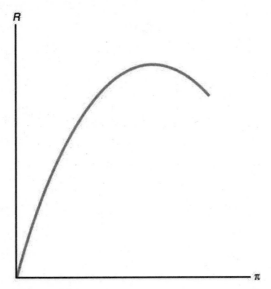

Figure 15.2

5. If governments raise money supply too rapidly, they may cause hyperinflation, but get less seignorage revenue than they would get with less money growth
   a. In Germany after World War I, inflation reached 322% per month
   b. Cagan estimated the inflation rate that maximizes seignorage at only 20% per month

■ Multiple Choice Questions

1. Government consumption expenditures equal
   (a) government outlays minus transfer payments.
   (b) government outlays minus net interest payments.
   (c) government purchases minus government investment.
   (d) the government primary deficit plus net interest payments.

2. Government purchases, transfer payments, and net interest payments are the three main categories of
   (a) the government deficit.
   (b) government outlays.
   (c) government investment.
   (d) the government primary deficit.

3. Compared with other countries in the OECD, U.S. government spending relative to GDP is
   (a) among the highest.
   (b) about average.
   (c) slightly below average.
   (d) among the lowest.

4. What portion of nondefense government purchases of goods and services is carried out by state and local governments?

    (a) Under 30%

    (b) About 50%

    (c) About 67%

    (d) Over 80%

5. The primary deficit is

    (a) the amount by which government purchases, transfers, and net interest exceed tax revenues.

    (b) the amount by which government purchases and transfers exceed tax revenues.

    (c) the deficit plus net interest payments.

    (d) total tax revenues minus net interest minus government expenditures.

6. The primary current deficit is

    (a) the deficit minus tax revenues.

    (b) the deficit minus net interest.

    (c) the current deficit minus tax revenues.

    (d) the current deficit minus net interest.

7. The U.S. government ran large primary surpluses during

    (a) World War II.

    (b) most of the 1970s.

    (c) most of the 1980s.

    (d) the late 1990s.

8. According to Keynesian economists, the primary problem with using fiscal policy as a stabilization tool is that

    (a) fiscal policy does not have the effect on output in practice that it should have in theory.

    (b) fiscal policy will be effective only if it is funded through lump-sum tax changes.

    (c) fiscal policy will be effective only if it is funded through permanent changes in taxes.

    (d) fiscal policy is inflexible because a large portion of government spending is planned years in advance and cannot be changed easily.

9. An example of an automatic stabilizer is

    (a) consumer spending.

    (b) inflation.

    (c) unemployment insurance.

    (d) discretionary fiscal policy.

10. The full-employment deficit is

    (a) the number of jobs needed to restore full employment.

    (b) what the government budget deficit would be if the economy were at full employment.

    (c) the increase in government spending that would be needed to return the economy to full employment.

    (d) the extra amount paid to government workers under the National Recovery Act.

11. The average tax rate is
    (a) the fraction of an additional dollar of income that must be paid in taxes.
    (b) the total amount of taxes paid divided by after-tax income.
    (c) the total amount of taxes paid divided by before-tax income.
    (d) the average amount of government spending that is financed by taxes.

12. An increase in the average tax rate, with the marginal tax rate held constant, will
    (a) increase the amount of labor supplied at any real wage.
    (b) not affect the amount of labor supplied at any real wage.
    (c) decrease the amount of labor supplied at any real wage.
    (d) increase the amount of labor supplied at any real wage if the average tax rate is above the marginal tax rate, but decrease the amount of labor supplied at any real wage if the average tax rate is below the marginal tax rate.

13. A decrease in the marginal tax rate, with the average tax rate held constant, will
    (a) increase the amount of labor supplied at any real wage.
    (b) not affect the amount of labor supplied at any real wage.
    (c) decrease the amount of labor supplied at any real wage.
    (d) increase the amount of labor supplied at any real wage if the average tax rate is above the marginal tax rate, but decrease the amount of labor supplied at any real wage if the average tax rate is below the marginal tax rate.

14. Assuming that market prices are efficient, imposing taxes on various economic activities creates
    (a) distortions.
    (b) a budget surplus.
    (c) an efficient tax system.
    (d) tax rate smoothing.

15. If a government is highly committed to tax rate smoothing, it will
    (a) require annually balanced fiscal budgets.
    (b) reduce tax rates during a recession.
    (c) tax every activity and every source of income at the same tax rate.
    (d) not change tax rates frequently to finance fluctuations in government spending.

16. Assume that the lost output due to tax distortions is proportional to the square of the tax rate. If the average cost of the distortion created by taxes is currently $500, and the tax rate is increased from 20% to 50%, the average cost of the distortion created by taxes will change to
    (a) $80.
    (b) $900.
    (c) $1,250.
    (d) $3,125.

17. The debt–GDP ratio in the United States
    (a) steadily fell after World War II.
    (b) steadily increased after World War II.
    (c) fell from the end of World War II until around 1970 and rose thereafter.
    (d) fell from the end of World War II until around 1980 and rose thereafter.

18. An expansionary fiscal policy will not cause an increase in the price level if the government
    (a) reduces the corporate income tax rate.
    (b) increases purchases in the classical model.
    (c). lowers taxes and Ricardian equivalence does not hold.
    (d) lowers taxes and Ricardian equivalence holds.

19. According to the Ricardian equivalence proposition, a government budget deficit created by a temporary tax cut
    (a) does not affect desired national saving.
    (b) does not affect expected future taxes.
    (c) reduces desired investment spending.
    (d) increases the real interest rate.

20. Suppose a temporary tax cut today is combined with a rise in tax rates on the next generation of taxpayers. This long delay in increasing future taxes would not in itself cause the Ricardian equivalence proposition to fail to accurately predict the effects of the tax cut, unless the
    (a) parents failed to leave bequests.
    (b) parents saved the tax cut.
    (c) parents invested the tax cut.
    (d) parents were farsighted in their expectations of future tax increases.

21. A decrease in taxes on the current generation would have no effect on consumption or national saving if
    (a) individuals face borrowing constraints.
    (b) individuals increase their consumption by less than the tax cut.
    (c) consumers bequeath all of the tax cut to the next generation.
    (d) consumers are not forward-looking concerning their future tax burden.

22. Which of the following would *not* be an argument that government debt imposes a burden on future generations?
    (a) Lump-sum taxes in the future may be raised to pay higher real interest costs.
    (b) Higher taxes in the future could increase the average cost of distortions to the economy created by taxes.
    (c) Higher taxes in the future to repay government debt will transfer resources from the poor to the rich.
    (d) Higher government deficits resulting from increased purchases may reduce savings, causing investment to fall.

23. If the deficit is 0.03 times GDP, the existing debt–GDP ratio is 0.3, and the growth rate of nominal GDP is 0.03, then the change in the debt–GDP ratio is
    (a) 0.
    (b) 0.003.
    (c) 0.009.
    (d) 0.021.

24. The revenue that a government raises by printing money is called
    (a) seignorage.
    (b) monetary revenue.
    (c) currency credit.
    (d) currency inflation.

25. Real seignorage revenue is most likely to be a significant source of revenue for
    (a) international development organizations.
    (b) developing countries during times of war.
    (c) developed countries during periods of slow output growth.
    (d) periods of disinflation.

26. Assuming that output is fixed, the real revenue raised by government from printing money in an all-currency economy is
    (a) the real money supply.
    (b) the inflation rate times the real money supply.
    (c) the real interest rate times the real money supply.
    (d) the tax rate times the increase in the growth rate of output.

27. The inflation tax is primarily a tax on
    (a) government bonds.
    (b) Social Security recipients.
    (c) money.
    (d) real income.

28. Consider an economy that has the following monetary data:

    Currency in circulation = $300
    Bank reserves   = $50
    Monetary base   = $350
    Deposits   = $700
    Money supply   = $1,000

    The monetary base and the money supply are expected to grow at a constant rate of 20% per year. Inflation and expected inflation are 20% per year. Suppose that bank reserves and currency pay no interest, all currency is held by the public, and bank deposits pay no interest. What is the profit to the banks from the inflation?
    (a) $130
    (b) $140
    (c) $190
    (d) $200

29. Real money demand in an all-currency economy in which real output and the real interest rate are fixed is given by

$$L = 0.3Y - 600i,$$

where Y is real income and i is the nominal interest rate. In equilibrium, real money demand L equals real money supply M/P. Suppose that Y equals 2,000 and the real interest rate is 5%. At what rate of inflation is seignorage maximized?

(a) 42.5%

(b) 45.0%

(c) 47.5%

(d) 50.0%

30. As inflation rises, real seignorage revenue _____ at first, and then _____.

(a) declines; declines

(b) declines; rises

(c) rises; rises

(d) rises; declines

■ Review Questions

1. How is the primary budget deficit related to the budget deficit?

2. Compare and contrast automatic stabilizers and discretionary fiscal stabilization policy in terms of flexibility and policy lags.

3. Compare and contrast the effects of automatic stabilizers during recessions on the budget deficit and on the full-employment deficit.

4. Why do economists endorse tax rate smoothing?

5. Why should governments smooth tax rates? If they do so, what happens to deficits over the business cycle?

6. Identify and briefly explain two reasons why a large government debt may not be a major burden on the future generation asked to pay it off.

7. State the Ricardian equivalence proposition.

8. Identify two conditions under which the Ricardian equivalence proposition may not hold.

9. State one argument in favor of a balanced budget amendment to the U.S. Constitution, and state one argument against a balanced budget amendment.

■ Numerical Problems

1. Suppose that for the economy of Chou,

    Tax revenues = 2,000 + 0.1GDP
    Transfers = 1,500 – 0.05GDP
    Government purchases = 3,000
    Interest payments = 200
    Full employment GDP = 15,000
    Actual GDP = 16,000

    (a) How much is the budget deficit?
    (b) How much is the primary budget deficit?
    (c) How much is the full-employment budget deficit?

2. Calculate the growth rate of debt–GDP ratio for each of the following cases, given that outstanding government debt = $5,000 billion and the primary budget deficit = $250 billion.

    (a) Nominal interest rate = 8% and nominal GDP growth = 2%
    (b) Nominal interest rate = 5% and nominal GDP growth = 2%
    (c) Nominal interest rate = 15% and nominal GDP growth = 4%

3. Calculate the real seignorage revenue in an all-currency economy, given each of the following conditions

    (a) inflation rate = 3% and M/P = $1,000 billion
    (b) inflation rate = 6% and M/P = $700 billion
    (c) inflation rate = 12% and M/P = $400 billion

■ Analytical Question

1. Compare and contrast the short-run effects of a tax cut on unemployment and output in the AD-AS model in which Ricardian equivalence holds, compared to a model in which Ricardian equivalence doesn't hold.

■ Answers

Multiple Choice

1. c	7. d	13. a	19. a	25. b
2. b	8. d	14. a	20. a	26. b
3. d	9. c	15. d	21. c	27. c
4. d	10. b	16. d	22. a	28. a
5. b	11. c	17. d	23. d	29. c
6. d	12. a	18. d	24. a	30. d

Review Questions

1. The primary budget deficit = $(G + TR) - T$. The budget deficit = $(G + TR + INT) - T$. The budget deficit exceeds the primary budget deficit by the value of net interest payments on government debt.

2. Automatic stabilizers have virtually no policy lags, and they are very flexible in creating changes in government spending and taxes, because these adjustments are automatic. In contrast, discretionary fiscal stabilization policy changes in government spending and taxes have long policy lags (e.g., eighteen months) and are not very flexible.

3. During a recession, automatic stabilizers increase government spending in the form of transfer payments and reduced taxes, thereby creating a budget deficit. In contrast, automatic stabilizers do not create a full-employment deficit, because automatic stabilizers do not create a deficit at the full-employment level of output. The full-employment deficit is the amount of the budget deficit created by discretionary fiscal stabilization policy. The difference between the budget deficit and the full-employment deficit is the deficit created by automatic stabilizers.

4. Tax rate smoothing reduces the output cost of raising a given amount of tax revenue over a number of years. Imposing a tax on the return to some factor of production, output, or asset typically creates a distortion. The overall distortion is smaller if tax rates remain fairly constant over time, rather than rising and falling over the business cycle. Business cycle fluctuations in output will create budget deficits in some years and budget surpluses in other years. But the distortions caused by taxes will be lower than if the government maintained an annually balanced government budget over the business cycle by raising the income tax rate in recessions when income declines and reducing the income tax rates in booms when income rises.

5. Governments should smooth tax rates because the increase in distortions from increasing the tax rate is larger than the decrease in distortions from reducing the tax rate by the same amount. Because of that, it's better to keep tax rates constant over time and run periodic deficits and surpluses rather than raise tax rates in times when the government needs extra revenue. This means running deficits in recessions and surpluses in booms.

6. Two reasons why a large government debt might not be a large burden on the future generation asked to pay it are: (1) this generation might have received bequests to cover the debt payments from the generation that incurred the debt; and (2) if the debt is "internal debt," then the future generation owes the debt to itself. Although some people are harmed by having to pay it off, others gain by receiving the debt payments.

7. The Ricardian equivalence proposition states that a tax cut financed by the sale of bonds is not expansionary, because the effect of bond financing on the present value of lifetime resources of the public is equivalent to tax financing. The Ricardian equivalence proposition assumes that the public does not face binding borrowing constraints and that future taxes will increase enough to pay off the bonds and the interest earned on the bonds.

8. The Ricardian equivalence proposition may not hold when either of its two principal assumptions is violated. If a significant percentage of taxpayers face binding borrowing constraints, they will spend some of the extra after-tax income they receive from the tax cut. Likewise, if people are shortsighted and consequently do not believe that their future taxes or their children's future taxes will be increased by enough to pay off the government debt, they will spend some of the extra after-tax income they receive from the tax cut. If the Ricardian equivalence proposition fails to hold, a temporary tax cut will increase aggregate spending, which is expansionary.

9. A balanced budget amendment to the U.S. Constitution would force fiscal policymakers to balance the government budget each fiscal year. One potentially positive effect cited by proponents of the amendment is that it would prevent the government from incurring huge deficits. One potentially negative effect cited by opponents of the amendment is that the government would have to stop using discretionary fiscal stabilization policy and would have to eliminate its automatic stabilizers.

Numerical Problems

1. (a) The budget deficit is $(G + TR + INT) - T = [3,000 + 1,500 - (0.05 \times 16,000) + 200] - [2,000 + (0.1 \times 16,000)] = 300$.

    (b) The primary budget deficit is $(G + TR) - T = [3,000 + 1,500 - (0.05 \times 16,000)] - [2,000 + (0.1 \times 16,000)] = 100$.

    (c) The full-employment budget deficit is what the budget deficit would be if output were at its full-employment level instead of its actual level, which is $[3,000 + 1,500 - (0.05 \times 15,000) + 200] - [2,000 + (0.1 \times 15,000)] = 450$.

2. The growth rate of debt–GDP ratio = (primary deficit)$/B + i -$ growth rate of nominal GDP, where $B =$ outstanding government debt and $i =$ nominal interest rate. The primary deficit = \$250 billion and $B =$ \$5,000 billion, so (primary deficit)$/B =$ \$250 billion/\$5,000 billion = 5%.

    (a) For $i = 8\%$, and the growth rate of nominal GDP = 2%, the growth rate of debt–GDP ratio = $5\% + 8\% - 2\% = 11\%$.

    (b) For $i = 5\%$, and the growth rate of nominal GDP = 2%, the growth rate of debt–GDP ratio = $5\% + 5\% - 2\% = 8\%$.

    (c) For $i = 15\%$, and the growth rate of nominal GDP = 4%, the growth rate of debt–GDP ratio = $5\% + 15\% - 4\% = 16\%$.

3. For an all-currency economy, real seignorage revenue is $R =$ (inflation rate) $\times M/P$, where M/P is the real money supply.

    (a) For an inflation rate = 3%, and $M/P =$ \$1,000 billion, $R = 3\% \times$ \$1,000 billion = \$30 billion.

    (b) For an inflation rate = 6%, and $M/P =$ \$700 billion, $R = 6\% \times$ \$700 billion = \$42 billion.

    (c) For an inflation rate = 12%, and $M/P =$ \$300 billion, $R = 12\% \times$ \$300 billion = \$36 billion.

Analytical Question

1. Given the Ricardian equivalence proposition, a temporary tax cut does not change national saving, so it doesn't shift the *IS* curve or *AD* curve, thus it has no output or employment effect. In the model without Ricardian equivalence, a temporary tax cut reduces national saving, which causes aggregate demand to increase, thus output increases and unemployment declines.